CHILD DEVELOPMENT IN ART

Anna M. Kindler, Editor

1997

National Art Education Association

About NAEA

Founded in 1947, the National Art Education Association is the largest professional art education association in the world. Membership includes elementary and secondary teachers, artists, administrators, museum educators, arts council staff, and university professors. The association provides membership benefits internationally. NAEA's mission is to advance art education through professional development, services, advancements of knowledge and leadership.

©1997 Copyright the National Art Education Association, 1916 Association Drive, Reston, Virginia 20191-1590

ISBN 0-937652-77-6

To my sons, Jan and Antoni

Acknowledgments

I would like to extend my sincere thanks to all individuals who have contributed to the publication of this anthology. I am grateful to the Past President of the NAEA, Mark Hansen; the NAEA Board of Directors; and the NAEA Executive Director, Thomas A. Hatfield for their support of this project. From the early stages of planning to the final editorial decisions, I was fortunate to benefit from the advice of many friends and colleagues. I would like to thank especially Bernard Darras and Ron MacGregor for their thoughtful comments and suggestions. I would like to express my appreciation to all the authors who contributed to this anthology, and whose professional expertise was matched by kindness and generosity. I am also indebted to my editorial assistant, Blane Després, and to Carol May in the NAEA office in Reston for their invaluable support. Finally, I would like to thank my family, and especially my husband Pawel, for all the encouragement and patience offered to me throughout the completion of this anthology.

TABLE OF CONTENTS

TABLE OF CONTENTS *(continued)*

CHILD DEVELOPMENT IN ART

PERSPECTIVES AND INTERPRETATIONS

One of the characteristics of the postmodern world is the increased interest in pursuit of multiple interpretations and meanings. Recognition of diversity, plurality of perspectives, and acceptance of the fact that the observed phenomena often acquire significance specific to the social and cultural contexts in which they occur allow for re-visiting of conceptions regarding child development in art from a different stance.

The present search for answers offering insights into the perceptual, cognitive, emotive, social, and cultural aspects of artistic development is guided by the ambition to focus on rules as much as exceptions; to describe and account for variations rather than dismiss them for lack of conformity to a universal model; and to accept relativity of some long standing assertions as a consequence of changing contexts and re-interpretations of the underlying concepts.

This change in focus is certainly worth acknowledgment in the field marked by tradition of a rather narrow understanding of artistic growth, defined to a large extent by the Western-culture-specific interpretation of what constitutes child art and by linear conceptualization of development in the artistic realm. Such culture-bound perspective, intrinsic to the accounts of child development in art in North America, should come as no surprise. "Ethnocentrism is at the same time a universal cultural characteristic and a psy-

ANNA M. KINDLER

chological process" which constitutes a prism, a convenient frame of reference commonly adopted across cultures (Lipiansky, 1995, p.206). It takes a conscious effort to overcome it and it requires a certain degree of decentration from habitual models of functioning.

Some of the difficulties related to the understanding of artistic development can perhaps be attributed to the semantic ambiguities embedded in the label describing the domain. Reference to "art," an open concept (Weitz, 1979) that is subject to change and re-definition as a function of time, space, and specific cultural and social circumstances, poses inherent problems in proposing a simple and stable model. When the underlying category is composed of members that often have little in common except for the status of art accorded to them by experts, it is clearly impossible to identify a single dimension, or even a set of universally common dimensions, that would allow for measuring growth in stage-like fashion or in terms of a continuous, linear incremental progress.

One of the great paradoxes in the modern Western conceptualization of the process of artistic development that has been embraced by the field of art education is the incongruity between the most cherished characteristics of child art on the one hand and the nature of the dimension identified to trace the developmental progress on the other. While characteristics such as originality, authenticity, spontaneity, freshness, and expressiveness were regarded as the prime attributes of child art, conceptualization of development in the domain remained focused on pictorial realism and the ability to mimic three dimensional reality on a two-dimensional surface.

Traditional focus of research on graphic production, and especially on drawing, imposed additional limitations to the discussion of artistic development. Several researchers, cognizant of this constraint chose to use more precise labels, such as graphic development, or development of pictorial representation. However, while much of the artistic production involves graphic media and is concerned with pictorial representation, not all graphic or pictorial production belongs to the category of art. Similarly, a vast territory of art lies outside the boundaries of graphic or pictorial representation. Yet, development in sculpture, architecture, or more recently, multimedia, has been very scarcely considered and remains an area of great need for future inquiry. The interchangeable use of terms "artistic development," "graphic development," or "development of pictorial representation" resulted from convenience, rather than from the direct equation of meaning.

This anthology offers a range of perspectives on child development in art and its value lies in the diversity, rather than the consensus of opinions. The authors contributing to this volume come from the fields of psychology, sociology, and art education in Australia, Canada, France, Switzerland, and the United States. Their research addresses various aspects of artistic growth. Together, they offer a wealth of knowledge invaluable to art educators, administrators of educational programs, policy makers, as well as parents and all those who are interested in better understanding of the ways in which children and adolescents develop in the artistic and aesthetic realms.

Rudolf Arnheim's reflections on "the century of growth" offer a unique perspective on the past decades of research on artistic development through the eyes of a scholar who has laid foundations for the new psychology of art and whose work has provided direction and inspiration for many other influential authors. Arnheim's dynamic conception of visual perception and his understanding of artistic process as guided by a graphic logic involving construction of pictorial equivalences rather than literal representations, has revolutionized thinking about the nature of growth in art. In this book, Arnheim revisits his work and places it in the context of other developments in the field while advocating the need for quality art education as "an indispensable instrument for training the mind" (p. 12).

The multiplicity of vectors along which artistic growth occurs is presented in Chapter 3, which describes a map-like model of the emergence and development of pictorial imagery. Congruent with findings of Wolf and Perry (1988), this model departs from a linear conception of development and describes a territory of possibilities. It regards development of pictorial imagery as a semiotic process that is affected by the sociocultural context in which it occurs and highlights links with other means of communication, such as verbal and gestural language. The model that Bernard Darras and I propose is essentially three-fold. One segment describes the gestation, birth, and development of pictorial imagery in early childhood years. The second component addresses the phenomenon of "initial imagery," a basic, commonly accessible system of pictorial representation that exhibits a remarkable resistance to change and often persists into adulthood. The third segment presents the range of vectors that can chart further artistic development. The role of art education in making selection among these vectors is emphasized and implications of our model to art education practice are carefully considered.

The following two chapters extend the discussion of development in drawing from a psychological perspective. Jessica Davis describes the objectives and research agenda of the Harvard Project Zero, focusing, in particular, on studies related to the production-perception paradox, an apparent decline of "artistry" in graphic production of children that is accompanied by increased sensitivity to it in the perceptual realm. Davis' conceptualization of artistic growth is centered around the expressive dimension, where progress or decline are defined in terms of the presence or absence of expressive attributes conforming to criteria often used in appraisal of professional art.

In contrast, Emiel Reith focuses on artistic development in terms of the unfolding of abilities to produce realistic depictions. He argues that the course of development is here determined by the increase in awareness of the dual reality of pictorial representations. A careful review of stages in drawing development and identification of factors considered as responsible for age-related changes is followed by a discussion of children's drawing activity as a function of their understanding of the "theory" of pictorial representation. Reith claims that such understanding involves distinguishing between the identity of an image as a thing in itself and its identity as a representation of an external referent. He highlights the importance of understanding of the correspondence between the features of marks on the picture and attributes of the object being represented. Reith also offers art educators advice regarding the choice of activities that promote awareness of the dual reality of pictures.

A sociocultural perspective on child development in art is explored in the next section of the anthology. Brent Wilson returns to the definition of child art pointing to the cultural determinants of this concept. Among the many perspectives that can be considered in addressing child art, Wilson focuses on three—those of the art world, the child, and the world of education. Wilson demonstrates how the diverse interpretations are signs that inform about assumptions, aesthetic theories, and the beliefs on which they are based. He points to the relationships between the child's work, the reality to which the child refers, and the aesthetic traditions that affect his or her work, as well as interests, experiences, and values of interpreters as factors defining the meaning of child art. The author cautions art teachers and researchers about the bias that their personal experiences, cultural traditions, and belief systems bring into shaping understanding of child art and, in consequence, guide their professional practice. He encourages more consideration of children's values and interpretations in art education.

The importance of the sociocultural perspective in discussion of artistic development is further stressed by Kerry Freedman who argues that many aspects of drawing are connected to culture and socialization. Her analysis of stage-by-age as well as novice-expert models stresses their deficiency in consideration of the sociocultural context. Freedman advocates art curriculum that acknowledges cultural influences on artistic knowledge and production, one that allows for interdisciplinary integration of content, respects intertextuality, and maintains relevance to students' life experiences.

The role of socialization referred to by Freedman, is further explored by Paul Duncum in his discussion of subjects and themes in children's unsolicited drawings. Noting a general stability of themes in a historical perspective, Duncum highlights gender differences and points to the close relationship between children's choices of drawing themes and their broad interests. Duncum regards these choices as both reflective of gender socialization and contributing to adaptation of culturally-defined gender roles.

David Pariser extends discussion of systematic changes in acquisition of drawing skills by offering an account of the artistic development of exceptional children. Early in his chapter, Pariser cautions that the notion of giftedness is a cultural phenomenon and that children are deemed exceptional only if they excel in a culturally defined and valued domain and their work conforms to the expectations of experts in this domain. Pariser's analysis of three categories of artistically exceptional children: those who suffered from neurological or psychological anomalies and who manifested outstanding drawing abilities at an early age; children who were artistically precocious, but whose adult artistic success is yet to be determined; and great masters who drew precociously and whose early displayed talents eventually lead them to artistic fame, leads to identification of seven common characteristics of graphic production of artistically gifted children. Pariser also highlights the fact that diverse sets of skills are relevant to the development of aesthetic and artistic competence cross-culturally as a function of the changing value and salience of specific characteristics in each cultural context. The recognition of the need to rethink conceptions of artistic giftedness in the light of the types of imagery recognized as art outside of the Western artistic tradition is followed by a call to restructure the notion of artistic development to account for the variety of possible vectors that can chart the course of artistic development.

Artistic development is clearly not limited to the development in graphic representation. While the amount of attention accorded to consideration of age-related changes in pictorial representation in this book is significantly greater than that given to the development in other artistic media, this is a direct reflection of trends in research. Work in 3-D media, for example, has received, to date, only limited attention. One of the very few scholars who has pursued research concerned with children's development in clay is Claire Golomb. In her chapter, Golomb presents results from recent studies concerned with representational strategies in children's clay construction and their relationship to task demands. Her work provides evidence of children's three-dimensional approach to modelling already in the early childhood years and offers additional support to the claim that the "primitive" representations of young children do not result from cognitive immaturity, but rather are related to the problems inherent in the nature of the medium and the lack of experience and practice that modeling technique requires in order to be mastered.

The past three decades have brought an increased interest of researchers in aesthetic development. The curiosity about the nature of artistic production of young children and the development of abilities in representation
involving visual signs and symbols became paired with interest in the ways
children, adolescents, and adults respond to works of art and attend to aesthetic qualities of objects in their environment. While there is some evidence
that the development of aesthetic perception does not go hand in hand, nor
does it closely parallel the growth in artistic production (e.g., Carothers &
Gardner, 1979, Davis, this book) both of these domains need to be considered
in a comprehensive look at human development in the realm of the arts.

Two chapters of this anthology are specifically devoted to the discussion of aesthetic development. Judith Smith Koroscik explores the question
of understanding of works of art, focusing on the differences between novices and experts in terms of their knowledge base and knowledge-seeking
strategies, dispositions, and abilities to transfer previously acquired knowledge, as appropriate, to new tasks. Advocating for more inquiry into the potential that young people have for understanding works of art, she points to
the usefulness of the novice-expert model in art education as a framework
facilitating development of assessment strategies for diagnosing learning problems.

A comprehensive review of research in aesthetic development is offered by Larry Kantner and Connie Newton. These authors highlight the need
for multicultural and cross-cultural investigations as a means to acquire a
more complete understanding of phenomena associated with aesthetic growth.
This chapter includes a discussion of studies exploring development of perception and response to art, aesthetic sensitivity and preference, from a perspective of postmodernist appreciation of the intricate relationships between
art and its cultural contexts.

The closing chapter of this anthology considers implications of research
in artistic development to art education. Ronald MacGregor reflects on the
nature of art education and its relationship to teachers' and policy makers'
understanding of artistic development. He points to the fact that controversies generated about the nature of artistic development are largely due to the
different emphasis and interests of the involved parties. MacGregor proposes
a list of factors or circumstances which can affect both the movement along
the developmental continuum and the interpretation and understanding of this
progression, devoting special attention to the personal, cultural, and economic
determinants. While he contends that artistic learning is like a map (Kindler
and Darras, this book), he notes that it is also like a river, traveling in a direction over time. Consequently, he advocates the need for comprehensive rather
than fragmented look at art curriculum as a program that unfolds in time and

maintains a close relationship to the developmental changes propelled by biological maturation, as well as social and cultural conditions. MacGregor notes that learning outcomes and standards in art education need to reflect recognition that artistic development is "as much a response to conditions as it is a genetic imperative" (p. 191). He invites researchers and art education practitioners to draw on and complement each others' expertise and contributions in order to further develop educational approaches that advance aesthetic and artistic learning.

Child development in art has long been of interest to art educators as its understanding provides bases for the practice of art pedagogy. How artistic growth is conceptualized bears heavily on how (and even if) art is taught. Consciously, as well as subconsciously, these conceptions guide educators' decisions about the content, sequence, and instructional methodology. This anthology offers an overview of current knowledge about artistic and aesthetic development. It brings to the reader historical perspective, as well as recent research in this field, presented in the form that highlights their implications for the educational practice. The inclusion of multiple perspectives allows for a broad view and empowers the reader to consider the psychological, cultural, and social aspects of artistic growth in a unified fashion. This anthology constitutes an account of what is known about child development in art while at the same time demonstrating how much there is still to be discovered. I hope that this anthology, while informing and enriching readers' understanding of artistic and aesthetic development, will also serve as an invitation to further inquiry into this fascinating realm of human experience.

References

Carothers, T. & Gardner, H. (1979). When children's drawings become art: The emergence of aesthetic production and perception. *Developmental Psychology, 15*(5). 570-580.

Lipiansky, E. M. (1995). La communication interculturelle. In D. Benoit (Ed.) *Introduction aux sciences de l'information et de la communication.* Paris: Les Editions D'Organisation. 187-216.

Weitz, M. (1979). The role of theory is esthetics. In M. Reader (Ed.) *A modern book of esthetics.* New York: Holt, Rinehart & Winston. 434-443.

Wolf, D. & Perry, M. (1988). From endpoints to repertoires: New conclusions about drawing development. *Journal of Aesthetic Education, 22*(1), 17-35.

A LOOK AT A CENTURY OF GROWTH

Art education and research on the development of children's art are essentially products of the century that is now completing its final years. Because this period coincides roughly with the course of my own life, I may be permitted to center this paper on the place of my work in its relation to progress in the field as a whole. My contributions dealing with the theoretical aspects of child art are very few, but they have had reverberations in the work of some influential authors, and some of my other writings on artistic representation and visual thinking have found applications in the field here under discussion.

A good way of getting to our subject is to remember that the human mind acquires its own experiences in two ways which run opposite to each other. On the one hand, comprehension of the world around us starts with broadly generic notions and becomes only gradually more specific. On the other hand, the exploration takes off from local details which come to take their place in the broader context that reveals their meaning in the world as a whole. The intricate give and take between the two mental developments reflects itself in the experiences of every individual person and in manifestations such as art activity.

I found myself at the crossroads of these two complementary progressions as I was approaching the middle of my life. I was beginning to become more aware of broader principles and to group together things I had been gathering piece by piece from art history, philosophy, and psychology. At the same time I was getting more concretely familiar with particular areas of experience, of which I had barely a nodding acquaintance. One of these areas was the artwork of children. I greatly welcomed the encounter because I recognized it as a strong testimonial for my conviction that one cannot do

R<small>UDOLF</small> <small>ARNHEI</small>M

justice to the nature and value of the visual arts by looking simply at how mechanically faithful they are to nature. While in an overall sense Western art has indeed moved toward increased naturalism, this development was counteracted throughout by strongly opposite tendencies. The modern art of our century had largely abandoned the demands of naturalistic correctness. And the spontaneous work of young children clearly ignores them.

The artwork of children reflects the early developmental stages of the human mind during which the multiformity of the world is synthesized in a few generalities. Stating this means accepting a fundamental shift in our psychological notion of how the mind copes with the world. Traditionally it had been taken for granted that the senses of vision, hearing, touch, and so forth, initiate their primary task by recording, piece by piece and more or less faithfully, what hits them from the outer world. The early experiences were supposed to reflect this inventory of particulars. Only secondarily was this raw material taken hold of by the higher cognitive functions of the mind. Thinking extracted general concepts which cleared the way for language because words, of course, are labels for concepts.

The older ones among us well remember how this psychological prejudice blocked any ready understanding of why the early artwork of children does not limit itself to the imprints of sensory recording. The battle we had to fight against the absurd, auxiliary theory, according to which children draw from intellectual concepts, echoed in my chapter on "Growth" in my *Art and Visual Perception* (Arnheim, 1954/1974).

By then it was already clear that the grasp of generalities, with which human cognition starts, would take in the arts the form of the overall shapes known from geometry. They lead to gradual differentiation and refinement, as the sense of observation matures. Less obvious, however, but in my view equally fundamental was the fact that children have a spontaneous respect for any particular medium they choose to work in. This respect, essential to every successful art work, makes for rules obeyed by children and other styles of art through the ages and all over the world. In drawing and painting it makes for the clear displaying of shapes on the surface, the avoiding of overlap, and for inventing special devices to cope with the depth dimension.

This led me in a later study on the representation of the third dimension (Arnheim, 1972a) to show that the deviations from traditional central perspective were misinterpreted in art theory as errors. They were, instead, perfectly logical ways for children and other artists to display on the pictorial surface aspects of three-dimensional objects which mechanical projection would have hidden.

The upshot of these findings is that the representation of experiences does not consist in copying or extracting or selecting from the observed facts but in creating equivalents of them in the given medium. This holds for the artwork of children as well as for that of adults, but also for the use of language. It is a translation rather than a reproduction, and it made me distinguish in an early paper (Arnheim, 1947) between two kinds of concepts. Perceptual experience such as vision consists in the formation of perceptual concepts. A child grasps with his eyes, say, the shape of a human figure or a rabbit. But to show it in a drawing, a second translation is necessary. Perceptual concepts have to be accounted for by representational concepts derived from the resources of a medium. For example, the perceptual concepts of a human head becomes in a drawing a circular contour line; in clay modeling it may become a ball.

It will be evident that all these principles apply to cognition quite in general. They apply to all levels of art, even though they show with particular clarity in early art. It has always seemed pointless to me to ask whether something is art or not art. On no scale dealing with the understanding of art is there a cut-off level separating art from non-art. Art, in my opinion, is not a category of things but a quality or property of things and actions (Arnheim, 1972b). Art is the capacity to express the nature and meaning of something through its sensory appearance. Whenever a child's product exhibits this representational virtue it has the quality of art. Simple or complex, conscious or unconscious, this precious ability begins to show in early childhood.

Child art, then, profits from being recognized as an inseparable aspect of good human functioning. No society can afford to ignore the fact that the capacity for behaving artistically is inherent in every human being and cannot be neglected without detriment to the individual and to society as a whole.

Art is not the privilege of a few gifted people. We are only beginning to understand the particular conditions needed for talent to come to fruition (Golomb, 1995), but it is already evident that the early formal principles in the development of gifted children are those of all normal children. Common to them seems to be a keen sense of observation and an eagerness to reflect these observations in their artwork. Frequently there is, in addition, a strong visual imagination, the invention of rich shape and color patterns. The originality of composition may show up quite early, although in our particular culture the precocity of gifted children may manifest itself mainly in an early ability to handle the devices of naturalistic representation, such as foreshortening and other aspects of spatial depth.

I need to mention here that my own concern with children's art, as indeed with the arts in general, has been mostly with its cognitive function. Not that I underrate in any way the psychological importance of the work's content or the personal attitudes it may reveal. See, for example, the drawings done by children during the Spanish Civil War (Huxley, 1938). I just happen to be mostly absorbed by the human mind's coping with the complexity and mysteriousness of the world we face, the problems raised by this confrontation, and the efforts of the mind to recognize and resolve these problems. I admire the mind's capacity to derive a pertinent order from the chaos of experience. This dramatic struggle starts at birth, and the art of children is an essential instrument of this need to recognize and create meaningful order.

Any successful coping with this fundamental problem presupposes an intimate cooperation of perception and thinking. I have referred already to the unfortunate separation in theory of these two components of the cognitive mind. The distinction is all the harder to handle when language does not provide terms to refer to their unity, as is the case in English. The German language, for example, provides the word"Anschauung," which stands for sensory experience comprising understanding and conceptualization. Henry Schaefer-Simmern (1948), in his pioneering book on the unfolding of artistic activity, helped himself with terms such as "visual conceiving," and I myself had to limit myself to speaking in English of "visual thinking" (Arnheim, 1969), even though such thinking amounts to much more than applying the purely optical recording of precepts to thought.

And yet this concept holds the key to what constitutes the principal value of art for human experience. When educators are asked to justify the study of art, they all too often talk more or less vaguely of the need to bring about a well-rounded personality, of responding to emotional needs, or of training certain manual and visual skills. No wonder they find it hard to persuade administrators and the authorities who decide on time and money for the curriculum. I have always been convinced that art education is an indispensable instrument for training the mind in the skills required for successful work in any area of learning whatever.

Because a piece of artwork is more directly grasped by the senses and surveyable as a whole, it serves as an ideal medium of training for tasks involving theoretical statements or lengthy verbal texts. The eyes have an easier time capturing the essentials demanded by a visual theme and to find and create order in a given complexity. There is no better preparation for learning to read microscopic images, to organize a mass of historical data, or to put a piece of prose in logical sequence. And the best time to begin such training is childhood, when the more demanding subjects of learning are not yet assailing the mind and the artwork is still simple.

In his influential work on multiple intelligences, Gardner (1983) refers to the arts in defining seven principal skills such as the musical, the bodily-kinesthetic, and the spatial; and from the days of Viktor Lowenfeld (1954) art educators are acquainted with the difference between more visually and more haptically inclined individuals. Gardner's theory is exerting an extremely wholesome influence on early education by pointing out that, from the beginning, children are disposed to learning most readily in particular areas of functioning and will depend on being educated with the individual emphasis on their special dispositions. I am hesitant to agree that these different dispositions are best called intelligences. I am inclined to believe that the notion of intelligence should not be split up into a variety of different manifestations. Gardner recognizes the ability to solve problems as a central virtue of intelligence, and it seems to me that the ability to group essentials, to see particulars in their broader context, to discover relations between distant realms, and thereby to view things in new ways, is a central, supreme distinction of intelligent persons. It is the same quality in a good painter, mathematician, or garage mechanic, even though it does not appear equally in all aspects of a person's mind. The cleverness of an intelligent child shows up early.

What I find particularly challenging in Gardner's work is the need for educators to discover ways of teaching different subjects in the perspective of a particular mental disposition. It is easy to teach a visual youngster art or geometry, but how does one give him or her a fitting access to prose or physics or history? Good teachers find ways of doing it, but it takes imagination.

In dealing with children's artwork, I have concentrated on the preschool years because, in early childhood, the root principles of the work, and in fact those of visual art in general, show up most purely. The steps of development from the simplest to more complex shapes have been analyzed by Schaefer-Simmern (1948), on whose approach I was able to base much of my own (1954/1974), and it has been usefully illustrated by Fein (1993). To Fein we also owe the most impressive case study on the development of a gifted child's artwork (1976), and hers was preceded by Hildreth's (1941) monograph on a boy drawing trains.

During the school years, the work becomes not only more complex but also more varied, depending on the style of the individual, the influence of teachers, and the conventions of the particular culture. I have just received the catalogue of the 7th Kanagawa Biennial World Children's Art Exhibition, illustrated with the prize-winning paintings selected from the entries of 135 countries (Kanagawa, 1993). Quite a few of the works still show some of the root features of child art, embedded in their makers' particular pattern of shapes and colors, but others do not. The overall quality, variety, and originality of the works chosen by the teachers and the Japanese jury are encouragingly high.

When I try for an overview of the theoretical assumptions by which educators and theoreticians deal with children in their artwork, I note a principal handicap. Too often, conditions due to our particular social environment are treated as though they were of the very nature of art. I referred already to the mistaken belief that the only objective of visual art aims at a naturalistic rendering of the images projected by the lenses of the eyes on the retinas. Another of these prejudices holds that the attention span of people, and particularly of children, is quite short. In consequence, the mass media, such as television, have popularized the notion that the only way to hold the attention of an audience is to feed it potpourris of various bits. This mischievous habit has trickled into art education, inducing teachers to prefer short lessons and confuse children with a bombardment of different techniques and assignments.

Nothing could be more averse to the natural behavior of an undisturbed person. A child, left alone, will spend endless time on a task that has caught his or her imagination. Just as centuries of observation have told us about the practices of artists, an absorbing task will not only occupy much time, it will also take over the initiative by replacing momentary whims with demands prescribed by the task.

A similar deviation from what comes naturally seems to me to have led to the slackening of the creative impulse and the decline of artistic quality that has been reported so frequently for the public school population. So widespread is this phenomenon that psychological speculations have related it to the onset of puberty. My own impression is that we are dealing with a cultural artifact. Not only is the attention of young adolescents deflected by powerfully promoted and prestigious occupation, but there is also little true affection for the arts in the population at large. Nor are the arts cultivated by such mass media as television, which also tempt youngsters to spend many hours on passive reception rather than active exploring, handling, and inventing of things. This grave threat to productive growth cannot fail to reverberate in the arts. It is also true that the popular insistence on naturalistic correctness in pictures stultifies inventiveness and originality.

Quite evidently, an undisturbed development of children's artwork flourishes when parents, teachers, and other influential persons protect them from environmental impediments. To be sure, few children grow up in a vacuum. They are affected by the standards and values of their social environment. We see children losing their spontaneous creativity when they copy comic strips and similar commercial imagery, and there have been art educators who neglected their mission by asking their pupils to faithfully imitate inferior models. But it is equally evident that children who trust their own style can produce beautiful responses when they look at models of bad or good quality. As an example, I mention experiments in which school-age children are asked to respond with paintings of their own to works shown them in a museum (Beeh, 1986).

Toward the end of a century in which a new conscious attention to the growth of the young mind has so greatly expanded our knowledge of the psychological principles that rule the development of visual creativity we find ourselves in unfailing presence of natural beauty in the spontaneous artwork of children all over the world. We have also become aware of the painful obstacles that hamper good art education everywhere. Those of us whose faith in the resources of the young mind is unbroken will not be deterred.

References

Arnheim, R. (1947). *Perceptual abstraction and art*. In Arnheim, 1966.

Arnheim, R. (1954/1974). *Art and visual perception*. Berkeley, CA: University of California Press.

Arnheim, R. (1966). *Toward a psychology of art*. Berkeley, CA: University of California Press.

Arnheim, R. (1969). *Visual thinking*. Berkeley, CA: University of California Press.

Arnheim, R. (1972a). *Inverted perspective and the axioms of realism*. In Arnheim, 1986.

Arnheim, R. (1972b). Art as an attribute, not a noun. *Arts in Society, 9*.

Arnheim, R. (1986). *New essays in the psychology of art*. Berkeley, CA: University of California Press.

Beeh, W. (Ed.). (1986). *Bilder und Figuren nach Vorbildern*. Darmstadt: Hessisches Landesmuseum.

Fein, S. (1976). *Heidi's horse*. Pleasant Hill, CA: Exelrod.

Fein, S. (1993). *First drawings*. Pleasant Hill, CA: Exelrod.

Gardner, H. (1980). *Artful scribbles*. New York: Basic Books.

Gardner, H. (1983). *Frames of mind*. New York: Basic Books.

Gardner, H. (1993). *Multiple intelligences*. New York: Basic Books.

Golomb, C. (1995). *The development of gifted child artists*. Hillsdale, NJ: Erlbaum.

Hildreth, G. (1941). *The child mind in evolution*. New York: King's Crown Press.

Huxley, A. (Ed.). (1938). *They still draw pictures*. New York: Spanish Child Welfare Assoc. of America.

Kanagawa Prefecture (1993). *The 7th Kanagawa Biennial World Children's Art. Exhibition*. Yokohama, Japan.

Lowenfeld, V. (1954). *Your child and his art*. New York: Macmillan.

Schaefer-Simmern, H. (1948). *The unfolding of artistic activity*. Berkeley, CA: University of California Press.

MAP OF ARTISTIC DEVELOPMENT

Stage theories of artistic development, rooted in Piaget's conceptualization of cognitive development, have guided our understanding of the artistic growth of children for several decades. The work of Luquet (1913) and Lowenfeld (1947) has greatly influenced art educators' understanding of how children grow in the artistic domain. Recently, however, an increasing number of researchers have raised concerns over the appropriateness of stage theories (e.g., Colbert & Taunton, 1988; De Meredieu, 1974; Freeman, 1980; Walsh, 1993; Widlocher, 1965; Wolf & Perry, 1988) and suggested the need for a revised conceptualization of artistic development.

In this chapter, we will discuss problems inherent in stage theories of artistic development and present an alternative model which has emerged as a result of our cross-cultural research, reflection on work of other researchers in the field, and personal experiences as art educators and parents over the past decade. We will also point to the significance of this new conceptualization for art education.

Problems with stage theories

Definition of artistic development
   The term "artistic development" implies that this phenomenon is concerned with human development in the domain of art. Consequently, it is impossible to consider it without reflecting on what constitutes art. While many definitions of art have been proposed over the centuries, the one which is embraced by the contemporary postmodern world centers around the notion of art as a concept with an "open texture" (Weitz, 1979, p. 438). If our understanding of art is not to be limited to any particular aesthetic theory,

ANNA M. KINDLER & BERNARD DARRAS

then conceptualization of artistic development needs to account for this breadth. Stage theories, however, are rather hermetic and thus are not sensitive to the open definition of art.

Linearity which does not account for diversity
　　Stage theories of artistic development are characterized by linearity, which does not account for diversity of work produced within particular stage boundaries. Wolf and Perry (1988) observed that at each "stage" children construct a range of visual languages. They observed that children are competent in making conscious choices in regard to the use of these languages by matching drawing systems available in their repertoire to the purposes which drawings are supposed to serve. This notion of a choice, rather than a single rule guiding a child's pictorial production, was also documented in studies by Bremmer and Moore (1984). These researchers demonstrated how children who possess skills to produce visually realistic drawings do not make consistent use of them. A linear conception of growth focuses attention on one category of pictorial production, and manifestations of pictorial activity outside its boundaries are not addressed within the framework of stage theories.

Concentration on realism
　　Progression through the stages is largely defined in terms of the increased ability to make isomorphic representations of people and objects in the environment. In stage theories of artistic development, realistic representation is used as a reference point to define accomplishment or progress. This, however, is a misleading cue, when one considers the broad range of purposes of visual imagery, and the varying significance of the optical realism dimension in art in both historical and cross-cultural perspectives. Maps, logos, and decorative art are just a few examples of instances in which the criterion of realism is useless as a classification cue or as a device to assess quality or merit. Optical realism is not a cross-culturally preferred representational convention and, as art history demonstrates, it is not a consistent goal even within the boundaries of Western cultural tradition. In fact, the emphasis on the expressive rather than narrative properties in Western art of the 20th century and the resulting interest in art education in creativity and self-expression, as defined by Lowenfeld (1947) and Freinet (1969), discredited the notion of realism-oriented representations as superior to other pictorial manifestations (Wallon, 1945). Thus, realism-centered stage theories seem to use an irrelevant baseline for considerations of artistic growth.

Lack of generalizability beyond early childhood years
　　Stage theories attempt to carefully trace development in early childhood. A number of researchers have described and interpreted scribbling behavior of children that seems to be universally shared (e.g., Golomb, 1992; Kellogg, 1969; Lowenfeld & Brittain, 1970; Lurcat, 1979; Wallon, Cambier,

& Englehart, 1990). However, stage theories lack generalizability when addressing artistic development of adolescents and adults. What these theories suggest applies only to a small percentage of the population, those who are deemed artistically gifted or destined for art-oriented careers. The U-curve of artistic development as described by Gardner (1982) turns into an L-shaped model for the remainder of the population (Davis, this book). This L-model does not imply, however, that children, adolescents, or adults who do not follow the line of progress defined by the stage theories of artistic development cease to explore pictorial imagery in their lives. Diagrams, sketches, decorated notes, photographs, and home videos are just a few examples of their pictorial productions for which stage theories do not account.

Strong emphasis on psychobiological determinants of artistic development
Stage theories are founded on a culture-free assumption and either neglect to consider the implications of the cultural and social context, or view any extraneous influences as detrimental to the natural, biologically defined process of development (e.g., Lowenfeld, 1947). Artistic development does not occur in a social and cultural void, however, and several researchers have stressed the significance of sociocultural factors in the ways it progresses (e.g., Lelarge, 1978; Kindler, 1992b, 1994a, 1994b; Paget, 1932; Thompson & Bales, 1991; Wilson & Wilson, 1977, 1984). This emphasis on the sociocultural context is congruent with the post-Piagetian perspective on development in general (Inagaki, 1992). Brent and Marjorie Wilson (1977, 1982, 1985) argue that learning in the realm of graphic production is culturally mediated and provide in their work an abundant number of examples supporting their hypothesis. Even if one is willing to regard cultural and social factors as simply contributing to the variability within the general rule (Golomb, 1992), this variability needs to be acknowledged and addressed.

Our model provides an attempt to conceptualize the development of pictorial representation in a way which does not rely on any particular definition of art. It embraces a diversity of pictorial manifestations without implying value judgments on the artistic merit of any of them, allows for consideration of sociocultural variables, and is concerned with the process from its onset in the early childhood and on through the adult years.

Theoretical foundations of the proposed model

Semiotic foundations
One of the underlying assumptions of our model is that all art shares communication potential. This potential is a common denominator of all pictorial manifestations. Whether this communication is of thoughts, ideas, emotions, values, states, understandings, or realities, it occurs through the use of icons, indexes, and symbols, which, according to Peirce (1931-35) constitute

components of signs. In attempts to trace developments in pictorial representation, we relied on Peirce's semiotic theory. This becomes particularly evident in our use of terms "indexality" and "iconicity" in the discussion of artistic development in the early childhood years.

Our model considers development of pictorial production as a semiotic activity and, consequently, explores the impact of this activity on pictorial imagery produced by people at various points of their lives.

Sociocultural foundations
Our model is grounded in the assumption that artistic development is a phenomenon which occurs in an interactive social environment and that artistic learning involves a social component. We have relied on Vygotsky's (1978) conception of the nature of human development. According to Vygotsky,

> Within a general process of development, two qualitatively different lines of development, differing in origin, can be distinguished: the elementary processes, which are of biological origin, on the one hand, and the higher psychological functions, of sociocultural origin, on the other. The history of child behaviour is born from the interweaving of these two lines. (p. 46)

Vygotsky's understanding of the relationship between learning and development, highlighting the existence of the "zone of proximal development" which can be accessed only through interactions with others, focused our attention on the importance of socially mediated learning in artistic development. Also, an increasing number of studies in art education pointing to the role of social interactions in art explorations of children (e.g., Dyson, 1988; Kindler, 1992, 1992a, 1994a; Korzenik, 1977; Thompson & Bales, 1991) provided support for our perspective.

Our model takes into account the social nature of learning. It acknowledges the role of social and cultural context in both qualitative as well as quantitative changes in pictorial production.

Philosophical perspective
Our model rests on the hypothesis that artistic development is propelled by a dynamic conflict between two opposing forces of attraction and repulsion which exercise their influence in the world of iconic signs and contribute to the diversity of pictorial imagery (see Figure 1).

This notion of visual imagery rooted in a conflict of bipolar forces can be traced back to the debate initiated by philosophers in ancient Greece who attempted to discover the mechanisms of progress in the world. It was Heraclitus (in Janniere, 1985) who first suggested the presence of two univer-

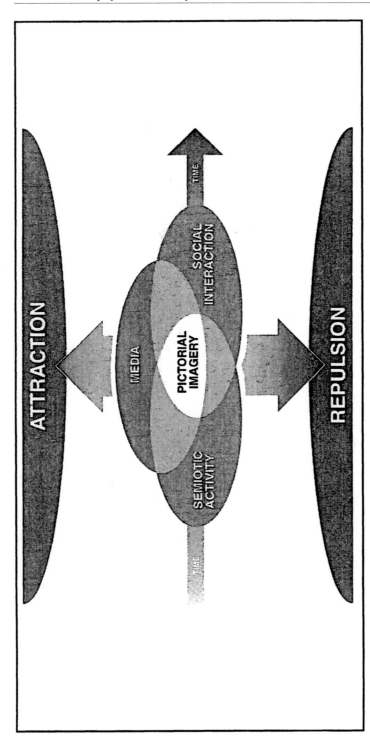

Figure 1
Emergence of Pictorial Imagery
©1994 Darras & Kindler

sal forces which, engaged in a continuing opposition and struggle, were responsible for change. In more recent times, Gombrich (1985) and Arnheim (this volume) explored a similar notion of duality in their accounts of the functioning of human mind.

On the one hand, we construct and organize knowledge through convergent thinking propelled by the "attraction" principle. On the other, constructs of human mind are derived through making distinctions, considering exceptions, and employing a divergent mode of processing resulting from the influence of the "repulsion" force. In the development of pictorial imagery we have identified two tendencies corresponding to these forces: the generic tendency, which favours rule, regularity, predictability, and order, and the individuate tendency which leads towards exception, uniqueness, and unpredictability.

In our conceptualization of artistic development we are also indebted to Thom's theory of catastrophe (1980). Where the system enters a state of disequilibrium which cannot be tolerated or ameliorated simply by quantitative improvements, a more dramatic change is required (Piaget, 1978). Following Thom's reasoning, we hypothesized that two distinct processes responsible for qualitative and quantitative changes lead to the diversity of pictorial representations encountered in the world. We suggest that diversification and the increase of complexity of images are due to two types of operation: incrementation and bifurcation (Darras & Kindler, 1993; 1994b). Incrementation defines gradual quantitative changes occurring within the same general framework and involves continuing, uninterrupted sequence. Bifurcation can be regarded as a sudden "catastrophe." At this point, the repulsion-attraction conflict results in a non-linear shift. Together, incrementation and bifurcation processes lead to the development of a map of artistic development which we propose.

Pluri-media conception of pictorial development
Our model is free of assumptions that pictorial activity is an isolated, self-contained phenomenon. While the concept of an artist as one who operates exclusively within the range of visual media often prevails within mainstream Western conceptualization of fine arts, this notion has also been challenged. Art of dadaism, pop art, happenings, instances of folk art, and, very clearly, much of children's production cross the boundaries of a single medium and embrace visual, vocal, and gestural elements in the creation of a piece.

In the analysis of drawing development, several researchers have indicated a link between language and graphic activity (e.g., Colbert, 1984; Dyson, 1982; Korzenik, 1977; Wallon, Cambier, & Englehart, 1990). Many drawings are incomplete and reveal little about intentions or abilities of those who produced them if they are detached from a context which includes words, sounds, and gestures. Dyson (1988) brought attention to this issue by stating that:

> Educators and researchers tend to talk about each kind of symbol separately. But when children sit together around a work table, the teacher will most likely see drawing, talking, movement, and quite possibly singing and writing as well. (p. 26)

We argue that pictorial activity not only can be supported by or supportive of other forms of communication and expression, but that in fact it can be regarded as an integral part of a pluri-media process (Kindler & Darras, 1994). Consequently, we suggest that consideration of growth within the artistic domain needs to be addressed in a more comprehensive manner, where proper attention to these other elements is accorded.

The Map Model of Pictorial Development

Our model is essentially three-fold. It describes artistic development in three segments of a map. The first segment deals with the gestation, birth, and development of pictorial imagery in the early childhood years. The second segment is concerned with the phenomenon of "initial imagery" (Darras, 1986, 1988, 1992a), a basic, stable, and efficient system of pictorial representation which seems to be commonly accessible. The third segment describes the many roads which may be followed in the development of pictorial imagery. These roads are not to be regarded as mutually exclusive choices, since one may travel through many of them throughout one's life.

Development of pictorial imagery in the early childhood years

(This section provides a summary of a more detailed explanation of the early childhood component of our model. See Kindler & Darras, 1994).

In our description of the development of pictorial imagery in the early childhood years we used terms "Iconicity 1" through "Iconicity 5", to indicate points of bifurcations or instances where there seems to be a qualitative rather than a quantitative change in the nature of semiotic activity. These points, as well as intervals between them, should not be regarded as stages where movement from one level to another assumes discontinuity of the earlier graphic manifestations. As Figure 2 illustrates, incremental changes continue regardless of the new emerging strands.

Each iconicity level delineates a range of behaviors and possibilities, rather than describing a precisely defined norm.

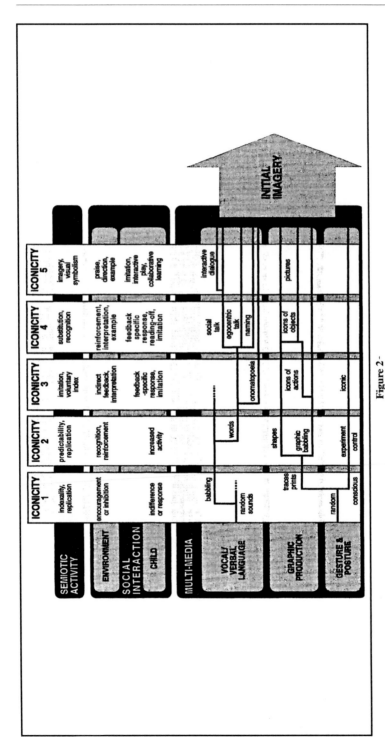

Figure 2 -
Development of Pictorial Imagery in Early Childhood
© *1994 Darras & Kindler*

Iconicity 1

Iconicity 1 delineates the beginning of the emergence of pictorial imagery. It is marked by the acquisition of the concept of basic relationship between actions and their traces. In terms of semiotic activity, Iconicity 1 signifies the recognition of ability to produce icons of actions (See Figure 3).

Repetition of realized kinetic acts constitutes a form of kinetic self-imitation of a child which initiates the understanding of resemblance, an analogy between actions and their traces. The influence of the individuate tendency is manifested in the very nature of indexality and the child's unending pursuit of new movements which hold iconic potential. At the same time, the generic tendency is evident in children's interest in replication and repetition of selected actions.

Figure 3
Olaver (11 mos.) notices traces left by his hand moving through spilled milk.

In terms of graphic evidence, Iconicity 1 encompasses what has been referred to as uncontrolled scribbling (e.g., Lowenfeld, 1947; Lansing, 1976). These early marks are sometimes accompanied by babbling, which may bring support to the notion that children are delighted in their new discovery. Yet, there is no evidence that, at this phase, vocal cues support the semiotic process. While in their early scribbling experience children tend to be oblivious to adults' attempts to have them focus more closely on their marks (Darras & Kindler, 1993, 1994b; Kindler & Darras, 1994), the influence of social interactions may begin to surface, as a response to feedback which children receive to their behavior. As Hurwitz and Day (1991) suggested, children's early explorations with mark making can be inhibited or discouraged if they involve messy play.

Iconicity 2

Iconicity 2 delineates the phase when a child's attention shifts from causing an effect to the effect itself. Marks and traces begin to matter beyond their mere existence and a child begins to explore relationships among them. Recognition of correspondence between certain gestures and their particular traces, and of similarity among some graphic forms indicate the presence of a basic classification mechanism centered around the principle of family resemblance (Rosh & Mervis, 1975).

The impact of the generic tendency which favors global generalizations and leads to predictability of outcomes is evident in this phase. At the same time, the emergence of repeated, predictable graphic forms allows for more than just an increase in regularity. Recognition of rules intrinsically offers the possibility of consciously exceeding them and the individuate tendency manifests itself in invention and experimentation with an increased number of visual forms.

The increased regularity and predictability of marks (See Figure 4), and especially the emergence of first shapes, are usually welcomed by adults, at least within the boundaries of Western culture, as signs of advanced picture making. Pictorial production influenced predominantly by the generic tendency is often received with more enthusiasm and encouragement than graphic production reminiscent of earlier pictorial attempts. The socially transmitted message seems to indicate to a child that organization, order, and predictability are the desirable outcomes of pictorial efforts. While children do not cease to engage in less organized "graphic babbling" (which can later be retraced in adolescent and adult spontaneous scribbles), through the feedback that they receive they begin to shape their understanding of the relative merit and value of various types of marks.

Figure 4

Iconicity 3

Adult reading of scribbles has traditionally been influenced by the notion that pictorial images represent things rather than dynamic events. Yet, children's early pictorial substitutions seem to be concerned with recording actions, not static objects (Darras & Kindler, 1993, 1994a; Kindler & Darras, 1994).

Analysis of vocal and gestural manifestations which accompany image making of two and three year old children, including the temporal and rhythmic correspondence between sounds, movements, and marks production, supports the hypothesis that the produced drawings are likely trajectories of people and objects in motion, rather than representations of tangible forms (Darras & Kindler, 1993, 1994a). Pictorial imagery emerges here as a result of a game, a story telling, a fantasy which is inscribed in time and space in a pluri-media fashion and which, at the instances where a drawing instrument touched the paper's surface, acquired some permanence. This new form of substitution marking Iconicity 3 draws on the connection with initial indexality; this time, however, the kinetic self-imitation extends to the understanding that imaginary actions can be pictorially recorded.

The significance of social interactions dramatically increases during this phase. Children begin to mimic each other's iconic gestures and sounds, this simulation activity being a manifestation of the generic tendency. Adult feedback is also very important, conducive in fact to the compression of this phase. Adults' insistence on decoding images as objects and things may communicate to the child that there is something illegitimate in making substitutions for actions only, or at least that they have less value than icons of things. This may prompt children to pursue the possibility of changing the focus of their pictorial attempts.

Iconicity 4

When a child realizes the potential of graphic forms rather than graphic actions to stand for objects and things rather than dynamic events, the substitution process continues through a pluri-media channel, with iconic gestures and verbal indicators still playing a significant role. This new discovery often emerges in combination with representations that characterized Iconicity 3 phase (see Figure 5).

Recognition of similarity and ability to sort, classify, and form associations which are fundamental in the emergence of these pictorial substitutions are guided by the generic tendency. The conception of equivalence and the understanding of "stand for" relationships do not rely on the identity of elements, but rather on prototypical, abstract properties and broad family resemblance (Arnheim, 1974; Rosh, 1978).

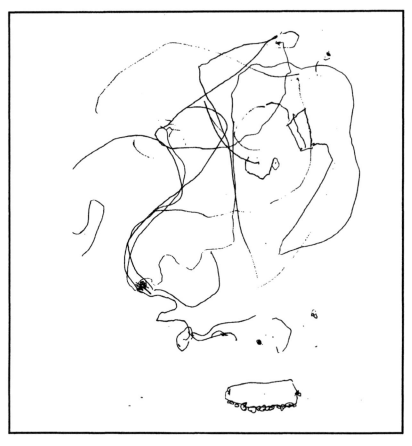

Figure 5
"A car for daddy who crashed his car." Quentin (2 yr. 10 mos.) made this drawing a few days after witnessing his father's car accident. He first drew the large scribble and then added the "new car" at the bottom of the page.

Iconicity 4 is marked by two strategies of substitution which children alternatively explore.

On one hand...the shapes they (children) produce in their controlled manipulations remind them of objects in the environment. On the other hand, the dawning realization that marks or shapes can convey meaning, together with the newly acquired skill to produce them at will, may prompt them to create their own symbols. (Hurwitz & Day, 1991, p. 72)

The tendency to "read-off" marks and attribute meaning to forms and shapes based on perceived associative visual cues (See Figure 6) coexists with the strategy according to which selected attributes of objects, visual or functional, guide production of images with defined, preselected meaning.

Children's drawings are at this point often generic in nature: a round, slightly differentiated shape may function as a mother, bus driver, or a cat. However, the substitutions, of which pictorial imagery is only a component, are far from being generic. Individualization successfully occurs through a vocal channel. A generic human, schematically represented by a closed, rounded form becomes a particular member of a family, often in particular time, place and circumstances, thanks to the verbal narrative which accompanies pictorial attempts. This individualization through the verbal channel also allows for easy changes in meaning without the need of additional graphic manipulations. The same form may take on a different identity, one which would best suit the flow of the child's thought or which can match best the perceived expectations of the audience.

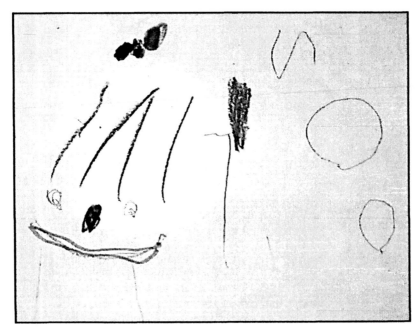

Figure 6
"My mom." Drawing by Jan (2 yr. 6 mos.)

During the Iconicity 4 phase, children increasingly acquire understanding that images can communicate socially shared meanings. They also realize
that the quality of such communication can be greatly enhanced by a pluri-
media approach. Opportunity to share drawings with peers and adults, and
the praise received when marks on paper can be explained as depictions of
people and objects, further encourage children to interweave visual, verbal,
and gestural cues.

While graphic production of children during the Iconicity 4 phase encompasses shapes which acquire meaning through some basic resemblance
along visual or functional attributes, geometric and informal scribbling and
marks-imprints of actions continue to permeate pictorial imagery.

Iconicity 5

Iconicity 5 phase is marked by a competent use of semiotic process and
extensive explorations in the realm of visual imagery. From an observer's
perspective, children's drawings begin to successfully carry meaning which
can be shared socially and appear to be independent of verbal narrative or
supporting gestural cues. Images produced by children increasingly share visual
characteristics and properties of objects which they represent. This, accompanied by an increase in complexity, detail, consideration of spatial organization of elements, and the evident, improved control over a drawing tool results in images that conform more closely to the common societal expectations of what a drawing should be like.

Even if pictorial imagery can function as a self-sufficient statement for
the possible interpreters, it often is just a part of pluri-media production. In
the Iconicity 5 phase, children readily engage in both egocentric and social
speech during their pictorial work (e.g., Darras & Kindler, 1992-1994; Kindler,
1994a; Kindler & Thompson, 1994; Thompson & Bales, 1991) and volunteer
verbal commentary or use iconic gestures to ensure accurate understanding
of their drawings (See Figure 7).

Peer conversations which accompany graphic explorations also support collaborative problem solving of pictorial dilemmas. Children share their
solutions with friends and offer each other advice on how to improve their
drawings (Kindler, 1994b). They spontaneously engage in imitative behavior
which involves re-interpretation and reinvention of popular culture themes
and other images produced by peers and older children (See Figures 8 and 9).

While from the Western cultural perspective art making is often conceived of as a solitary experience, children do not exhibit the need for such an
autonomy in their pictorial efforts. Neither are they particularly concerned
with the notion of individuality or uniqueness, nor "creative" merit of their
pictures. Instead, they focus on the efficiency with which their pictorial

Figure 7
Antoni (5 yrs. 1 mo.) explains his drawing to Jan using gestures and toys to complete the story

Figure 8
Johanna's (5 yrs. 6 mos.) drawing of the Little Mermaid

Figure 9

Antoni (4 yrs. 10 mos.) drew this scene of fire fighters in action (bottom drawing) inspired by the picture made by his older brother (8 yrs. 3 mos.)

representations function as carriers of intended meaning. They are more concerned with visual graphic logic which dictates what parts need to be drawn for a specific figure and how this is to be done (Golomb, 1992) than with the "artistic" merit of their work.

An interesting interplay between generic and individuate tendencies can be observed during Iconicity 5. A synthetic selection of defining features and attributes and increased reliance on pictorial representations of others is balanced by curiosity in the particular, the unusual, and the special. Consequently, even within very schematic drawings some degree of individualization can be detected. Children's pictorial production of this phase usually elicits praise and appreciation within contemporary Western culture, and children's drawings attain the preferred forms of "child art".

While we have identified the five Iconicity phases characterized by the emergence of new representational strategies, it is important to keep in mind that artistic development in the early childhood years cannot be conceptualized as a simple linear movement along a well defined continuum. As children grow, they develop an expending repertoire of strategies of pictorial representation which they apply according to the perceived needs and functions of their drawings and the context in which their work is produced (Wolf and Perry, 1988). Often, the difference between work created at school and at home, or between drawings made spontaneously and those completed in response to specific tasks can be significant, in terms of the used representational devices. The same child, within the span of a few hours, may produce images demonstrating great concern about visual resemblance of the drawn elements to their referents, as well as drawings that remain very synthetic and schematic. This is a reflection of the continuing struggle between the individuate and generic tendencies and provides strong evidence that children's strategies of pictorial representation are broader and more diverse than any linear model could account for.

Initial imagery
When drawings of nine- or ten-year-old children are mixed with those of adult art novices, it is often difficult to classify them according to age categories (Darras, 1994). Visual characteristics of these images are very similar and they seem to be guided by the same rules of representation (see Figure 10).

A conclusion which may be drawn from this phenomenon is that somewhere in the middle childhood years there is a point in the development of pictorial imagery which is universally accessible, but which cannot be crossed without additional stimulation, focused learning, and effort.

Figure 10
Drawing by an 82-year-old woman representing the farm where she grew up

If artistic development in early childhood can be regarded, at least to some extent, as a process of spontaneous emergence of pictorial abilities which is encouraged by social and cultural context and is guided by an internalized need to improve and expand the functional visual vocabulary, this clearly is not the case later in life. Acquisition of "initial imagery" (Darras, 1986; 1992a) marks this critical point of basic sufficiency. Attainment of this point, especially when accompanied by lack of motivation to move beyond this basic competency level, leads to stagnation in the development of pictorial imagery.

Initial imagery is an iconic system heavily influenced by the generic tendency and is characterized by the presence of simple but stable schema (See Figure 11) which seem to satisfy the basic needs of pictorial representation (Darras, 1992b; Darras & Kindler, 1993, 1994a, 1994b).

Initial imagery does not involve individualization. It is concerned with the generic, rather than the specific. One may speculate that this is related to the function and purpose of visual images in everyday lives of people whose careers do not demand a particular artistic involvement. In the case of direc-

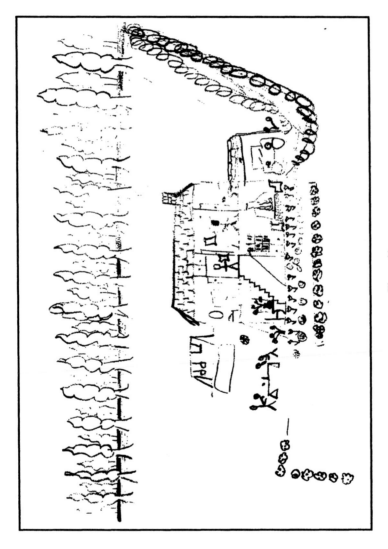

Figure 11
Drawing by a 25-year-old woman

tional maps, diagrams, or visual depictions which are often destined to simply complement vocal or written narrative, the need for increased complexity
is reduced, and the represented objects or people are sufficiently defined in
terms of global, rather than specific characteristics.

The perceived lack of need to be proficient in the use of visual vocabulary, especially in terms of image production, may be another factor which
inhibits the move beyond the initial imagery system. In contemporary Western cultures oral and written languages are assumed to be the dominant modes
of communication. While there are abundant examples of ways in which visual
imagery impacts human communication (e.g., traffic and directional signs,
color coding of hospital floors, sport team emblems, Valentine's Day hearts,
images of flowers on a greeting card, company logos, and diagrams which
accompany instructions to install home appliances, etc.), people tend to regard themselves as recipients rather than initiators of these one-way communications. Also, the symbolic way in which these images function de-empha-
sizes the need for increased individualization and differentiation of pictorial
imagery.

Furthermore, the lack of skills necessary for production of more elabo-
rate imagery perpetuates the idea that more sophisticated pictorial activity is
a privilege of the few who are destined for artistic future. The ethos of the
artist as one who possesses a unique talent, combined with lack of quality art
education which would allow for the development of abilities and confidence
in the realm of pictorial production, are conducive to keeping people locked
in the initial imagery system.

The cross-roads: Generic and individuate realms of pictorial imagery
Initial imagery provides a base from which, through cultural and social
influences including formal education, new forms of pictorial imagery emerge
(Darras & Kindler, 1994b). This new realm includes several alternative pictorial systems which are governed by either generic or individuate tendencies
(see Figure 12). The family of generic images includes representations which
display a tendency towards generalization. In contrast, the individuate family
is governed by attention to the unique and particular.

In traditional Western understanding, artistic expression tends to be associated with functioning within the individuate realm. Yet, an open-ended
definition of art and the multiplicity of possible cultural perspectives permit
consideration of pictorial production within both domains as relevant in the
discussion of artistic development.

Generic tendency
Within the pictorial realm governed by the generic tendency two streams
can be distinguished. We have called the first one writing tendency.

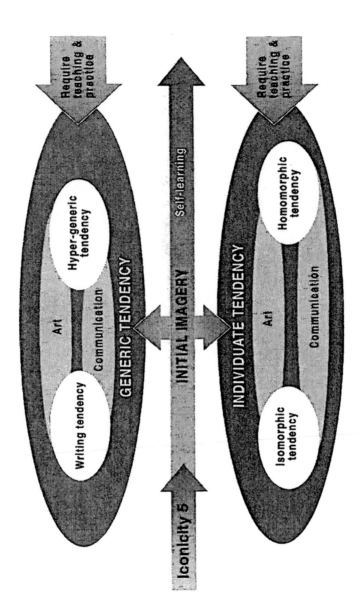

Figure 12

Development of pictorial imagery in adolescence and adulthood ©1994 Darras & Kindler

Writing tendency. This family of images includes schematic representations and pictograms. Synthetic substitution and capturing the essence of meaning through a very modest repertoire of marks characterize this type of pictorial production. Silhouettes of humans and animals in prehistoric cave drawings, pictorial narratives capturing ritual chants of Cuno Indians of Panama, as well as pictograms which were precursors of the Chinese writing system provide examples of this category of imagery.

The connection of this type of pictorial representation with the initial imagery system is close and evident (Darras, 1992b). Depending on one's historical and cultural perspective, these forms of pictorial representation can be considered as instances of "writing," or instances of "art," or both.

Hypergeneric tendency. At the extreme of the influence of the generic tendency lies the hypergeneric family of images. Here, the ambition is to create pictorial systems which define the perfectly generic, insensible to any transformations or variations. The pursuit in the ancient Greek art of the essence of the ideal, evident in artists' attempts to overcome reality and create instead representations of its ideal, provide a good example of hypergeneric tendency.

Similarly, some abstract geometric models as well as encyclopaedic and medical illustrations are governed to the extreme by the generic tendency. The rationale for their existence is to describe a rule or universal pattern and any attempts to individualize them would in fact be contradicting their purpose. This quest for condensation, synthesis, and compression of information in a pictorial icon was also evident in the drawings which were taken to outer space by the Pioneer 10 satellite to provide possible extraterrestrial spectators with some idea of human kind.

Individuate tendency

On the opposite side of the initial imagery continuum a territory governed by the individuate tendency can be found. This universe, influenced by principles of individualization and attention to particularities is also very rich and diversified. In our model we propose to organize it into two segments: imagery guided by homomorphic and isomorphic tendencies.

Homomorphic tendency. This realm of imagery encompasses work where artists' emotions, moods, or states of mind take precedence over considerations of visual realism. The creative process is propelled by individual rather than shared experiences and is concerned with interpretation rather than objective reality.

Within the imagery guided by the homomorphic tendency it is possible to further distinguish two branches. The first one, idiosyncratic, describes artistic production which is characterized by the artist's self-focus and search within, expression of individuality, or even eccentricity. Work of some expressionist artists, as well as images produced by the mentally handicapped, provide examples of pictorial production dominated by this tendency.

The second branch mirrors the evidence of the impact of sociocultural context on a personal narrative. This context may define both the subject matter of imagery, as well as its stylistic properties, but the particular rather than the global perspective is maintained by the artist. Much of 20th century art that is free of the obligation of visual realism and where interest in the reality lies not in the generalizability of experience but rather in the particular and unique, falls into this category of imagery.

Isomorphic tendency. Imagery which is concerned with close depiction of reality in its accidental nature demonstrates the influence of isomorphic tendency. Here, the artist is concerned with capturing the reality in a particular instant to account for an experience in its immediacy and uniqueness and with representing it in the most faithful manner. The ambition to seek correspondence between the real world and its pictorial representation leads to preoccupation with visual similarity and to experimentation with various perspective systems as means to achieve the illusion of depth to accurately account for three-dimensional objects within the constraints of a two-dimensional picture plane.

The invention of camera obscura opened the door to the development of photography as a medium of pictorial representation which allows to "imprint" the reality and provides the perfect means of substitution concerned with visual resemblance. Holography, cinematography, video, and Omnimax projections mark further advances in pictorial representation within the isomorphic family of imagery. The addition of sound, smell, temperature and kinaesthetic effects in the presentation of visual stimuli echoes the pluri-media world of representation which young children so masterfully explore. At the frontier of isomorphic imagery lies the territory of virtuality, where creation of a new reality, a cyber universe, is the goal.

Implications to art education

Our conceptualization of artistic development as a map, rather than a process of linear unfolding, provides new context for consideration of art education. The fact that it accommodates a broad definition of art and moves from often rhetorical considerations of diversity to recognition that there is more than one way to grow and develop in the artistic domain, makes this model particularly relevant in the context of multiculturalism and global education. By identifying the broad categories of imagery within which artistic growth can occur, our model is more cross-culturally relevant than the traditional stage approach. While we do not suggest that it is culture-free, it is culturally flexible and adaptable.

The realization of the usefulness of the continuing interplay between the generic and individuate tendencies in the development of pictorial imagery necessitates pedagogical approaches which help support and maintain this dynamic relationship. Neither of the tendencies should be discounted in the educational process, even if emphasis given to each of them may vary in time. Art education should provide children with opportunities to experiment with pictorial imagery on either side of the generic-individuate continuum. This, however, requires a suspension of value judgments which strongly favor production only within the selected realm.

Children who engage in "copying" behavior or who seem to be influenced by schemata developed by their peers or mediated by popular culture should not be regarded as less creative or dysfunctional, as Lowenfeld (1947) suggested. While they need to be challenged and exposed to a variety of pictorial interpretations of themes which surface in their drawings and to understand the value of personal, unique interpretation, their pictorial efforts within the generic realm should be acknowledged and validated. Especially when the initial imagery system has already emerged, art education curriculum should actively support both analytic and synthetic approaches to image making and recognize that pursuit of excellence can progress along several rather than single dimension.

Without negating the validity of efforts contained exclusively within the visual media, our model insists on the acknowledgment of the possibility of the pluri-media nature of artistic development. In early childhood art education more emphasis should be given to strategies which recognize the social nature of art explorations and which recognize contributions of language and gesture in the development of graphic production. Similarly, art education in middle-childhood and adolescence should be comprehensive of opportunities for pluri-media explorations and this should also be reflected in assessment and evaluation strategies.

Recognition of the significance of the sociocultural context, and, in particular, social interactions in artistic development, supports the need for art education which recognizes the positive potential and contribution of peer and child-adult interactions in the artistic development of an individual. Rather than centering on innate potential, our model leads to the recommendation of learning strategies which can be applied within Vygotsky's "zone of proximal development" (1978, p. 86). Our conceptualization of artistic development implies that, with very few exceptions, acquisition of pictorial abilities on either side of the initial imagery axis is dependent on purposeful, guided learning and practice, which quality art education needs to deliver.

We realize that it is often difficult to establish a very direct link between a theoretical model and classroom practice. We hope, however, that the conceptualization of artistic development which we propose in this chapter, with its account for diversity of imagery and attempt to systematically organize it, will provide teachers with new bases for curriculum considerations. We also hope that it will encourage further research in the complexity of artistic growth and ways in which it can be furthered through art education.

References

Arnheim, R. (1974). *Art and visual perception.* Berkeley, CA: University of California Press.

Bremmer, J., & Moore, S. (1984). Prior visual inspection and object naming: Two factors that enhance hidden feature inclusion in young children's drawings. *British Journal of Developmental Psychology, 2,* 371-376.

Colbert, C. B. (1984). Strategies of representation: Observational drawings of 4- and 5-year-old children. *Proceedings of the Arts and Learning Special Interest Group, American Educational Research Association, 2,* 112-117.

Colbert, C. B., & Taunton, M. (1988). Problems of representation: Preschool and third grade children's observational drawings of three dimensional model. *Studies in Art Education, 29*(2), 103-114.

Darras, B. (1986). L'audiovisual initial. *Panoramique, 2,* 82-87.

Darras, B. (1988). L'espace et son traitement dans les productions cinématographiques des débutants. *CERTEIC, 9,* 145-148.

Darras, B. (1992a). *L'Image de l'art: Livre 3.* Montreal, Canada: Editions Image de L'Art.

Darras, B. (1992b, August). The power of figurative writing. Keynote address at the International Society for Education through Art European Congress. Helsinki, Finland.

Darras, B. (1994, April). Initial imagery as an iconic communication system: A cross-cultural perspective. Paper presented at the Symposium on Artistic Development. University of Illinois, Champaign, IL.

Darras, B., & Kindler, A. M. (1992-1994). Unpublished data from a longitudinal comparative case study.

Darras, B., & Kindler, A. M. (1993). Emergence de l'imagerie. *MScope, 6,* 82-95.

Darras, B., & Kindler, A. M. (1994a, April). Image et l'éducation. L'AGIEM Rencontres Academiques. Bordeaux, France.

Darras, B. & Kindler, A. M. (1994b). Emergence de l'image et strategies cognitives. *Les Actes du 28e Congres mondial de la Societe internationale pour l'education artistique.* Montreal, Canada: INSEA. 119-123.

De Meredieu, F. (1974). *Le dessin d'enfant.* Paris: Editions Universitaires.

Dyson, A. H. (1982). The emergence of visible language: Interrelationships between drawing and early writing. *Visible Language, 6,* 360-381.

Dyson, A. H. (1988). Appreciate the drawing and dictating of young children. *Young Children,* 25-32.

Freeman, N. H. (1980). *Strategies of representation in young children.* New York: Academic Press.

Freinet C. (1969). *L'Apprentissage du dessin.* Neuchatel, Switzerland: Delachaux et Niestle.

Gardner, H. (1982). *Art, mind, and brain.* New York: Basic Books.

Golomb, C. (1992). *The child's creation of a pictorial world.* Berkeley, CA: University of California Press.

Gombrich, E. H. (1985). *Meditations on a hobby horse and other essays on the theory of art.* Chicago: University of Chicago Press.

Hurwitz, A., & Day, M. (1991). *Children and their art* (fifth edition). New York: Harcourt, Brace, Jovanovich.

Inagaki, K. (1992). Piagetian and post-Piagetian conceptions of development and their implications for science education in early childhood. *Early Childhood Research Quarterly, 7*(1), 115-133.

Janniere, A. (1985). *Heraclite, traducation et commentaire des fragments.* Paris: Aubier.

Kellogg, R. (1969). *Analyzing children's art.* Palo Alto, CA: National Press Book.

Kindler, A. M. (1992a, August). Reflective art explorations: Reaching into the zone of proximal development in early childhood artistic growth. Paper presented at the International Society for Education through Art Research Conference. Tampere, Finland.

Kindler, A. M. (1992b, August). Artistic process in early childhood: Implications of social context. Paper presented at the International Society for Education through Art European Congress, Helsinki, Finland,

Kindler, A. M. (1994a). Children and the culture of multicultural society. *Art Education, 47*(4), 54-60.

Kindler, A. M. (1994b). Artistic learning in early childhood: A study of social interactions. *Canadian Review of Art Education. 21*(2). 91-106.

Kindler, A. M., & Darras, B. (1994). Artistic development in context: Emergence and development of pictorial imagery in the early childhood years. *Visual Arts Research. 20*(2). 1-13.

Kindler, A. M., & Thompson, C. (1994, April). Social interactions and young children's artistic learning. Paper presented at the National Art Education Association National Convention, Baltimore, MD.

Korzenik, D. (1977). Saying it with pictures. In D. Perkins & B. Leonard (Eds.), *The arts and cognition.* Baltimore: Johns Hopkins University Press.

Lansing, K. (1976). *Art, artists, and art education.* Dubuque, IA: Kendall/Hunt.

Lelarge, R. (1978). Pourquoi Wallon aujourd'hui? *Millieux et Activities Graphique, Vers L'éducation Nouvelle, 322,* 4-9.

Lowenfeld, V. (1947). *Creative and mental growth.* New York: Macmillan.

Lowenfeld, V. & Brittain, W. L. (1970). *Creative and mental growth.* (5th Edition). New York: Macmillan.

Luquet, G. H. (1913). *Les dessins d'un enfant.* Paris: Alcan.

Lurcat, L. (1979). *L'activité graphique a l'école maternelle.* Paris: ESF.

Paget, G. W. (1932). Some drawings of men and women made by children of certain non-European races. *Journal of the Royal Anthropological Institute, 62,* 127-144.

Peirce, C. S. (1931-35). *Collected papers.* Cambridge, MA: Harvard University Press.

Piaget, J. (1978). *La formation du symbole chez l'enfant.* Paris: Delachaux.

Rosh, E. (1978). Human categorization. In N. Warren (Ed.), *Advances in cross-cultural psychology*, Vol. 2. London: Academic Press.

Rosh, E., & Mervis, C. B. (1975). Family resemblances: Studies in the internal structure of categories. *Cognitive Psychology, 7*, 573-605.

Thom, R. (1980). *Modèles mathématiques de la morphogenèse*. Paris: C. Bourgeois.

Thompson, C., & Bales, S. (1991). "Michael doesn't like my dinosaurs": Conversations in a preschool classroom. *Studies in Art Education, 33*(1), 43-55.

Vygotsky, L. S. (1978). *Mind in a society*. Cambridge: Harvard University Press.

Wallon, H. (1945). *De l'acte à la pensée*. Paris: Flammarion.

Wallon, P., Cambier, A., & Engelhart, D. (1990). *Le dessin d'enfant*. Paris: Presses Universitaires de France.

Walsh, D. J. (1993). Art as socially constructed narrative: Implications for early childhood education. *Art Education Policy Review, 94*(6), 18-22.

Weitz, M. (1979). The role of theory in esthetics. In M. Rader (Ed.), *A modern book of esthetics*. New York: Holt, Rinehart, & Winston.

Widlocher, D. (1965). *L'Interprétation des dessins d'enfants*. Bruxelles, Belgium: Dessart.

Wilson B., & Wilson, M. (1977). An iconoclastic view of the imagery sources in the drawings of young people. *Art Education, 30*(1), 5-11.

Wilson, B., & Wilson, M. (1982). The case of the disappearing two-eyed profile: Or how children influence the drawings of little children. *Review of Research in Visual Arts Education, 15*, 19-32.

Wilson, B., & Wilson, M. (1984). Children's drawings in Egypt: Cultural style acquisition as graphic development. *Visual Arts Research, 10*(1), 13-26.

Wilson, B., & Wilson, M. (1985). The artistic tower of Babel: Inextricable links between culture and graphic development. *Visual Arts Research, 11*(1), 90-104.

Wolf, D., & Perry, M. (1988). From end points to repertoires: New conclusions about drawing development. *Journal of Aesthetic Education, 22*(1), 17-35.

THE "U" AND THE WHEEL OF "C"

DEVELOPMENT AND DEVALUATION OF GRAPHIC SYMBOLIZATION AND THE COGNITIVE APPROACH AT HARVARD PROJECT ZERO

The 5-year-old child drawing an unhappy flower creases her brow into a sad furrow and stoops over her crayons and paper. The 35-year-old professional artist steps back from the charcoal drawing she is creating at her easel and assumes the position of the model who is standing before her.

The 5-year-old's free-wheeling arm motion spreading crayon on paper is so fluid and sensual that observers suspect she is more involved with the exploration of the medium than the creation of the picture of the flower. Indeed, the down-turned tangles of lines on her paper may really just be scribbles that the child has, after-the-fact, decided to call a sad flower.

The 35-year-old artist is wildly scratching her charcoal on newsprint. Disappearing with apparent abandon into a black cloud of charcoal dust, she looks more like a child in a dustbin than a professional at work. Is it possible that the emerging mountain of dark moving lines has anything to do with the shape of the model? Don't think to dismiss these swarms of lines as scribbles. The marks on the artist's paper comprise what is called a gesture drawing.

JESSICA DAVIS

Young children and adult artists alike create abstract drawings (some that look like scribbles); they employ visual metaphors (like flowers that express sadness); they may seem viscerally attached to the works of art they create (through their facial expressions or stances as they work); they obviously experience and enjoy the medium in which they work; and they explore that medium to create with apparent confidence and ease.

The behaviors I describe are examples of the characteristics that have led various individuals (from romantic philosophers to cognitive developmentalists) to make serious comparisons between the artistic behaviors of young children and adult artists (e.g., Arnheim, 1969; Gardner, 1973, 1979, 1980, 1982; Read, 1945; Schaefer-Simmern, 1948; Winner, 1982).

Certainly there is at least as long a list of behaviors that separate the playful artistry of 5-year-old children from the skillful work of professional artists. But the discovery and exploration of similarities has generated a line of research that not only points to an intriguing course of development, but also raises some challenges to those arbitrators of education who ultimately chart our course to cultural survival (Davis, 1991; 1993; Davis & Gardner, 1993a; Gardner, 1973).

Harvard Project Zero

Harvard Project Zero was founded at the Harvard Graduate School of Education in 1967 by the philosopher Nelson Goodman. The project emerged on the crest of the wave of what is known as the cognitive revolution. This revolution of thought emerged in the mid-1950s and challenged the behaviorist approach that had dominated American psychology since the 1920s.

In response to the limitations of a behavior-based model which attended to individuals' visible response to stimuli, cognitivists were eager to explore what happened beyond sight, where individuals' thought processes actually transpired. Intrigued by the interchange between human problem-solving and the creation of the electronic computer, cognitivists were interested in how human beings process information, as well as the ways in which they construct and represent knowledge through various systems of symbols.

Music is one system of symbols (notes); language is another (words); and the graphic symbols of drawing (images) comprise yet another. The Symbol Systems Approach was the cognitive perspective that prevailed at Harvard Project Zero. Children's artistic development in the various symbol systems was the object of the project's research (Davis, 1992; Davis & Gardner, 1992, 1993; Ives, Silverman, Kelly, & Gardner, 1981).

Characteristic of cognitive initiatives, Harvard Project Zero was an inter-disciplinary effort from the start. Embracing the philosophical tenets of Nelson Goodman (1976, 1978), the project also found inspiration in arts research done by psychologist Rudolf Arnheim (1966, 1969, 1974) and the research into children's construction of knowledge done by genetic epistemologist Jean Piaget (e.g. Piaget & Inhelder, 1948). Early Project Zero researchers wondered whether children's development in the aesthetic dimensions discussed by Goodman and Arnheim would resemble the linear hierarchical stages proposed by Piaget (Davis, 1992; Davis & Gardner, 1992; Gardner, 1973).

Project Zero's early research was intended to inform practice in a new brand of art education, one which focused on the arts as cognitive processes of constructing and comprehending understanding. More traditional approaches had focused on the arts as a means for children to express and release energy or emotion (Lowenfeld, V. & Brittain, W.L. 1964). The "zero" in the project's title represented a playful assessment of the current state of knowledge about an arts education, which viewed the arts *not* as separate extracurricular activities to be *appreciated* (as opposed to science which was to be *understood*) but as serious intellectual arenas, important domains of learning.

Project Zero researchers in the Development Group were impressed by the apparent similarity that exists between the early performances of young children in visual art, language, and music, and the work of professional artists, writers, and musicians. Young children who were creating "sad flowers" on paper were metaphorically expressing the trip down in an elevator as "melting," and setting their vivid experiences to music of their own design. Project Zero's careful observation of these artful processes of thought inspired them to label the age of five as "the golden age of creativity" (Gardner, 1982).

Taking the comparison between child and artist seriously, Project Zero researchers framed their developmental studies around the same aesthetic criteria that were applied to the work of professional artists. For example, early research considered the extent to which young children's drawings were balanced, according to Arnheim's criteria for balance (Winner, Mendelsohn, Garfunckel, Arrangio, & Stevens, 1981). Based on Goodman's definition of repleteness (Goodman, 1976), researchers considered the extent to which children exploited the aesthetic potential of line: whether they, for example, varied the width and direction of lines in order to express different meanings (Carothers, & Gardner, 1979; Ives, 1984).

Project Zero researchers considered the development of facilities in the construction and communication of meaning through art as the acquisition of a kind of literacy. Through internal symbols or representations, the individual child or producer of art constructs a world view. Through external symbols or representations, the individual shares a world view. This happens when that construction of meaning is recognized or reconstructed by a receptive, equally active meaning-maker, the perceiver of art.

This view of active construction of meaning by producer and perceiver required that study of the development of aesthetic literacy address both parts of this cognitive construction: production and perception. Project Zero's early research into the development of these mutually informative processes uncovered a curious portrait (Gardner, 1980, 1982; Ives, Silverman, Kelly, & Gardner, 1981; Rosenblatt & Winner, 1988; Winner & Gardner, 1981).

Production - Perception Paradox
At the same time that children's own *production* of art work is declining in such aesthetic dimensions as balance and expression (in the period of middle childhood deemed the "literal stage") children's *perception* of these aesthetic properties seems to be on the rise (Carothers & Gardner, 1979). Project Zero researchers explored this curious portrait in and across symbol systems

It is preschool children's drawings that are most often thought to contain the expressive quality of work of adult artists. The symbols employed have universal appeal and they are often organized into balanced or unified compositions (see Figure 1).

Between ages 8 through 11, what Project Zero researchers described as the "flavorfulness of children's drawing" is, however, on the decline. Because children seem dominated in their productions by a quest for the replication of photographic reality or stereotypical equivalencies thereof, their work appears more slavishly executed, less unified or balanced, and too constrained to be truly expressive of emotion. (Rosenblatt & Winner, 1988). Lines that are replete with emotion are often replaced with stick figures and written words. (see Figure 2).

Nonetheless, at the same time that the child's own drawings begin to show less expressive use of line, the child is becoming better able to recognize that aesthetic element in the drawings of others. Although the child's own drawings appear to be fragmented, the child is now able to recognize unity or balance in the drawings of others (Davis & Gardner, 1993; Gardner, 1980, 1982, 1990).

Figure 1
A 5 year old's drawing of "happy."

Figure 2
An 11 year old's drawing of "angry."

This phenomenon may be more explanatory than discrepant. Indeed, a more developed experiential awareness of the aesthetic potential of drawings may account for the "literal stage" child's disappointment in his or her own work (Rosensteil & Gardner, 1977). The inhibition that new awareness may cultivate can be seen as intruding on the child's freedom to produce a "flavorful" drawing. Experienced expectations of perception may translate into constraints on production.

It has also been suggested that children aged 8-11 have become so ensconced in the symbol systems embraced by the culture of school that they now want their drawings to accomplish what words and numbers can do: to more precisely describe. Although the power of aesthetic symbols may lie in the trueness of imprecision, school children are being enculturated to celebrate the clear-cut edges of right and wrong. They want their drawings to tell the real *story* and enumerate the *correct* number of details. Their literal bent lowers their tolerance for the abstract. "A flower cannot be sad. It has no feelings." "Scribbles are messy!"

In any case, while the professional artist is covered with charcoal dust around an abstract drawing that is vested with animation and apparent abandon, the "literal stage" child is reaching for rulers and erasers in hopes of achieving exactitude. The dreariness that drawing has acquired may account for the fact that by adolescence, most individuals have abandoned the activity completely (Winner, 1982; Davis, 1991, 1993b).

The U-curve of artistic development

What emerges from these observations of artistic thinking in the symbol system of drawing is the view of a course of development quite different from the hierarchical progressions advanced by Piaget. In Piaget's structure, the young child is at the bottom of a steep linear ascent to the pinnacle of thought represented by mature exemplars. With young children producing drawings that seem similar to the work of professional artists, and children in middle childhood declining in that facility, the course of development in graphic symbolization looks more like a "U" (Davis, 1991, 1993b; Davis, in press; Davis & Gardner, 1993; Gardner & Winner, 1982).

In U-shaped cognitive development, early facilities appear, disappear or submerge, and reappear (Strauss, 1982). In drawing development, the early appearance marks one high point of the "U," the submersion in middle childhood, the floor or trough of the "U," and the full development of the capacity, the other high point of the "U." As most individuals stop drawing after middle childhood (transforming the "U" to an "L"), it is only the artistically persistent (a choice that appears to be made by adolescence) who seem to ascend in their development to the other high point of the "U" (see Figure 3).

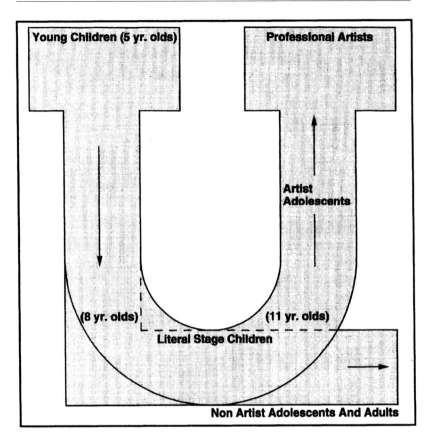

Figure 3
U-curve of graphic development.

In recent research, I tested this hypothesis of U-shaped development in graphic symbolization through a comparison between child and adult art (Davis, 1991; 1993a; 1993b; Davis, in press). Prior comparisons between the artwork of young children and adult artists seemed to have been made haphazardly. Proponents would compare, for example, *any* Miro drawing with *any* drawing by a 5-year-old child (Gardner, 1980). In my study, I put constraints around the comparison by giving the same drawing tasks to young children and to artists.All subjects in the study were asked to draw, howsoever they pleased, the target emotions of "happy," "sad," and "angry." Subjects were grouped by age and experience. There was a group of 5-year-olds; two groups of children in the "literal stage" (one group of 8-year-olds; the other of 11-year-olds); a group of adolescents (14-year-olds) who considered themselves to be artists, a group of adolescents (14-year-olds) who considered themselves to be non-artists; a group of non-artist adults, and a group of professional working artists. Each group consisted of twenty subjects.

Four hundred and twenty drawings of the three target emotions were scored by expert judges on the following aesthetic criteria: overall expression; overall balance; and the use of line and composition, as appropriate to the target emotion being expressed. These criteria reflect the view from which the expression of emotion through line and composition is considered a cognitive achievement of the thoughtful construction of meaning.

Overall, the results confirmed the hypothesis of U-shaped development in the production of graphic symbolization. On all criteria, the 5-year-old children's scores, like those of the adolescent artists, were most like those of the professional artists. For each of the four dimensions, the professional artists' scores were significantly different from all other groups; but *not* significantly different from the scores of the adolescent artists and the 5-year-old children (in post hoc comparisons <.05). These observations confirmed the placement of 5-year-old children and professional artists at the two high ends of the "U."

The "trough" of the U was occupied by the low scores of the literal stage 8- and 11-year-old children. Charting development on the other side of the literal stage, the artistically persistent adolescents were seen to go on to reclaim and/or surpass the scores of the 5-year-old children; but the non-artist adolescents did not. Indeed, on overall expression and overall balance, the non-artist adolescents scored lower than the children in the literal stage and the non-artist adults scored even lower than that. These observations point to the dissolution or loss of some early abilities to construct meaning out of graphic symbols.

Children possess an early gift in artistic production that bears similarities to the artistry of professional artists and seems to be lost to most of them by middle childhood. What causes the loss and how and why might skills of graphic symbolization be developed and marshaled into the service of developing understanding?

Some challenges to arbitrators of education

There are those who charge the rude intruder of school with the loss of the child's early gift of artistry and the onset of literal expectations which challenge free creative expression (Davis, 1993a; Davis & Gardner, 1993). Certainly the contextual difference between 5-year-olds and children in the literal stage is the more extensive experience of school, a place in which many (but not all) children congregate through adolescence.

Some educators regard young children as empty vessels who come to the school house to be filled with the gifts of knowledge that schooling affords. This attitude too often harbors a disregard for the gifts of knowing which preschool children already bear. The ability to produce an expressive and balanced drawing is one of these gifts. And the lack of continued artistic training to develop these early skills represents a devaluation of both the preschool child's state of knowing and the cognitive arena of artistic expression. There has not been much research into the implications such negative experience may have across symbolic domains. But more recent research at Harvard Project Zero points to the possibility that artistic learning may have a positive impact on students' experience in school. Twenty-five years after Project Zero's early developmental research, researchers are now observing children as artists within the contexts of school and beyond school walls: in museums and community art centers. Resonant narratives attest to the power of arts production to provide students with positive habits of learning from the realization of cultural roots and individual potential to the discipline of seeing a project through from beginning to end (Davis, Soep, Maira, Remba, Putnoi, 1993).

If educators were to embrace the cognitive view of arts production underlying the research described in this chapter, they might take more seriously the loss of the early gift of artistry. If graphic symbolization were to be regarded as an important venue for the making of important meaning, the place of the arts in students' daily education would have to be rethought.

Traditionally, this loss of artistry is dismissed as the loss of a facility that really only needs to be developed by the minority, those of us who will go on to become professional artists. How bleak for our educational system if we were to embrace that approach across disciplines and only teach writing to those who will become professional writers, or math only to those who will become mathematicians.

Most importantly, the ability to make meaning out of symbols entitles the individual to active participation in the cultural conversations through which human beings individuate and unite themselves. By acknowledging and developing children's early gifts in this area, educators have the power to enrich the conversation that perpetuates our cultural survival.

If educators could be convinced of the importance and prevalence of this early gift of thought, how might they reconfigure students' experience in school so that loss could be avoided? The easy and clear reply is that drawing would be taught as regularly as any of the other symbol systems valued and transmitted through school. Every day along with math and science (and of course dance and music), drawing would be taught in a curriculum that might have as its objective the cultivation and continuation of human culture. We might even call this new approach a "culturriculum."

Charting a course to cultural survival

A "culturriculum" would respect the culture or world view represented by every child in the classroom and the power of the arts to give form and to connect that individual world view to: the world view of cultures referring to families, communities, schools; cultures referring to nationalities, races, and ethnicities; and ultimately culture referring to the common humanity that all of us share. That universal culture directly informs and is informed by the culture of the individual child. The wheel that connects these different manifestations of culture is motored by that which humans uniquely do (the creation of meaning through symbols), the source and fruits of artistic thinking, the ongoing cognitive activities of production and perception (See Figure 4).

We can consider this interconnectedness in terms of specific symbolic constructions. For example, the culture or world view of the individual child is imprinted on the child's drawing which reflects and informs the cultures of families, schools, and communities as they are imprinted on the art (e.g. representational reproductions or colorful murals) that is or is not displayed at home or school or in the community. Certainly that art informs and is informed by the world views imprinted on the artistic productions of cultures of nations (e.g., Chinese brush paintings or Chicano murals) and ultimately humankind in the universal potential of art to embody our shared humanity. And perhaps nowhere is that universal expression more evident than in the drawings of young children.

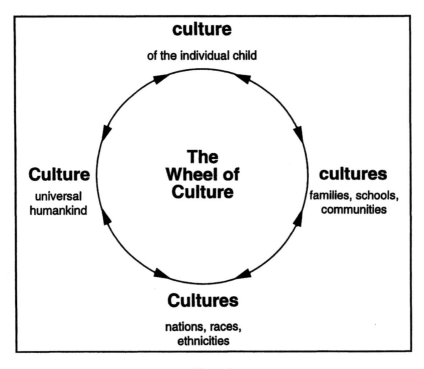

Figure 4
Culturriculum attends to The Wheel of Culture

Conclusion

Extending the image of the wheel, the discussion ends where it began with a look at the construction of meaning through symbols as the distinct feature of humankind. This recognition drew cognitivists away from a behaviorist approach which centered on the activities humans share with animals. It is a view of symbols as the legislators of human knowledge that informed a body of arts research at Harvard Project Zero and the study of similarities between the playful productions of young children and the work of professional artists. The story that has unfolded is one of promise and loss and cultural devaluation of a process of meaning-making.

It will be the work of educators to translate this knowledge into practice that can rewrite the story. Educators need to find ways to celebrate and develop early gifts and to recognize the power of aesthetic symbols to frame knowledge that is unique. I end with a challenge to educators reminiscent of the challenge that confronted arts researchers early on at Harvard Project Zero. It is the challenge that emerges from a recognition of artistic production and perception as serious cognitive activities worthy of respect and cultivation.

The author is grateful for the support of the Bauman, Dodge, Ford, and Nathan Cummings Foundations.

References

Arnheim, R. (1966). *Toward a Psychology of Art.* Berkeley, CA: University of California Press.

Arnheim, R. (1969). *Visual thinking.* London: Faber & Faber, Ltd.

Arnheim, R. (1974). *Art and visual perception, A psychology of the creative eye.* Berkeley, CA: University of California Press.

Carothers, T., & Gardner, H. (1979). When children's drawings become art, the emergence of aesthetic production and perception. *Developmental Psychology, 15*(5), 570-580.

Davis, J. H. (1991). *Artistry Lost: U-shaped development in graphic symbolization.* Doctoral dissertation. Harvard Graduate School of Education.

Davis, J. H. (1992, August). *The History of the Arts at Harvard Project Zero.* A paper prepared for the Annual Meeting of the American Psychological Association, Division 10, Washington, DC.

Davis, J. H. (1993a). Why Sally Can Draw: An Aesthetic Perspective. In E. Eisner. (Ed.), *Educational Horizons , 71*(2), (pp. 86-93).

Davis, J. H. (1993b). *Drawing's demise: U-shaped development in graphic symbolization.* Adapted from a paper presented at SRCD Biennial Meeting, New Orleans, LA.

Davis, J., & Gardner, H. (1992). The cognitive revolution: Its consequences for the understanding and education of the child as artist. In R. A. Smith. (Ed.), *1992 Yearbook of the National Society for the Study of Education.* Chicago.

Davis, J., & Gardner, H. (1993). The arts and early childhood education: A cognitive developmental portrait of the young child as artist.. In Spodek, B. (Ed.), *Handbook of research in early childhood education.* Second Edition. New York: Macmillan.

Davis, J., Soep, E., Maira, S., Remba, N., Putnoi, D., Gardner, H., & Gonzalez-Pose, P. (1993) *Safe Havens: Portraits of Educational Effectiveness in Community Art Centers that Focus on Education.* Cambridge, MA. Project Co-Arts. Harvard Project Zero.

Gardner, H. (1973). *The arts and human development.* New York: John Wiley & Sons.

Gardner, H. (1979). Entering the world of the arts: The child as artist. *Journal of Communication, 29*(4), 146-156.

Gardner, H. (1980). *Artful scribbles.* New York: Basic Books.

Gardner, H. (1982). *Art, mind, and brain.* New York: Basic Books.

Gardner, H. (1990) *Art Education and Human Development.* Los Angeles: Getty Center for Education in the Arts.

Gardner, H., & Winner, E. (1982). First intimations of artistry. In S. Strauss. (Ed.), *U-Shaped behavioral growth.* New York: Academic Press.

Goodman, N. (1976). *Languages of art.* Indianapolis, IN: Hackett Publishing Co.

Goodman, N. (1978). *Ways of worldmaking.* Indianapolis, IN: Hackett Publishing Co.

Ives, S. W. (1984.) The development of expressivity in drawing. *British Journal of Educational Psychology, 54*(2),152-159.

Ives, S.W., Silverman, J., Kelly, H., & Gardner, H. (1981). Artistic development in the early school years: A cross-media study of storytelling, drawing, and clay modeling. *Journal of Research and Development in Education, 14*(3), 91-105.

Lowenfeld, V., & Brittain, W.L. (1964). *Creative and mental growth.* New York: Macmillan Co.

Piaget, J., & Inhelder, B. (1948). *The child's construction of space.* New York: Norton.

Read, H. (1945). *Education through art.* New York: Pantheon (reprinted without date).

Rosenblatt, E., & Winner, E. (1988). The art of children's drawing. *Journal of Aesthetic Education,* 22(1).

Rosensteil, A.K., & Gardner, H. (1977). The effect of critical comparisons upon children's drawing. *Studies in Art Education, 19*(1), 36-44.

Schaefer-Simmern, H. (1948). *The unfolding of artistic activity.* Berkeley, CA: University of California Press.

Strauss, S. (Ed.). (1982). *U-shaped behavioral growth.* New York: Academic Press.

Winner, E. (1982). *Invented worlds. The psychology of the arts.* Cambridge, MA: Harvard University Press.

Winner, E. & Gardner, H. (1981). The art in children's drawings. *Review of Research in Visual Arts Education, 14*,18-31.

Winner, E., Mendelsohn, E., Garfunkel, G., Arangio, S., & Stevens, G. (1981). *Are children's drawings balanced? A new look at drawing: Aesthetic aspects.* Unpublished symposium presentation at the Society for Research in Child Development. Boston.

DRAWING DEVELOPMENT

THE CHILD'S UNDERSTANDING
OF THE DUAL REALITY OF
PICTORIAL REPRESENTATIONS

Pictures are unique among objects in that they have a dual reality. They are both flat surfaces covered with marks and representations of real or virtual three-dimensional worlds. Picture perception, identifying what a picture represents, is a spontaneous process that does not require a conscious differentiation of the two realities. But picture production does. Making a representational drawing or painting involves purposeful manipulation of marks on a surface to denote real objects in the world. Success in such activity depends on the extent to which the artist can render explicit to himself the visuo-spatial properties of physical objects, the layout of the marks on the picture surface, and the relationships between them. In this chapter I argue that the course of development in children's drawing is determined by a growth of awareness of the dual reality of pictorial representations. Children's skills in making realistic depictions improve as they become able to differentiate and reflect upon the relationships between picture content and picture surface.

First, I will briefly summarize the stages in drawing development and discuss some of the explanations put forward by psychologists to account for these stages. I will argue that an integrated model of the drawing process and drawing development must take into account the child's comprehension of pictorial representation. I will then describe the main components of an understanding of the dual reality of pictures, showing via examples of empirical studies the importance of these components in the development of drawing skills.

EMIEL REITH

Stages in drawing development

Since the turn of the century, cognitive psychologists have been concerned with describing and explaining the development of representational drawing in children (for a review of the major findings and issues, see Cox, 1992; Freeman & Cox, 1985; Lange-Kuettner & Thomas, 1995; Thomas & Silk, 1990). As far as the description of the age-related trends is concerned, there is a wide consensus. Children start producing marks on paper sometime between the ages of one and two when they have acquired sufficient motor coordination to experiment with moving a marker over a surface. The child's scribbles gradually differentiate into specific, discrete forms such as curved and jagged lines, straight lines, dots, and eventually closed elliptical forms. Representational drawing emerges at about age three when children notice that the marks on the page look like something, which leads them to label their productions. From this moment on they initiate their drawings with the intention to portray a particular object. The child's early depictions are both schematic and generic: a simple graphic figure, such as a circle with a few added lines and dots, stands for the object as a whole, and the child will use the same figure to represent a wide range of objects. At first, the forms on the page are merely juxtaposed instead of being coordinated into unified wholes. For instance, a hat is placed well above the head, and buttons alongside the body. The figures denoting objects are not organized in any systematic fashion with respect to the axes of the page. By about age 5, children join the elements of a figure to show the part-whole relationships within an object. They organize and locate the figures in a non-random fashion on the page.

One of the aspects of drawing development that has caught the interest of many psychologists is the passage from "intellectual realism" to "visual realism" (Luquet, 1927). After age five, children become progressively more concerned with depicting all the relevant features and details of objects. At first they do so without considering whether or not the features might actually be visible simultaneously from a particular view point (e.g., a face in profile with two eyes), or from any view point at all (e.g., food in the stomach). Only after the age of 8 or 9 do children attempt to portray the view-specific appearance of objects and scenes. They include only those features that are visible from a particular perspective and adjust the location, shape and size of figures on the page to match what an observer might see. For instance, only one leg of a horseman and only the top of a tree behind a house are shown; objects in the background are made smaller than objects in the foreground, etc. Although children now show a heightened interest in adult techniques of realistic depiction, such as vanishing-point perspective, foreshortening and shading, it is rare, and usually not until adolescence, that children become skilled in using these pictorial devices to produce something close to a photographic likeness.

Whereas there is a general agreement among psychologists about the nature of the stages in the development of children's drawing, there is considerable debate about how these age-related changes can be best explained. To summarize the literature, I will mention the main factors that have been invoked and point out the problems that each factor leaves unresolved.

Many theories stress the role of *knowledge about objects*. Drawings are believed to reflect the subject's mental representations and conceptual knowledge about the objects they draw. Drawings become more accurate and detailed as children's mental models of the world become more extensive and differentiated. This perspective on drawing has led some psychologists to devise drawing tests for measuring intellectual development (Goodenough, 1926; Harris 1963). More recently, however, authors have stressed the *negative* influences of knowledge on drawing. It has been shown that reference to the known physical structure of an object prevents young children from portraying its view-specific appearance (e.g. Cox, 1989; Crook, 1985; Freeman & Janikoun, 1972; Luquet, 1927). They actually make more accurate depictions when they are asked to represent unfamiliar objects, or meaningless forms (e.g. Reith, 1988). Thus, we see that the role of knowledge about objects is ambiguous: it can be conducive to the production of more differentiated drawings and, at the same time, it can hinder visual realism. What a theory of drawing development needs to explain is why young children tend to portray their knowledge about the relevant, invariant features and structure of objects, whereas older children are more likely to depict the variant, view-specific appearance of objects.

In this context, some authors have argued for the role of *spatial cognition*, that is, children's ability to mentally represent, manipulate, and reason about spatial relationships (Piaget & Inhelder, 1956; Piaget, Inhelder & Szeminska, 1960; Lange-Kuettner & Reith, 1995). Thus, the schematic and unorganized drawings of young children are associated with an inability to construct explicit spatial relations between objects, whereas the more structured drawings of older children show children's mastery of simple spatial relationships such as proximity, separation, enclosure, continuity and closedness between objects or parts of objects ("topological space"). Visual realism becomes possible when subjects understand that the appearance of the environment depends on one's location within it and are able to construct explicit mental representations of objects seen from different vantage-points ("projective space"). Most authors have referred to the development of spatial cognition only to explain changes in the way subjects mentally represent the objects they draw. They have not considered its role in ability to manipulate lines on the page and in understanding the correspondence between the structure of the two-dimensional line configuration and the features of the real objects in three-dimensional space.

Some authors have related the stages in drawing skills to changes in *perceptual processes*. Young children's drawings are global, schematic, and unorganized because their perception is *syncretic*: objects are perceived either as unitary wholes or as ensembles of unrelated parts (Claparède, 1938; Meili, 1931). The more articulated drawings of later stages (intellectual realism) reflect *synthetic* perception in which the parts composing the whole are integrated in a hierarchical fashion. The emergence of visual realism has frequently been associated with a growth in ability to shift from the natural mode of perception, in which one attends to the visual world, seeing objects as solid, bounded and functional entities in their true physical shape and size, located in three-dimensional space, to a pictorial mode of perception in which one attends to the visual field, that is, the perspective of the environment from a fixed vantage point (Gibson, 1971, 1986; Edwards, 1979). In this mode of perception one treats the visible world as if it were a picture projected in front of the eyes. One notices that distant objects project smaller images, that surfaces of far objects are hidden by those of closer objects, and that the parallel edges of surfaces recede in depth converge. Artists have devised technical aids to facilitate this way of processing visual information. One of these devices, called a da Vinci Window after its inventor, consists of a sheet of glass placed like a window between oneself and the scene to be drawn. While viewing with one eye from a fixed position, one traces the edges of the model directly onto the glass. By thus treating the drawing surface as a projection plane, one obtains a picture in perfect perspective (see Figure 1).

Although visual realism in drawing emerges at age 8 or 9, recent research provides evidence that younger children can portray certain aspects of the visual projection of objects when they are given clear instructions (e.g., Barrett, Beaumont & Jennett, 1985; Reith, 1988) or are provided with a facilitating device such as a da Vinci Window (Reith, Steffen & Gillieron, 1994; Lange-Kuettner & Reith, 1995). When using this device, five-year-olds produce perspective drawings of objects that are virtually identical to those of adults. If children, just as adults, have access to the visual projection of the world, then why do they not attend to it spontaneously? Clearly there seems to be a conceptual problem rather than a perceptual deficit. Children may have difficulty making a distinction between appearance and reality (Flavell, Green & Flavell, 1986), between an object as a meaningful, three-dimensional "thing" and as a two-dimensional visual image (Reith, 1988, 1994; Reith & Dominin, 1997; Reith & Liv, 1995). Since attending to the visual image of objects or scenes is useful only for making pictures, it is likely that children's readiness to do so depends on their understanding of pictures and on their own drawing experience.

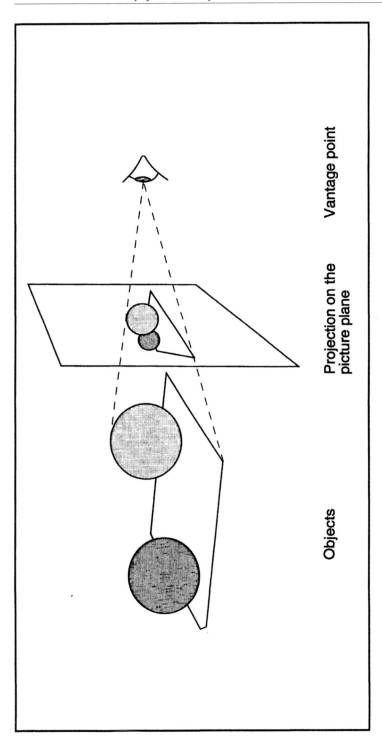

Vantage point

Projection on the picture plane

Objects

Figure 1
In a perspective drawing, the picture surface is used as a projection plane.

Most contemporary researchers, inspired by the work of scholars of pictorial representation such as Gombrich (1960) and Arnheim (1956), have shifted their attention away from general psychological processes, such as mental representation and perception, toward the role of knowledge and skills that pertain specifically to drawing (e.g., Freeman, 1980; Golomb, 1992; Willats, 1985, 1995). Vivid mental representations and the ability to attend to visual projection are helpful for drawing but they do not guarantee success: A subject may conjure up a very precise image of her house or the face of a familiar person, yet be unable to draw a good likeness of them. She requires in addition the *depiction skills* for translating what she imagines or perceives using lines on paper. According to this perspective, learning to draw is a matter of learning a language with its own vocabulary and syntax. The stages in drawing development reflect the steps in which children acquire through experience and practice a repertoire of schemata or structural equivalents for portraying objects and their features, as well as rules for combining these schemata on the page. Many authors consider the main problem of drawing to be that of "mapping" or "projecting" three-dimensional reality onto lines on the two-dimensional picture surface. As we shall see, there are various ways of doing this and children of different ages tend to use different methods or systems. The main shortcoming of these views is that they do not account for the *sequence* in which children learn different systems of representation. In our modern day world, true-to life pictures are very common. Children are confronted with them from an early age and actually often prefer realistic drawings to schematic ones. If drawing development is a question of learning depiction methods, why do visual realism and perspective drawing emerge so late? Why are such styles of representation difficult to learn?

A final factor that has been considered to account for drawing development is *planning and organizational skills*. Drawing is conceived of as a problem solving activity that involves anticipating, planning, and sequencing actions. While knowledge about objects, perceptual abilities and a repertoire of graphic means are all prerequisites to the production of a drawing, the child also needs to be able to organize his graphic actions according to a set of goals and subgoals: What to draw? Where to start the drawing? Which object to draw first and which last? Research shows that there are developmental changes in the way children implement, monitor, and judge the execution of a project (e.g. Freeman, 1972, 1980; Friedman, Scholnick & Cocking, 1987; Gardner & Wolf, 1979; Van Sommers, 1984). For instance, in copying tasks, older children explore the model longer than younger ones and check the adequacy of their efforts by more frequent movements between the model and the drawing (Stambak & Pécheux, 1969). Although this approach to drawing development has the advantage of being nonreductionist, recognizing that drawing is a complex activity involving numerous interrelated processes, it leaves some essential questions unanswered: What determines the nature of the subjects' representational goals and methods? According to what principles do they monitor and judge their drawing activity? Why do these principles evolve with age?

Towards an integrated model of drawing development

Clearly, mental representations of objects, spatial cognition, perception, depiction skills, and organization abilities are all part and parcel of the drawing process. To arrive at an integrated model of drawing and its development we need to know how these aspects are coordinated with each other in the production of a drawing. What are the general principles that control the drawing process? I have come to believe that children's drawing activity is a function of their understanding or "theory" of pictorial representation. In recent years psychologists have discovered that many aspects of children's social and cognitive behavior can be explained by their "theories of mind," that is, by their level of understanding that people have mental states, such as beliefs and desires, and that people's actions depend on their representation of the world rather than on the way the world actually is (see Astington, 1993 for a review). In a similar way I believe that the development of children's drawing behavior can be explained by their growing awareness about pictures. Although it has been shown that children's understanding of pictorial representation evolves with age, this understanding has not been related to children's own skill in producing pictures. I hypothesize that children's level of understanding about pictures governs the type of knowledge they conjure up when setting out to draw, the way they visually explore model objects, the depiction techniques they comprehend and implement, the way they sequence the production of a drawing, and the criteria they use to evaluate the adequacy of their depictions.

Awareness of the dual reality of pictorial representations

Understanding pictorial representations comprises two main aspects: a) *distinguishing* between the two realities of a picture, that is, between its identity as a thing in itself, a surface covered with marks, and its identity as a representation of something else, the referent; b) understanding the *correspondence* between the features of the marks on the picture surface and the features of the referent.

Research shows that the ability to distinguish the two realities of pictures is achieved at progressively higher levels of mental functioning (eg., Beilin & Pearlman, 1991; Nye, Thomas & Robinson, 1995; Perner, 1991; Sigel, 1978). At a very basic level, it involves making a perceptual discrimination between a picture of an object and the real object. Infants as young as six months respond differently to a photo of an object and the real object; they do not confuse them perceptually. They also recognize the similarity between a picture and the object it represents. These early abilities to discriminate and perceive similarities between pictures and their referents do not imply that infants have a reflective understanding about pictures as representations. Indeed, they seem to consider that pictures are a variety of the real thing they represent. For instance, a one-and-a-half-year-old child might try to put on a picture of a shoe (Perner, 1991). By about age 3 or 4, children have a conceptual understanding that a picture does not share the same properties or the same fate as its referent: they will deny that a picture of an ice-cream cone is cold, or that milk in a picture of a glass will disappear when the milk in the real glass is drunk. By age 5, children acquire a reflective understanding of pictures as representations. They know that figures on the page denote or stand for objects. This implies the ability to construct a mental model containing two substructures and their relationship: one structure representing the picture as a physical entity and the other what the picture depicts. The model also includes links between the two structures that specify how the picture relates to the depicted content. An important consequence of such dual coding abilities is that children can now understand misrepresentation, that is, cases in which a picture denotes a certain reality wrongly or inaccurately. As children's perceptual skills and spatial knowledge develop they become progressively better equipped to analyze the exact nature of the correspondence between the marks on the page and their referents. In comparing the spatial properties of the layout of marks on the page with the visual and spatial properties of the depicted objects, children come to recognize that there can be both similarities and difference between the configuration of marks and the objects they represent. For instance, they now understand that contiguous graphic forms on the picture surface do not necessarily imply contiguity of their referents. By the age of 9 or 10, children gain the ability to measure two- and three-dimensional space using a system of coordinates and to determine the shape, size and location of objects using notions such as length, rectilinearity, parallelism and angle (Piaget & Inhelder, 1956). This allows them to analyze the marks on the picture surface and their relationships to the spatial properties of real objects in an even more differentiated manner. For instance, they can compare and reflect upon different systems for depicting depth and perspective.

In two studies (Reith, 1987, 1990), I analyzed the relationships between children's ability to differentiate the two realities of pictures and their performance in drawing production. In one of these studies, 5-to 11-year-old children's understanding of pictorial representation was measured on the basis of their procedures and verbal commentaries in a task requiring comparison and classification of a set of drawings (Reith, 1990). The drawings, made by children of different ages, were all representations of the same two objects. These models were presented to the subject along with the drawings. The results indicated very clear age-related trends. Five-year-olds showed interest only in the content of individual drawings and made no systematic attempt to relate them to the models. Seven-year-olds, however, did take the models into account. They classified the drawings according to the model they believed the drawings represented. They were also concerned with the resemblance of drawings to the models, using criteria such as the shape and presence of relevant features. Nine-year-olds' responses evidenced an increased awareness of the stylistic and structural aspects of the drawings. They compared drawings to each other, not just to the models, and grouped them according to the types of details of the models that were included. Eleven-year-olds showed an even more sophisticated awareness of the surface structure of drawings. They commented explicitly on the different methods of representation present in the set of drawings. For instance, they distinguished between drawings made with contour lines and those composed of juxtaposed schematic forms. In other words, they showed ability to focus on the line patterns of the drawings and to reflect upon the nature of the correspondence between lines and the models.

Children's level of awareness of pictorial representation in the drawing classification task correlated significantly with the types of drawings they produced themselves when required to represent real objects (Reith, 1990). Five-year-olds, who focused mainly on depicted content, produced highly schematic drawings composed of discrete forms denoting the parts and features of the models. Seven-year-olds, who grouped drawings according to their resemblance to the models, were also concerned with the accuracy of their own drawings, making sure that they included all the relevant features of the objects. Nine- and eleven-year-olds, who reasoned about the different ways in which an object can be depicted, produced drawings that were more stylistically coherent than those of younger children. Usually, they represented the view-specific presentation of objects, using lines to denote the contours and edges of the model's surfaces. Significant correlations between representational awareness and drawing performance were also obtained within age groups: children who showed a more advanced level of representational awareness than their age mates also tended to produce more sophisticated drawings.

Another study (Reith, 1987) showed that changes in ability to differentiate the two realities of a picture determine not only children's skills in depicting model objects but also in copying drawings made by others. In these studies, children were asked to copy, as accurately as possible, two types of drawings: representational and non-representational (Figure 2). They were instructed to proceed as if they were tracing the drawings using transparent paper. The results showed that until the age of 7, children copied the representational models less accurately than the nonrepresentational ones. The reproductions of the representational drawings contained more errors with respect to the form and connection of lines than the reproductions of the non-

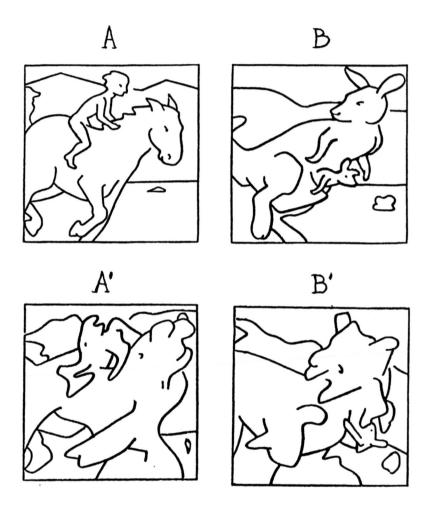

Figure 2
*Representational (A, B) and corresponding non-representational (A', B') line drawings used
as models in copying tasks (Reith, 1987)*

representational drawings, in spite of the fact that both kinds of drawings were equally complex. Evidently the depicted content in the representational drawings hindered young children's ability to focus on the line pattern. Since, at this age, they do not yet conceive of picture content and picture surface as two distinct entities, they are unable to direct their attention voluntarily to the shape and connection of the lines of the drawings. Comparison of performance at different ages revealed a gradual improvement in this area (see examples in Figure 3). Four- and five-year-old children focused alternatively on the content or the surface structure of pictures but were unable to relate one to the other. Thus, their drawings were usually composed of schematic forms inspired by the content of the picture and some disparate lines copied directly from the line pattern of the model. At 6 and 7, children still focus mostly on the models' content, but their productions show attempts to adapt the shape and location of graphic forms to match the layout of lines and the enclosed surfaces of the model. By the age of 8 and 9, subjects replicated the models very accurately. An analysis of the sequence in which they copied the models (see Figure 4) showed that they decomposed the line configuration in terms of its depicted content: they would first draw the lines making up the figures, and then those making up the background, or vice versa.

Relating picture content and picture surface

These two studies show that changes in ability to differentiate picture surface and picture content go hand in hand with changes in ability to deal with the relationships between the marks on the page and the signified object. These relationships involve several aspects: a) the denotational status of lines, that is, what do lines stand for; b) the rules for connecting lines; and c) the relations between the layout of figures on the page and the layout of objects in the environment.

A line in a drawing can stand for many different things: a whole object, such as an arm or a strand of hair; a feature of the physical structure of an object, such as the concave corner or the convex edge formed by two intersecting surfaces; an occluding contour of a curved surface; an abrupt discontinuity in the color, reflectance, or texture on a surface; a horizon or skyline; a crack in a surface, and so forth (Gibson, 1986; Kennedy, 1974). It follows that a graphic form can have many referents in the world depending on what the lines making up the form stand for. A circle, for example, can represent a ring, a head, a sphere, a disk, a hole in a surface, or a polka dot. To produce recognizable and detailed depictions of different objects, children must posses an active understanding of these possible functions of lines. They must be aware of the possible ambiguities of a drawing, especially when lines with different denotational status are combined within the same drawing.

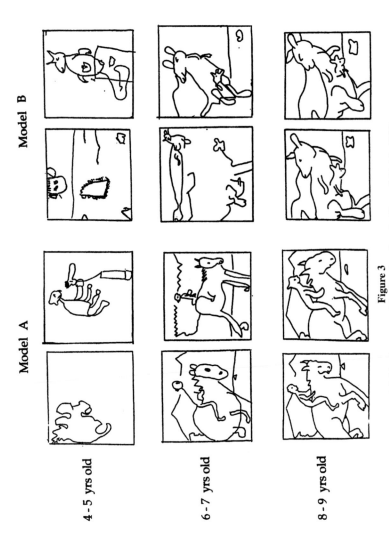

Figure 3
Examples of children's copies of the line drawings in Figure 2 (Reith, 1987)

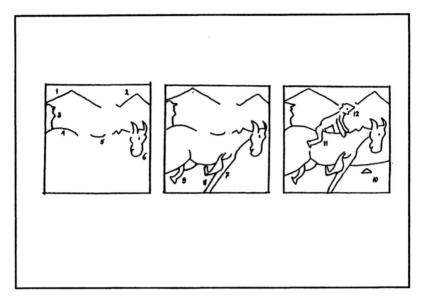

Figure 4
The construction sequence of a drawing by a 9-year-old child, showing deconstruction of the model's configuration into lines representing the figures and the background (Reith, 1987)

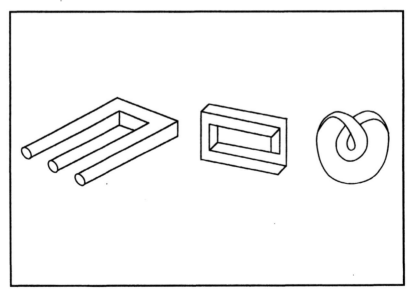

Figure 5
Impossible objects resulting from incompatible connection of lines.

The meaning of lines and enclosed surfaces in a drawing can often be inferred from the way they are connected. This is because the rules for connecting lines depend on what the lines denote. When lines are used to create closed forms that symbolize whole objects, such as in the schematic drawings of young children, the main constraint for correct depiction is that the relationships of proximity, connection, separation, and enclosure between the graphic forms match those of the referent. For instance, the arms should be connected to the trunk, not the head; the eyes and the mouth should be placed within the form denoting the head. The constraints are more complex when lines represent corners, edges and occluding contours of curved surfaces. Violation of the rules can lead to ambiguous representations. Figure 5 shows some examples. The referents of these drawings could not exist in reality, they are "impossible objects." This is because of an incompatible connection of lines. In the three-pronged tuning fork, lines specifying occluding contours of curved surfaces on the left run directly into lines specifying the concave edges formed by intersecting planes on the right (Gibson, 1986).

Interestingly, children's drawings often display similar errors (Reith, 1988). Some examples are given in Figure 6a. In these representations of a three-dimensional model made of clay, lines representing the outer contours are not closed appropriately, such that the circumscribed spaces representing the figure are open onto the background. Schematic forms symbolizing details of the object are tacked onto the inside and outside of the contour lines. These errors suggest that while executing their drawing children lose track of which portion of the drawing space constitutes the figure and which part is background. Their attention shifts in an uncontrolled fashion from the projective silhouette of the model (while producing the contour line) to its three-dimensional structure and distinctive, meaningful parts (when attaching schematic forms to the contour). Such line connection problems and sudden perceptual shifts would not arise if the children were fully aware of the denotational status of the lines in their drawings. Children use lines to produce symbol-like forms long before they are able to use line to create the outline of a figure (Fucigna & Wolf, 1981; Spielman, 1976). It is not until about nine or ten years of age that children can portray complex solid objects by embedded contour lines, which implies the ability to explore the visual projection of the object and to monitor the execution of the drawing using fixed reference points (Reith, 1988) (see Figure 6b).

In many cases, the child intends to depict scenes comprising several objects rather than a single object. This entails additional problems concerning the correspondence between the location of forms on the page and the location of the real objects in the scene. Just as there are various ways of using lines to represent the structure of an object, there are several possibilities for arranging the forms on the page to portray a collection of objects.

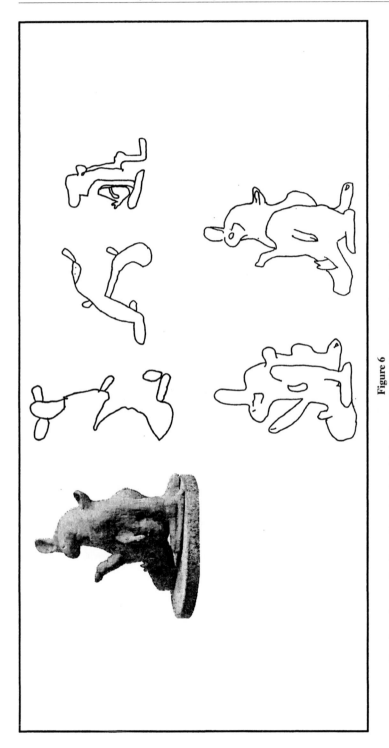

Figure 6

Drawings of a complex three-dimensional model showing incoherent use of contour lines by 5- and 6-year olds (above), and successful use of embedded contour lines by 8- and 9-year olds (below). (Reith, 1988).

Figure 7 shows various strategies for representing a scene composed of a ball and a box resting on a table. In the first stategy, the presence of the three objects is symbolized by three shapes placed haphazardly on the page. No explicit information about the location of the objects relative to each other or to the observer is provided. The second drawing portrays the relationship "on top of" between the objects and the table: the figure representing the table is placed near the bottom of the page, the ball and the box are fixed to the top of the table. In this solution the vertical axis of the page represents the vertical axis of real space. The third strategy uses height on the picture plane in a different way: it denotes depth, or distance from the observer. Positioning of an object down on the page signifies "near" and upper placement stands for "far." The fourth drawing depicts depth by partially "overlapping" the shape representing the far object by the shape representing the near object. This technique provides information about the location of the objects by specifying an aspect of their visual appearance, visual occlusion, at an observer's vantage point. The fifth strategy, a perspective drawing, portrays the spatial relations in the scene by replicating as closely as possible the scene's projection at the eye of the observer. The drawing represents the projective shape, size and location of objects in the visual field. In this system of representation, which rests upon the laws of optical geometry, the drawing surface is treated as a projection plane or a cross section of the visual array arriving to the eye. The page is like a window through which we perceive a scene. In short, each strategy constitutes a different drawing system with its own set of rules for relating the composition of graphic forms on the page to the layout of objects in the world.

Developmental studies on children's depiction of spatial relationships evidence stages that correspond approximately to the order of the drawings illustrated in Figure 7 (e.g., Lewis, 1963, Freeman, Eiser & Sayers, 1977; Willats, 1977). This evolution can be better understood if we take into account the degree of differentiation between picture surface and picture content that each strategy supposes. Three- and four-year-olds tend to place figures haphazardly within the confines of the page (strategy 1). They are not concerned with the orientation of the forms on the page, nor with the orientation of the page to themselves. The drawing surface simply "contains" graphic forms, just as the world contains objects. This reflects a simple understanding of pictures, in which discrete forms on the page are merely construed as symbols for objects in the world. Young children's drawing procedures consist in creating a one to one correspondence between real objects in the world and forms on the page, drawing one object after the other. Children draw what they see of the world, but what they see is a collection of meaningful, unitary "things," not a structured visual array. At five and six, children place figures along the bottom of the page or on a horizontal base line drawn across the page (strategy 2). They manipulate the relative location of forms to match

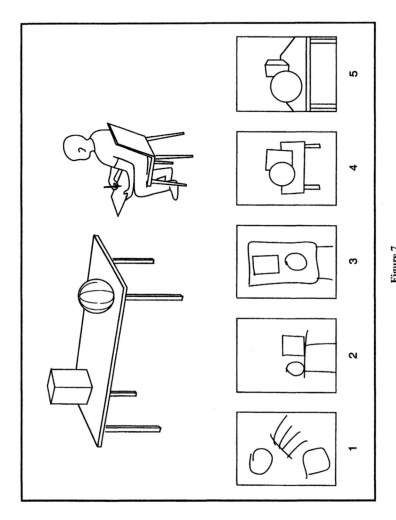

Figure 7

Some strategies for depicting the spatial relationships between objects

that of the referents. This shows that they now recognize a requirement for the resemblance between the spatial arrangement of forms on the page and their referents in the real world. It also shows that children have objectivized the axes of the page. They use these axes to produce and evaluate the resemblance of the picture to the referent. Seven- and eight-year-olds tend to use the vertical axis of the page to suggest depth (strategy 3). This suggests that they might construe the picture surface, which is usually placed horizontally during the drawing process, as the ground of the real world (Klaue, 1992). In nine-year-olds' drawings, production of overlapping forms becomes more frequent (strategy 4). This indicates an increased sensitivity to visual projection at a vantage point. The axes of the page are now related to the vertical and horizontal axes of the visual field rather than to the ground of real space. By the age of 11 or 12, children vary the size of figures to indicate distance and depth, and use foreshortening, and oblique or converging lines to show the surfaces that recede from the observer (strategy 5). This type of drawing evidences an increased ability to manipulate the form, orientation, and interconnection of lines. It also indicates a more abstract understanding of the relationships between the surface structure of the drawing and the referent. Children now recognize that the forms on the page can refer to the visual projection of an object's surfaces, not just to its invariant physical structure. Repeated efforts to render the visual appearance of objects and an increased awareness that pictures are flat are probably what bring children to recognize the need for adopting a pictorial mode of perception and to construe the visible world somewhat like an image projected on a plane in front of one's eyes.

The work of professional draftsmen and artists is the fruit of knowledge and ideas about the relationships between the form and content of pictures which are far more complex and abstract than those displayed by children. However, by the age of 12, children are already equipped with some basic concepts that can serve as a foundation for developing a more sophisticated comprehension of pictorial representation. Unfortunately, only a small percentage of children develop advanced pictorial skills. If it is true that the development of drawings is a function of awareness of the dual reality of pictures, then one of the goals of art education might be to engage children in activities that facilitate such awareness. Some examples might be to discuss, in highly explicit terms, the differences and similarities between the features of pictures and the properties of the real objects they represent, to demonstrate different ways of using line and alternative methods for depicting spatial relations, to encourage children to verbalize their intentions and procedures while they are engaged in drawing, and to provide children with the experience of drawing on a da Vinci Window. Such activities might provide a useful support for improving pictorial skills and for fostering critical appreciation of works of art.

Author notes
    Preparation of this paper was supported by a grant from the Jean Piaget Foundation for Epistemological and Psychological Research (Geneva, Switzerland). I thank John H. Flavell for his helpful comments on an earlier version of this paper.

References

Arnheim, R. (1956). *Art and visual perception: A psychology of the creative eye.* London: Faber & Faber.

Astington, J. W. (1993). *The child's discovery of the mind.* Cambridge, MA: Harvard University Press.

Barrett, M. D., Beaumont, A.V., & Jennett, M.S. (1985). Some children do sometimes do what they have been told to do: Task demands and verbal instructions in children's drawing. In N.H. Freeman & M.V. Cox (Eds.), *Visual order: The nature and development of pictorial representation* (pp. 176-187). Cambridge, England: University Press.

Beilin, H., & Pearlman, E.G. (1991). Children's iconic realism: Object versus property realism. In H.W. Reese (Ed.), *Advances in Child Development and Behavior, Vol. 23* (pp. 73-111). San Diego, CA: Academic Press.

Claparède, E. (1938). A propos d'un cas de perception sycrétique. Archives de Psychologie, 26, 367-377.

Cox, M. V. (1989). Knowledge and appearance in children's pictorial representation. *Educational Psychology, 9,* 15-25.

Cox, M. V.(1992). *Children's drawings.* London: Penguin Books.

Crook, C. (1985). Knowledge and appearance. In N.H. Freeman & M.V. Cox (Eds.), *Visual order: The nature and development of pictorial representation* (pp. 248-265). Cambridge, England: University Press.

Edwards, B. (1979). *Drawing on the right side of the brain.* Los Angeles: Thatcher.

Flavell, J., Green, F., & Flavell, E. (1986). Development of knowledge about the appearance-reality distinction. *Monograph of the Society for Research in Child Development, 51*(1, Serial No. 212).

Freeman, N. H. (1972). Process and product in children's drawing. *Perception, 1,* 123-140.

Freeman, N. H. (1980). *Strategies of representation in young children: Analysis of spatial skills and drawing process.* New York: Academic Press.

Freeman, N. H., & Cox, M. V. (Eds.). (1985). *Visual order: The nature and development of pictorial representation.* Cambridge, England: University Press.

Freeman, N. H., & Janikoun, R. (1972). Intellectual realism in children's drawings of familiar objects with distinctive features. *Child Development, 4,* 1116-1121.

Freeman, N.H., Eiser, C., & Sayers, J. (1977). Children's strategies in producing three-dimensional relationships on a two-dimensional surface. *Journal of Experimental Child Psychology, 23,* 305-314.

Friedman, S. L., Scholnick, E. K., & Cocking, R. R. (1987). *Blueprints for thinking: The role of planning in cognitive development.* London: Cambridge University Press.

Fucigna, C., & Wolf, D. (1981). *The earliest two-dimensional symbols: The onset of graphic representation.* Paper presented at the Eleventh Annual Conference of the Jean Piaget Society, Philadelphia. Copyright by Harvard Project Zero.

Gardner, H., & Wolf, D. (1979). First drawings: Notes on the relationships between perception and production in the visual arts. In C. Nodine & D. Fischer (Eds.), *Perception and pictorial representation*, (pp. 361-387). New York: Praeger.

Gibson, J. J. (1971). The information available in pictures. *Leonardo, 4,* 27-35.

Gibson, J. J. (1986). Pictures and visual awareness. In *The ecological approach to visual perception* (pp. 267-291). Hillsdale, NJ: Erlbaum.

Gombrich, E. H. (1960). *Art and illusion*. London: Phaidon Press Ltd.

Golomb, C. (1992). *The child's creation of a pictorial world*. Berkeley, CA: University of California Press.

Goodenough, F. L. (1926). *The measurement of intelligence by drawing*. New York: World Books.

Harris, D. G. (1963). *Children's drawing as a measure of intellectual maturity*. New York: Hartcourt, Brace & World.

Kennedy, J. M. (1974). *A psychology of picture perception*. San Francisco: Jossey-Bass.

Klaue, K. (1992). The development of depth representation in children's drawings: Effects of graphic surface and visibility of the model. *British Journal of Developmental Psychology, 10,* 71-83.

Lange-Kuettner, C., & Reith, E. (1995). The transformation of figurative thought: Implications of Piaget and Inhelder's developmental theory for children's drawing. In C. Lange-Kuettner & G.V. Thomas (Eds.), *Drawing and looking: Theoretical approaches to pictorial representation in children* (pp. 75-92). Hemel Hempstead, England: Harvester Wheatsheaf.

Lange-Kuettner, C., & Thomas, G. V. (Eds.). (1995). *Drawing and looking: Theoretical approaches to pictorial representation in children*. Hemel Hempstead: Harvester Wheatsheaf.

Lewis, H. (1963). Spatial representation in drawing as a correlate of development and a basis for picture preference. *Journal of Genetic Psychology, 102,* 95-107.

Luquet, G. H. (1927). *Le Dessin Enfantin*. Paris: Alcan.

Meili, R. (1931). Les perceptions des enfants et la psychologie de la Gestalt. *Archives de Psychologie, 23,* 25-44.

Nye, R., Thomas, G., & Robinson, E. (1995). Children's understanding about pictures. In C. Lange-Kuettner & G.V. Thomas (Eds.), *Drawing and looking: Theoretical approaches to pictorial representation in children* (pp. 123-134). Hemel Hempstead: Harvester Wheatsheaf.

Perner, J. (1991). *Understanding the representational mind*. Cambridge, MA: MIT Press.

Piaget, J., & Inhelder, B. (1956). *The child's conception of space*. London: Routledge & Kegan Paul.

Piaget, J., Inhelder, B., & Szeminska, A. (1960). *The child's conception of geometry*. London: Routledge & Kegan Paul.

Reith, E. (1987). *Attitude intellectuelle et attitude visuelle dans la copie de modèles tridimensionnels et bidimensionnels chez des enfants de 4 à 10 ans*. Unpublished doctoral dissertation, University of Geneva, Switzerland.

Reith, E. (1988). The development of use of contour lines in children's drawings of figurative and non-figurative three-dimensional models. *Archives de Psychologie, 56,* 83-105.

Reith, E. (1990). Development of representational awareness and competence in drawing production. *Archives de Psychologie, 58,* 369-379.

Reith, E., & Liv, C.H. (1995). What hinders accurate depiction of projective shape? *Perception, 24*, 995-1010.

Reith, E., & Dominin, D. (1997). The development of children's ability to attend to the visual projections of objects. British *Journal of Developmental Psychology, 15.*

Reith, E., Steffen, C., & Gillièron, C. (1994). Children's drawing of water level: Operatory knowledge, attention to visual image, and depiction skills. *Revue Suisse de Psychologie, 53*(2), 86-97.

Sigel, I. E. (1978). The development of pictorial comprehension. In B.S. Randhawa & W.E. Coffman (Eds.), *Visual learning, thinking, and communication* (pp. 93-111). New York: Academic press.

Spielman, K. S. (1976). Development of the perception and production of line forms. *Child Development, 47*, 787-793.

Stambak, M., & Pécheux, M.G. (1969). Essai d'analyse de l'activité de reproduction de figures géométriques complexes. *Année Psychologique, 69*, 55-66.

Thomas, G. V., & Silk, A. M. J. (1990). *An introduction to the psychology of children's drawings*. New York: Harvester Wheatsheaf.

Van Sommers, P. (1984). *Drawing and cognition: Description and experimental studies of graphic production processes*. London: Cambridge University Press.

Willats, J. (1977). How children learn to draw realistic pictures. *Quarterly Journal of Experimental Psychology, 29*, 367-82.

Willats, J. (1985). Drawing systems revisited: The complementary roles of production systems and denotation systems in the analysis of children's drawings. In N.H. Freeman & M.V. Cox (Eds.), *Visual order: The nature and development of pictorial representation* (pp.78-98). Cambridge: University Press.

Willats, J. (1995). Learning to draw: An information processing account of pictorial representation in children. In G. Thomas & C. Lange-Kuettner (Eds.), *Drawing and looking: Theoretical approaches to pictorial representation in children* (pp. 27-43). Hemel Hempstead: Harvester Wheatsheaf.

CHILD ART, MULTIPLE INTERPRETATIONS, AND CONFLICTS OF INTEREST

Child "art" is a product of the modernist era. Indeed, the art of the child gained its art-world toehold at the very beginning of modernism when Champfleury claimed that the artistic innovations of the adult painter Courbet were directly attributable to the creative juices that flowed undiluted from the child Courbet (Schapiro, 1979 pp. 47-85, Wilson, 1992, p. 15). To the modernist art educator and psychologist, artistic development was essentially a natural unfolding process that led to individual expression. This belief was not unlike the preferred modernist view of the artist as an individual with the obligation, perhaps the moral imperative, to develop a unique style of expression unconstrained by artistic convention. Although there is still controversy regarding the question of whether we live in the modern or postmodern era, it seems quite certain that the modernist ideologies and expressionist theories of art that shaped our conceptions of child art for well over a century are not nearly so compelling as they once were.

For just a moment, I wish to attend to definitions. Like the entire category, *art, child art* is an *open concept* that continues to be defined and redefined in light of changing conditions (Weitz, 1959, pp. 145-156). A brief working definition will, at the very least, permit me to dispense with the troublesome practice of placing the art in child "art" inside quotation marks. Child art refers to objects and events, made by young people between the ages of 1 or 2 and the middle-teen years, which adults (and children who are influenced by them) classify as art because they often look and function somewhat like the things that adult artists create. In other words, objects and events become child art when they are so interpreted. As Danto says, "for an object is an art work *at all* only in relation to an interpretation. It transforms objects into works of art" (1986, p. 44). When expressionist artists in *Der Blaue Reiter* group included the works of children in their almanac in 1912, (Miesel, 1970,

BRENT WILSON

p. 44) or when Victor D'Amico organized exhibitions of child art at the Museum of Modern Art during the 1940s, these events reinforced the status of child-made objects as art.

There are two distinct but related points I wish to make regarding the status of child as artist. First, the boundaries of art continually expand; individuals who call themselves artists make things that may not, at one time, have been classified as art but which have become art works because they have been interpreted as such by individuals within the art world. Child art is also a product of this process. From the Renaissance to the beginning of the modern period, the mastery of conventions such as the skillful depiction of the world through linear perspective, drawing the human figure with anatomical correctness, and the depiction of complex mythical and allegorical scenes were among the criteria used to judge whether or not something was art. Because most children were unable to master these rigorous conditions, the things they could do, their drawings on walls, for example, were probably viewed by adults and children alike as little more than play. When modernist artists rejected Renaissance conventions and their work began to look more like children's graphic play, it was possible for the drawings and paintings of little children to gain at least a marginal status as art.

The second point relates to the processes of interpretation that transform children's objects into art. Every art-like thing created by a child may be seen as a sign which contains a collection of other signs. When individuals with different sets of interests and values interpret children's objects differently, those objects are transformed into very different things, things that are sometimes works of art and sometimes not. If we examine different classes of children's creations from different aesthetic or ideological positions, our interpretations lead to quite different conceptions about what is classified as child art, how it develops, and the functions it plays in children's lives.

Perspectives on Child Art

It will be useful to illustrate some of the different perspectives from which almost any drawing, painting, construction, or other art-like thing made by a child might be interpreted. Here are three perspectives from which child art might be interpreted:

- The art world, the complex of art forms, aesthetic theories, individual artists and their works; the historians and critics who interpret, study, and evaluate works of art; institutions such as galleries and museums which house and conserve works of art, etc.
- The world of the child, the interests and motives of the child; the social, cultural, and psychological realms in which the child exists; etc.

- The world of education, the institutions in which the child is expected to learn specific things based on educational goals, school curricula, specific subjects, and instructional programs; teachers, educational and psychological researchers who try to understand how children develop as artists, why they make art, and what it contributes to their development; etc.

When children's art-like creations are viewed as signs, the resulting interpretations tell us about art world values, about the child and his or her motives, cognitive and developmental states, and about the educational programs and conceptions of children as artists. Our interpretations are also signs (Bal, 1992, p. 215); when we watch ourselves and others in the act of interpreting child art, we learn something about the assumptions and aesthetic theories on which our interpretations are based. Just as in the interpretation of adult art, the meaning of the art of the child becomes possible through relationships created among: (1) the text (the child's art work); (2) the pretext (Pollock, 1993, p. 530) to both the dimensions of reality to which the child refers and the artistic traditions that affect the work; and (3) the post-text to the interests, values, and assumptions of the interpreters of child art (including both children and adults). If we are to understand child art we must look at what the child has represented and expressed, the conditions under which child art is made, and ourselves and others in the act of studying it.

Multiple Interpretations of Child Art

I wish to present three cases in which the art-like things of children are interpreted in different, even contradictory, ways. These brief analyses will take us to contemporary Japan, 19th century Pennsylvania, and early 20th century Austria. These cases illuminate some of the issues that surround contemporary conceptions of child art.

Japanese Children's Story Drawings: Doraemon's Problematic Artistic Status

I have tried to understand Japanese children and their art through the study of the things they make both in and out of school. In 1989, I traveled throughout Japan asking children to draw stories, a familiar task because virtually every Japanese child is a reader of comic books called *manga* and countless numbers of Japanese children also form *manga* clubs, create their own versions of comic books, share them with friends, and sell them in *manga* conventions organized specifically for young people.

When I asked Japanese children to draw stories, I found that many of the 5-, 6-, and 7-year-old children didn't bother to create a new character. They merely borrowed a character from *manga*. Hundreds of children drew

Figure 1: *In this six-frame graphic narrative drawn by an 11-year old Japanese child, Doraemon, the "famous" atomic-powered cat, enters the "No. 1 everywhere door" that will take him anywhere he wishes to go. In the final frame, he finds the "where" he has gone is indeed a threatening place.*

Doraemon, a little atomic-powered cat who materialized from the top drawer of his friend Nobita's desk one day, while the drawer became the gateway to the fourth dimension. Like Japanese children, I, too, was intrigued by Doraemon's kangaroo-like pouch from which an amazing variety of gadgets were produced and used to solve problems and resolve difficulties (Schodt, 1983, p. 14). Why did so many Japanese children draw the Doraemon character? What might children's drawings of Doraemon tell us about Japanese children and Japanese culture?

I would argue that there are a number of obvious reasons why children like Doraemon: He is little, like a child, and he's also "cute." More importantly, he is clever, and although Doraemon is childlike, he has power, freedom, and mobility that enable him to travel wherever he wishes. Doraemon's characteristics, his capabilities, and the things he does are signs. Perhaps the places to which he travels represent the unknown, the future, a whole series of possible futures. These futures are filled with endless surprises and challenges. Nevertheless, when Doraemon gets into difficulty, he possesses the inner resources needed to solve the problem, the gadgets in his pouch.

When children draw their own Doraemon stories, I think that they are symbolically rehearsing ways to overcome difficulties that they might encounter as they grow older. Doraemon provides children with powerful and exciting ways to symbolically fulfill their wishes and plan their lives.

My speculation about children's Doraemon stories has led me, in turn, to speculate about the entire Japanese *manga* industry, with its savvy creators of mass media who know that kids will be attracted to a cute little character with marvelous powers. Doraemon's creators also know that the exploration of the fourth dimension, with its relentless stories of what happens and what happens next, of tension and release, of equilibrium lost and regained, will attract an eager audience for each new publication. Perhaps it is the case that the very features that make the Doraemon *manga* attractive to children are also the features that help children practice coping with problems.

In their own graphic narratives, through the employment of Doraemon and countless other *manga* characters, either co-opted or invented, Japanese children experiment with life's themes. They can invent situations that enable them to observe such things as cause and effect, growth and development, threat and overcoming, good versus evil, the process of creating and destroying, and on and on. They reconstruct their own little graphic worlds along *manga* lines and then experiment endlessly with how these worlds are, with how they might be, and with the many ways in which individuals encounter life's joys and cope with its challenges.

I have concluded that creating new fourth dimension worlds (futures), overcoming difficulty after difficulty, and symbolically solving endless problems is very good practice for children in Japan, a country with few natural resources such as coal, timber, steel, and oil. Japan is a country whose very survival of which depends on the development of the one natural resource it has in abundance, the minds of its young people. The nation must assure, when its young people enter the work force, that they will contribute to the prosperity of the country by creating, for example, a never-ending series of technological miracles. I think that Doraemon provides a model for invention, ingenuity, creativity, problem solving, and imagination. Indeed, from my outsider vantage point, I see Doraemon as a sign of the creative problem solving and technological wizardry needed to keep Japan competitive in the international marketplace. If I am correct, the little character makes a vital contribution to the well-being of Japan. I should quickly add that it is doubtful that either the adult creators of Doraemon or their young imitators have a conscious understanding of the role the little character might play in furthering their national well-being.

In America the comics have, at best, marginal status within the world of art; the same is true of *manga* in Japan. When asked about *manga*, most Japanese art teachers replied that it was a form of crass mass media entertainment hardly worthy of attention, although a few schools did assist the children in forming after school *manga* clubs. While thousands of Japanese children aspire to become manga artists, their art teachers, most of whom closely follow the national curriculum, base their lessons on high-art models that leave no place for *manga*. It is doubtful that the children think of their *manga* drawings as art either, certainly not the kind of art they do in schools and see in art museums. Nevertheless, I, an art educator, went to Japan, collected thousands of story drawings, analyzed them, and noted the great skill with which Japanese children narrate graphically, depict characters and their actions, show emotional states, represent three-dimensional space, and show changing points of view to illustrate the kinds of difficulties characters get into and out of. I view the *manga* drawings as a class of child art and claim that these popular art-like story drawings provide Japanese children with ways to understand themselves, their society and its values, and ways to construct the "prophetic reality", the very cognitive functions that Kreitler and Kreitler (1972, pp. 325-358) attribute to works of art. The children's art-like *manga* probably lead to important educational outcomes, to my mind a more important outcome than the highly expressive but less idea-laden art they make in schools, and yet their *manga* do not have art status in the eyes of most of their teachers. To Japanese children, making graphic narratives is stimulating and rewarding; to their teachers making *manga* is little more than low entertainment; and to a visiting art educator *manga* is a form of child art that shapes children's conceptions of themselves and their world in profound ways.

The Pictographs and School Drawings of the Students at the U.S. Indian
School in Carlisle, Pennsylvania: A Series of Interpretations

Conflicting interpretations of children's art work are sometimes rooted in cultural differences that are far deeper than those existing between the popular and high arts. In the late 1870s, young Plains Indians were brought to the Carlisle Indian Industrial School in Carlisle, Pennsylvania. After classes were finished for the day, the young Indians drew, sometimes subversively. Luther Standing Bear later told of the drawing activities of the young boys.

> We were marched into the schoolroom where we were each given
> a pencil and a slate. We soon discovered that the pencils made
> marks. We covered our heads with our blankets, holding the slate
> inside, here we would draw a man on a pony chasing a buffalo, or
> a boy shooting birds, or one of our Indian games.(in Smith 1988,
> p. 100)

The Indian students brought with them the drawing style of one of several Plains tribes. In their drawings they depicted the hunting of buffalo and groups of mounted warriors in full battle dress (and an occasional cavalryman). They drew horses with a bobbed tail, stylized phallus, a definite peak that marked the point at which the rump began to slope to the tail (Young, 1986, p. 58). Their horses have had long arching necks, the small heads, and the carefully defined fetlocks and hoofs seen on hide paintings and in ledger book pictographs. Before they arrived at Carlisle, young Indian boys were well on their way to mastering one or another of Plains Indian tribes' drawing styles.

It is possible to speculate about the young Indians' drawings from theirs and their teachers' perspectives. For the young Plains Indian, the drawings could be signs for the following: (1) the way of life of the Plains Indian people from which they had been removed, (2) a way of remembering aspects of Plains Indian culture that was being destroyed, (3) things that could be possessed symbolically which were not present in actuality, things such as manhood and bravery, (4) themes of life and death, of animals giving up their lives so that a people might live, (5) the style used by elders of the tribe when they drew and painted on hides, muslin, and in ledger books and (6) the kinds of drawings that the young Plains Indian boys wished to make of their own free will, not because their teachers assigned them.

What might the image mean to teachers whose job it was to "civilize" the young Indians and prepare them to make a livelihood in the white man's world? The Carlisle images were like those drawn by the Kiowa, Comanche, and Cheyenne Indian prisoners at Fort Marion, Florida, curiosities which had attracted the attention of white collectors (Young, 1986, pp. 59-60). They

Figure 2: *Alvin Goodboy, a Commananche, drew this buffalo hunt during the 1880s while he was a student at The Indian Industrial School at Carlisle, Pennsylvania. His drawing reflects a way of life that he and his people had lost.*

were also signs of: (1) a way of life with ponies, buffalo, hunting, and warfare that were totally unrealistic (and undesirable) for Indians to expect to have either at the time or in the future, (2) ideals of manhood and bravery which had no place in the contemporary (white-man's) world in which Indians should have been prepared to live, (3) symbols of the past and perhaps even unhealthy reminders of a culture that must change, that must be changed, (4) a form of art that had no usefulness in preparing young Indians for a vocation, (5) the kind of drawing that young Indian boys should *not* have been encouraged to make, (6) a sign of the industrial school teachers' failure, a sign that they had not succeeded in properly educating these young Indians to the ways of white men, and (7) a sign that teachers will impose artistic styles and subject matter on students.

It appears that the teachers at the industrial school acted on their reading of the drawings as signs of continuing savagery. Consequently, a different form of art education was instituted. During the 1880s and '90s, Carlisle Indian Industrial School students were assigned to make carefully shaded drawings of pots and bottles drawn from life. How might these drawings be interpreted? The Plains Indians' light and shade drawings might indicate the following: (1) that students are obedient, that they are willing to do almost anything teachers ask them to do; (2) the drawings are a sign of trust on the part of students, implicit trust that teachers know what is good for students; (3) an indication that young Indians could excel in the white man's ways of drawing, the drawings are skillfully done; and (4) to a viewer in the late 20th century, a sign that the teachers failed to value the cultural interests of the young Indians.

There was a third phase in the art program at the Carlisle School. According to Smith,

> by the end of the nineteenth century, the new sociological movement was shaping American perceptions of Indian education. Redeeming aspects of Indian culture, in particular the native arts and crafts, were encouraged. In 1906 the first native art course was taught at the Carlisle by the well-respected Indian artist, Angel de Cora Dietz (1988, p. 104).

The irony is that although the art program dealt with Native American subject matter, during the first and second decades of the 20th century the Plains Indian students (and students from tribes throughout North America) were assigned to make stylized border designs and designs for weaving and pottery, the "art" associated with Navajo, Pueblo, and Zuni tribes, but not with Plains Indians. This kind of art was probably taught at the school because it had commercial potential and because it was a safe, domesticated Indian art far removed from warfare, acts of bravery, and hunting found in the early Plains Indian drawings.

Of the many conclusions that might be drawn from an examination of the art program at Carlisle, three are of greater significance: (1) that teachers customarily make decisions about the kind of art children should make in art school; (2) teachers have almost complete control over the subject matter, styles, expressive qualities, and forms of school art; and (3) teachers' art assignments are pervaded with values and artistic ideologies.

Lowenfeld and the Making of Haptic Art
    The assumption that school art is as much a creation of the teacher as of the student merits a closer look. The genesis of Viktor Lowenfeld's ideas about child art and art education can perhaps best be seen in *The Nature of Creative Activity*, first published in 1939. As a young man, Lowenfeld was fascinated with the art of the blind, so much so that when he was unable to obtain formal permission to work in an institution for blind children, he smuggled in clay on visiting days (Lowenfeld, undated). From his work with blind students, he discovered two distinct approaches to working with clay. He claimed that some blind and partially sighted children were visual types; when they modeled heads, they approached the task as spectators working face to face as if they were relying on their sight for information. Other children were haptic types who worked from behind the head so that their fingers formed the features almost as if they were feeling their own faces. The haptic individual, according to Lowenfeld, "is primarily concerned with his own body sensations and with the tactual space around him" (1939, p. 87).

Connections among the haptic creative type, expressionist art, and the art of "primitive" people formed Lowenfeld's theory of child art.

> The relation of the art of children to that of primitive peoples, the relation of both these to the mode of expression used by the weak sighted and the blind, the common mode of representing space in early and archaic works of art and the presence of the same form symbols and means of expression in the case of emotionally expressive representation, all showed clearly that in these forms of creative activity the experiences of the visual sense had to relinquish their primacy. (1939, p. 9)

Although Lowenfeld presents the work of both visual and haptic creative types in *The Nature of Creative Activity*, there is little doubt that he had preference for the haptic. In the book, only about a dozen art works of human heads are by visual and over 50 are by haptic creative types. The titles of the works, which represent the art assignments Lowenfeld gave students, are revealing: *Man Trembling with Fear, The Cry for Help, A Father Hears of the Death of his Son, Exhausted Proletarian Woman, Moses Hears the Jews Dancing Round the Golden Calf.* To be sure there are other heads with titles such as *Officer, Listener,* and *Chess Player,* but like the drawings of visual types, they are in the minority.

The paintings and modeled heads Lowenfeld used to illustrate the haptic creative type are powerfully moving. Some humans cry out in anguish and pain and others are filled with brooding pathos. They reflect the style of German expressionist artists such as Emil Nolde and Ernst Ludwig Kirchner and August Macke. Indeed, Macke, like Lowenfeld, praised the art of children and aborigines "who have their own form, strong as the form of thunder." And in a letter to Macke, his fellow artist, Marc, proclaimed,

We must be brave and turn our backs on almost everything that until now good Europeans like ourselves have thought precious and indispensable. Our ideas and ideals must be clad in hairshirts, they must be fed on locusts and wild honey, not on history, if we are ever to escape the exhaustion of our European bad taste. (Wiedmann. 1979, p. 223)

It seems apparent, from our late-20th century perspective, that Lowenfeld wished to transform children into expressionists. Indeed, the emergence of expressionism and its ideological attachment to the art of "primitive" peoples and children legitimized the haptic attributes in art produced by young people when furnished with thick tempera paint and wide bristle brushes and encouraged to paint subjects such as what a headache feels like. Expressionism was obviously Lowenfeld's preferred style and he was not adverse to doing what was necessary to assure that students produced "haptic" art. For example, in the third edition of *Creative and Mental Growth* on page 344 (Figure 47), Lowenfeld shows a drawing which he characterizes as a "stiff, academic representation of [a] head by Frank Stewart." On the opposite page, in Figure 48, there is a loose expressive haptic-like drawing characterized as a "free representation made by the same student, Frank Stewart, *after applying correct stimulation*" [italics added].

I do not wish to be critical of either Lowenfeld's teaching methods or his artistic tastes. After all, is it not appropriate for an art teacher to take advantage of the educative power of a particular style of art? I am, however, critical of the fact that teachers and researchers are not sufficiently aware of the consequences of their aesthetic theories. Researchers, like art teachers, have artistic preferences and aesthetic theories that influence the way they interpret children's art. Gardner (1980, pp. 94-142) and Davis (1991, 1993), for example, have analyzed children's drawings and paintings in terms of artistry and concluded that their artistic development can be described as a U-shaped curve. Through their studies they show that young children express emotions, such as anger, in their drawings and paintings (Davis, 1993) which they claim most older children cannot. Their conclusion is that the initial artistry of children is lost and retained or regained by only a few young people. Of course Lowenfeld was highly successful in assuring that older children's power to create emotionally expressive art did not decline. It should also be noted that the Davis and Gardner findings are plausible primarily when viewed through abstract expressionist lenses. While children may lose some of their intuitive artistic abilities relating to the expression of emotion, the National Assessment data show a general increase in students' abilities to do such things as design, represent space, and draw human figures in action (National Assessment of Educational Progress, 1978, pp.142-167). A decline in one artistic skill is apparently accompanied by gains in other skills, albeit in areas where expressiveness plays a less crucial role. Research conclusions about child art are inextricably tied to particular aesthetic theories.

Some Concluding Thoughts About the Future of Child Art

Japanese children's *manga*-like story drawings, because they are associated with the popular arts and because they are obviously derived from adult art, have little connection to traditional forms of child art, and little status as child art. Ironically these non-child-art things demand that the children who produce them exercise a high degree of drawing, designing, and narrative skill. Moreover, they fulfill many cognitive orienting functions associated with art.

The three kinds of art, the Plains Indian style and subject matter, carefully shaded still life drawings, and decorative "Indian art", found over a 40-year period at the Carlisle Industrial School show that teachers and school administrators either consciously or unconsciously saw students' art in ideological terms. In their well-intentioned efforts to help their students, teachers suppressed the art that signaled continuing "savagery," used school art as a form of cultural hegemony, and encouraged culturally bastardized forms of Indian art. The Carlisle teachers were not the first to use child art for ideological purposes, nor the last.

Lowenfeld's teaching and research shows just how much the child art of a given period is influenced by contemporary art styles and aesthetic theories. He assumed his theory to be universal when it applied primarily to the modernist/expressionist realm. Nevertheless, his brilliant work also helps us to realize that school art is almost always the result of a collaboration, willing or unwilling, knowing or unknowing, between teacher and students.

If we were to view these findings as cautionary tales, what morals might we extract from them? They illustrate how we shape child art. We art teachers and researchers frequently do not recognize the power of our individual tastes for certain types of child art; we do not fully understand the control our teaching methods exert over children's schooled images; we do not yet see clearly all the subtle and pervasive ways in which society and culture shape the art of young people; and we do not realize that our research findings are always framed by our assumptions about what art is and what we think it ought to be.

We are told that child art will change. We might expect that as art teachers become familiar with the various new forms of art, performance, installation—conceptual, environmental, etc.—and current artistic interests relating to things such as feminism, gender, political issues, and the environment, that new forms of child art will emerge. As new forms of popular art emerge, children will emulate them and when they do, child art will change. Although we educators will probably resist the changes, children will continue to entertain and educate themselves through their self-initiated art.

These cautionary tales teach us about conflicts of interest. We should expect that art teachers and students will frequently attach different meanings to child art. These differences, rather than being undesirable, can provide the opportunity for achieving mutual understanding if we teachers are willing to recognize and discuss our artistic and aesthetic interests, try to understand students' motives, and try to develop instructional activities that reflect both our own aesthetic value and our students' artistic interests.

References

Bal, M. (1991). *Reading "Rembrandt": Beyond the word-image opposition.* Cambridge, England: Cambridge University Press.

Danto, A. (1986). *The philosophical disenfranchisement of art.* New York: Columbia University Press.

Davis, J. (1991). Artistry lost: U-shaped development in graphic symbolization. Doctoral dissertation. Harvard Graduate School of Education. Harvard University. Cambridge, MA.

Davis, J. (1993, June). *On lost artistry: Is the U-shaped development in graphic symbolization unnecessary.* Paper presented at the meeting of the Piaget Society, Philadelphia, PA.

Gardner, H. (1980). *Artful scribbles.* New York: Basic Books.

Kreitler, H., & Kreitler, S. (1972). *Psychology of the arts.* Durham, NC: Duke University Press.

Lowenfeld, V. (1939). *The nature of creative activity.* London: Routledge & Kegan Paul.

Lowenfeld, V. (1957). *Creative and mental growth, 3rd edition.* New York: Macmillan.

Lowenfeld, V. (undated). *Viktor Lowenfeld speaks of his life.* Unpublished manuscript in the possession of B. Wilson, the Pennsylvania State University.

Miesel, V. H. (1970). *Voices of German Expressionism.* Englewood Cliffs, NJ: Prentice-Hall.

National Assessment of Educational Progress. (1978). *Art Technical Report: Exercise Volume* (No. 06-A-20). Denver, CO: Education Commission of the States.

Pollock, G. (1993). Review of Mieke Bal, Reading "Rembrandt": Beyond the Word-Image Opposition, *The Art Bulletin, 75*(3), 529-535.

Schapiro, M. (1984). *Modern art: 19th and 20th centuries.* New York: Braziller.

Schodt, F. L. (1983). *Manga, manga!: The world of Japanese comics.* Tokyo, New York, and San Francisco: Kodansha International.

Smith, L. F. (1988). Pictographic drawings from the Carlisle Indian Industrial School. *Cumberland County History, 5*(2), 100-107.

Weitz, M. (1959). The role of theory in aesthetics. In M. Weitz (Ed.), *Problems in aesthetics: An introductory book of readings* (pp. 145-159). New York: The Macmillan Company.

Wiedmann, A. (1979). *Romantic roots in modern art.* Surrey, England: Gresham Books.

Wilson, B., (1989). Children's schooled and unschooled images from the nineteenth and early twentieth centuries: art education, cultural hegemony, and the 'intentions' surrounding three sets of visual artifacts. In P. Amburgy, D. Soucy, M.A. Stankiewicz, B. Wilson, & M. Wilson. (Eds.), *The history of art education: Proceedings from the Penn State conference, 1989* (pp. 226-233). Reston, VA: The National Art Education Association.

Wilson, B. (1992). Primitivism, the avant-garde and the art of little children. In D. Thistlewood (Ed.), *Drawing: Research and development* (pp.14-25). London: Longman.

Young, G. A. (1986). Aesthetic archives: The visual language of the plains ledger art. In E. L. Wade (Ed.), *The arts of the North American Indian: Native traditions in evolution,* (45-62). New York: Hudson Hills Press in association with Philbrook Art Centre, Tulsa, C. Haralson (Ed.).

ARTISTIC DEVELOPMENT AND CURRICULUM: SOCIOCULTURAL LEARNING CONSIDERATIONS

Although educators generally agree about the importance of students' developmental considerations in the construction of curriculum, debate continues about the character of those considerations. What conceptions of development have influenced public school art curriculum? How should curriculum be structured based on recent shifts in conceptions of development? These questions are the focus of this chapter.

The first major section of the chapter provides an overview of two psychological perspectives of artistic development that have been prevalent and influenced curriculum. The first perspective led to "natural development" stage models. The notion of an innate, universal process of psychological development that is reflected in children's drawings and can be delineated in this type of model is a century old (Efland, 1990). From this perspective, at a given time, children are represented as located in one of several stages, which are internally consistent, formally logical, and intellectually revealing. These models of development have resulted in curriculum based on sequential activities tied to stage-by-age dependent behaviors and the assumption that children's growth is a naturally unfolding process that cannot be essentially changed (e.g. Golomb, 1974; Kellogg, 1969; Kershensteiner, 1905; Lowenfeld, 1947, 1957; Lowenfeld & Brittain, 1964; Schaefer-Simmern, 1950; Sully, 1895).

The second perspective, expert-novice models of development, is based on steps of learning required to advance from a novice level of knowledge to a complex, higher-order level of expertise. In contrast to the stage-by-age

KERRY FREEDMAN

approach, which involves the assumption that children can perform certain behaviors at certain times, expert-novice models represent learning in terms of increasingly complex levels of thought within a particular domain of knowledge. These stage models have influenced curriculum by shifting the notion of sequentiality from an age dependent conception of "natural development" toward a sequence based on expert experience. Although authors of both types of models refer to development as dependent to a greater or lesser extent on interaction with the world, these models fundamentally concern internally motivated behaviors (and to a lesser degree, thought processes) that demonstrate that learning has taken place.

The second major section of this chapter focuses on the recent movement toward a conception of development that increasingly takes into account social and cultural influences. Much of the current research suggests that development is more dependent on learning than previously thought, which has important sociocultural implications. I will refer to this movement as the sociological approach to the study of development, although it includes research by psychologists, and argue that sociocultural considerations should be an important dimension of curriculum. In the third section, I will discuss those considerations and make recommendations for curriculum planning.

Historical Trends in Artistic Development: Two Psychological Models

Twentieth century accounts of artistic development have largely focused on psychobiological explanations. The emergence of the professional field of psychology near the turn of the century provided a basis for research on the influence of innate factors of growth. This research has particularly shaped conceptions of development in terms of two general models: stage-by-age and expert-novice. Elementary school curriculum has been closely tied to these psychological conceptions of artistic development, first through child-centered curriculum beginning in the 1920s and then discipline-centered curriculum from about 1960. Secondary curriculum has drawn most heavily upon the expert-novice ideas about learning, as demonstrated by the open studio design problem-solving approaches to teaching used in high school art classes.

Stage-by-Age Models

Early in the century, child study psychologists supported the conceptualization of children's development in terms of stages of growth that depended on chronological age. The analysis of children's drawings was an important part of child study research (e.g., Barnes, 1908; Hall, 1911; Sully, 1895). These analyses of children's drawings tended to focus on representationality and formal qualities that were thought to illustrate natural development.

The mythological idea of "the normal child" was extremely important to this research. Although the social and political milieu of the United States directed the new psychology toward questions of individual difference, this milieu also supported the scientific conception of individualism as framed by standards based on group norms. For example, Edward L. Thorndike (1913), often referred to as the first behavioral psychologist, was interested in innate potentials for abnormal and outstanding behavior. His study of individual differences actually involved the collection of data from an array of behavioral tests, including drawing tests, that resulted in definitions of innate capabilities in terms of groups, such as gender. Thorndike and other researchers in the early part of the century saw drawing tests as illustrative of various mental capacities and several used children's drawings, particularly of human figures, as measures of intelligence (Cox, 1993).

The focus on behaviorism in psychology limited the study of learning (Anderson, 1980; Baars, 1986). The resulting theories of development were based heavily on analyses of behaviors that were assumed to reflect natural characteristics of growth. This focus on behaviorism reduced generalized statements about the implications of behaviors for predicting mental capacities; however, it gave increasing credibility to the idea of natural, universal models of development based on in sequential, behavioral stages.

Behaviorism and its related methodologies often resulted in analyses of artistic behavior generalized from small, homogeneous groups to large, heterogeneous populations. At the same time, researchers tended to allow group differences, such as gender differences, to become hierarchical in value. For example, psychologists, such as Thorndike (1913), claimed that gender differences in drawings reflected boys' greater intellect. Even into mid-century, researchers such as Gessell (1940) argued that differences between drawings by young boys and girls of the same age indicated that boys were inherently more creative than girls. However, later research indicated that few formal gender differences exist, and those that do may indicate that girls develop more quickly than boys (Cox, 1993). Therefore, it is reasonable to assume that differences in form and content between girls' and boys' drawings exist largely because they reflect gender socialization, rather than sex differences in innate creative or intellectual potential.

The stage-by-age models of artistic development are based on the assumption that growth is a predictably linear, unfolding process that naturally moves toward realism (Kellogg, 1969; Kershensteiner, 1905; cited in Werckmeister, 1977; Schaefer-Simmern, 1950). From this perspective, children progress from one stage to the next, some moving through the stages more quickly than others, but all moving in the same general sequence. The role of art teachers and curriculum has been to aid in that progression by enabling children to move through the stages freely, but in a timely fashion. This perspective of artistic development treated curriculum as a scientifically isolatable variable dependent on, rather than interacting with, "the normal child's" natural progression. The curriculum implications of stage-by-age development have typically resulted in a focus on production activities that are sequential by grade or age range.

Expert-Novice Models

Expert-novice conceptions of development did not begin to be studied seriously by psychologists until the 1960s, when they shifted from a focus on traditional behavioristic research to research concerning complex performances and, by the late 1970s, learning processes (Langley & Simon, 1981). In a sense, cognitive psychology re-opened the possibility of theorizing about internal psychological processes, which had been closed for a time by the focus on behaviorism.

Researchers in cognitive theory generally agree on the importance of prior knowledge in learning (e.g. Joyce & Weil, 1986; Marzano, 1992). Specifically, they indicate that "most of the learning that occurs in life is either incorporated within prior knowledge (Piaget's *assimilation*) or modifies prior knowledge (Piaget's *accommodation*)" (Vosniadou & Brewer; p. 1987: 51, italics in original). Although subtle changes in knowledge occur on a continual basis, radical restructuring of knowledge seems to emerge with age or expertise. This periodic restructuring of knowledge, considered by Piaget and others to be a global developmental change called a stage, involves interaction with the world. Researchers are in debate about whether a global approach to learning, such as Piaget's, should be replaced by one that is more domain-specific, in part, to explain developmental differences between novices and experts.

Expert-novice models suggest that age may not be the most important determining factor in development. Increased formal knowledge is also dependent on the structure of domain specific information. Formal knowledge is defined as knowledge "constrained by principles that govern a domain" (Resnick, 1987, p. 47). Experts in a field follow different strategies for learning and organizing formal knowledge than do novices (Larkin, 1981). For example, unlike novices, experts have multiple levels of knowledge from which they draw when solving problems. Expertise is tied to knowledge of form as well as content. Even adults who are proficient in the use of traditional media to produce art, use processes that reflect novice thinking when learning to employ a new art medium, such as a computer, to produce art (Freedman & Relan, 1992).

The research in expert-novice development has involved several disciplines. Particular attention has been given to expert-novice development in science and math education. The results of research indicate that theorists should move from the idea of global restructuring of knowledge suggested by the stage-dependent conception of development to a cognitive perspective of learning dependent on the integration of specific concepts (Novak, 1977, p. 473). This and related research suggests that any domain of knowledge has characteristics that are inherently interdisciplinary.

In art education, analyses of expert-novice development have been done concerning artistic production and response (e.g. Koroscik, 1990; Parsons, 1987). However, unfortunately, when precursors to the research-based expert-novice approach (i.e., general conceptions of artist-as-model or classroom-as-studio) were applied to curriculum, much of the complexity of the domain of art was lost in the application. As a result, two aspects of art have often been loosely translated from the professional fine art community and focused on in curriculum: the development of production skills and an intuitive leap to a complex level of artistic expression. Harold Rosenberg (1972) termed this reductionism "craft plus inspiration" (p. 47). He argued that the most essential aspect of art expertise, that is, the way to get from skill proficiency to the creation of art, was not handled effectively in education.

The mid-20th century cognitive revolution in psychology (Baars, 1986) was, in part, responsible for changes in curriculum. However, other influences also resulted in change related to expert knowledge. By 1960, theorists—such as psychologist, Jerome Bruner, and art educator, Manuel Barkan—became interested in making education resemble more closely its parent disciplines for social, political, and economic, as well as psychological, reasons. Scientific expert-novice models gained credibility as educators were pressed to create curriculum based on adult domains of knowledge. An understanding of the ways in which proficiency was gained in those domains was required if such curriculum was to be developed.

Stage-by-age models were and are still very influential in addressing some aspects of development important to curriculum planning. However, expert-novice models have helped researchers and educators understand more fully the character of learning and applying formal knowledge. Also, some of the research on which the psychological interpretations of artistic development have been based has helped to establish psychobiological conceptions of development, particularly concerning early childhood. Nonetheless, attempts to devise stage-by-age or expert-novice stage models have had inherent sociological problems on at least four levels. First, behavioral analyses resulted in positive and negative classifications of people by group. Second, the learning of informal knowledge, which is also an important aspect of schooling, was not taken into account. Third, the social attributes of image construction and recycling were not given serious attention (until the work of Wilson & Wilson, 1977). Fourth, the social construction of art disciplines was not analyzed in relation to expert-novice development.

The Sociological Perspective of Development

As psychologists became increasingly interested in cognition after the Second World War, the influences of society and culture on development and learning also became of interest. At the same time, the work of sociologists and anthropologists became more closely associated with psychological considerations and the boundaries between these and other social sciences began to blur. A new sociological conception of development emerged that accounted for the sociocultural influences that were previously ignored.

This sociological perspective of artistic development takes into account the particularly strong influence of psychobiological similarities between children before formal schooling. Gardner (1991) states,

> As I have already conceded, the category of 'natural development' is a fiction; social and cultural factors intervene from the first and become increasingly powerful well before any formal matriculation at school. The fiction seems a useful one to maintain in the pre-school years, however. (p. 105)

When children begin their social life, and the emergence of language occurs, their art becomes increasingly influenced by society and culture. This influence is seen not only in content, but also in structure. If sociocultural influences are, in fact, an essential part of artistic development, then differences in the structure of children's art, such as gender differences, may be socialized and should be considered an important part of any developmental theory.

In curriculum, children have often been viewed as entirely unique and without attributes of culture when not categorized by psychobiological stage. Such a conception of individualism supports the idea of a fictional, free self-expression in school (a social institution) through the teaching of art (a product of cultural communities). The focus on this conception of "natural" individualism in curriculum has resulted in a neglect of both cultural similarities and differences. Yet, the sociocultural attributes that confound this notion of individualism, such as the influence of schooling, mass media, and gender-specific/ethnic experience, have received little attention by researchers in art education.

However, by the 1970s, important sociological changes took place in research on children's drawing development. Wilson and Wilson (1977) formulated a conception of development based on the suggestion by Paget (1932) that drawing behaviors referred to social learning. These authors demonstrated that children learn to draw from many cultural sources, including other children, the mass media, and other adult forms of representation. They also rejected the notion of drawing schema, which Lowenfeld (1957) described as the symbolic forms children use to represent generic types of objects, such as a person or tree. For Lowenfeld, schema are stable concepts that do not change form until a child requires another mode of representation, at which time, the child will develop a new schema through experimentation. Wilson and Wilson (1977) state that the concept of a drawing program (somewhat like a computer program) is more apt. They argue that children develop thousands of symbolic programs for objects that may be called upon at any time to represent an object. The programs may be repeated several times, but often with certain changes, to make a generic form more particular.

In response to models of artistic development that have represented the characteristics of children's art as universal and psychobiological, developmentalists with a sociological perspective argue that many aspects of drawing are connected to culture and socialization. The notion of sequential stages has been questioned with the increasing diversity of school populations. As Wilson and Wilson (1977) and others have shown, forms of children's drawing development are not universal (see Cox, 1993, for a review). They differ to various extents cross-culturally and historically.

The relationship between social life and learning has been a topic of constructivist learning theory. Constructivist conceptions of development are based on research indicating that all learning is *situated*, or closely related to the circumstance in which it takes place. Development, then, is bound by the construction of knowledge by students as they learn. Students learn by appropriating information and restructuring it in relation to what they already know (Vosniadou & Brewer, 1987). Such restructuring actually influences the processes used to learn further information. If this information is consistent with previous knowledge, it is assimilated. If it is inconsistent, most often it will be rejected or changed to fit what is already known. Students continually interpret knowledge, which sometimes results in misinterpretations as they restructure the new knowledge to fit the old. Simple information is easiest both to assimilate and to reject, and highly complex new information will probably be rejected. As a result, constructivists argue that students learn best through deep engagement in activities with medium levels of complexity that reflect life experiences and provoke several levels of thought.

From a constructivist perspective, it is through curriculum that students develop. Students tend to learn disconnected bits of knowledge when they are taught that way. They cannot automatically put the pieces together or transfer knowledge to other situations. From this perspective, curriculum should be designed to help students make connections between various arenas of knowledge and experience. Some research has indicated that socially bound experiences, such as cooperative learning and whole-language education, advance knowledge beyond expected levels precisely because they do not involve a synthetic sequence of information.

Expert-novice conceptions of development are based on the devices of professional communities and therefore, are socially constructed. Professional communities claim certain areas of knowledge within their domain and construct certain representations of that knowledge to be considered appropriate to the community. For example, art history has traditionally been a domain of Western fine art. Although it deals with historical images, the domain of the professional community is not usually considered to extend to mass media images, for example. Mass media images are considered unrelated to art history to such an extent that they are studied in a different department at universities, usually called communications or media studies. Of course, art historians deal with visual communication and media. However, each professional community has claimed certain aspects of image-associated knowledge and represented those aspects as more different than similar. The differences are primarily related to the purposes the images fulfill for their makers and their audiences, which are social conditions.

Although previous conceptions of development have shaped the 20th century curriculum, the acceptance by educators and researchers of profound social and cultural influences on children has not been greatly reflected in curriculum.

Implications for Curriculum

Both the stage-by-age and expert-novice models help us understand something about artistic development. The first describes aspects of the presocial conditions of artistic growth; the latter aids us in understanding psychological processes of building on domain-specific knowledge. However, neither perspective can help us effectively design curriculum without attention to the social conditions that influence student development and the construction of domains of knowledge. An interpretation of development that takes into account social conditions requires a new conception of knowledge and knowing, including a move beyond the limitations of "formal" thinking (Kincheloe & Steinber, 1993).

Curriculum shapes not only what students know, but how they come to know. Therefore, attention to developmental considerations in curriculum concerns not only the organization of content for schoolwork. It also involves juxtapositions of language practices, cultural norms and ideals, student experience, and other social conditions that can influence the ways students restructure knowledge. However, references to subject areas in curriculum come from a variety of places outside of school (not only from the professional community of the parent discipline) and these fragmented external references may have more to do with student understandings of a subject than to formal thinking and logical, sequential written curriculum. Students' attitudes and beliefs about art, including their misconceptions, exist all around them and are dependent, in part, on the many contradictions about art that pervade contemporary culture. (Freedman, in press). Social contradictions are reflected in children's drawings, as well (Duncum, 1989). Such contradictions may not simply lead to a rejection of new information if students are socialized to approach them as a positive challenge (Prawat, 1989). These social conditions should be considered in curriculum planning.

Although educators have often tried to filter out experiences that are not considered legitimate curriculum content, many levels of such influence are reflected in children's apprehension and creation of art. For example, teachers and parents have tried to prevent children from copying images from each other and popular culture sources in the hopes of promoting creativity, individuality, and psychological health. However, as discussed above, children's spontaneous drawings rely on graphic sources ranging from media images, comic books, and other popular sources, to other children's drawings (e.g. Duncum, 1989; Kindler, 1994; Wilson & Wilson, 1977).

The new thinking about drawing in art education has included reconsiderations of other long-standing opinions about the ways in which children represent. For example, Duncum (1982) re-evaluated the assumption that Cizek's students in Vienna near the turn of the century created the beautiful, intricate, and stylized art without adult influence. He pointed out that although the children may not have been directed toward a particular style by their teacher, the images came from the many images the children saw in their daily life.

Although students are active learners and construct individual meaning from their daily experiences, some common meanings are constructed by children through the pervasive common experience. For example, many more students, from childhood through adolescence, watch the same television shows than are taught through the same school curriculum. Children attend to television in an organized fashion, typically scanning programs for the parts that have meaning for them. When representations of art become attached to popular culture objects and images that are interesting to children, children learn associations with art. Children, as well as adults, tend to focus even more direct attention on films than on other television shows. For these reasons, popular imagery should be included in curriculum.

Response theory from literary studies enhances understanding of the process of knowledge construction through the concept of *intertextuality*. Intertextuality is the reference a reader makes to various other texts the person has read in the past. The process of intertextuality might be said to take place in the conceptual space between texts. Rather than focusing on the text at hand, reading necessarily focuses on the conceptual space between various (written and verbal) texts. If this were not the case, we would have to learn to understand each new text that we read; we would not be able to relate one text to another; and text producers would not be able to use techniques like simile, analogy, and metaphor.

The same type of conceptual space exists for visual culture. This includes what traditionally has been called art in curriculum (Freedman, 1994). Our minds are capable of recalling and integrating a vast array of images and their associated meanings. When confronted with a new visual form, the focus of cognition often involves an interrelationship between dispersed references to other representations rather than a single object or meaning. The images we have encountered become attached to associations related to the context in which we saw them, including the context of thoughts about (or the conceptual space between) previous experiences. In a sense, the attached meanings are part of what is known about the images until we restructure or construct new knowledge through more experience. This *intergraphicality*, then, enables us to comingle images, make associations between them, recycle and change them, etc. as we restructure knowledge.

To understand the social conditions of knowledge restructuring, students need to be made aware of them through curriculum. Students can begin to understand how knowledge is constructed in professional communities and by individuals through experiences that focus them on creating meaning as well as products. Group activities through which students must discuss intepretations and group and individual reflections on learning that involve teacher and student responses to visual culture can aid student understanding and growth.

Conclusion

Part of what makes each of us individual is the many possible combinations of developmental responses to social groupings, some of which have emerged in relation to biophysics. (For example, gender is one such social grouping that has been created in relation to sex.) Each child is socialized to develop in ways that are consistent with the social groups to which the child belongs. Also, although students experience culture in different ways depending on gender, ethnicity, socioeconomic class, institutional environment, etc., American cultural boundaries and popular culture work to promote certain commonalities in thinking across social groups. In other words, students are always *situated*, and that situation influences development.

The debate about the relative influence of nature and culture is far from settled. Considerations, such as cultural influences on artistic knowledge and production, interdisciplinary language skills required for writing and talking about art, and the deliberate modeling of thinking processes in teaching are too often written out of public school curriculum. However, in creating curriculum based on the emerging sociocultural perspective of development, these influences must be taken into consideration.

References

Anderson, J. (1980). *Cognitive psychology and its implications*. New York: W. H. Freeman.

Baars, B. J. (1986). *The cognitive revolution in psychology*. New York: Guilford.

Barnes, E. (1908). Child study in relation to elementary art education. In J. Haney (Ed.), *Art education in the United States* (pp. 101-32). New York: American Art Annual.

Cox, M. V. (1993). *Children's drawings of the human figure*. Hove, UK: Erlbaum.

Duncum, P. (1982). The origins of self-expression: A case of self-deception. *Art Education*, September, 32-35

Duncum, P. (1989). Children's unsolicited drawings of violence as a site of social contradiction. *Studies in Art Education*, *30*(4), 249-256.

Efland, A. (1990). *A history of art education: Intellectual and social currents in teaching the visual arts*. New York: Teachers College Press.

Freedman, K. (in press). Representations of fine art in popular culture: Curriculum inside and outside of school. *Journal of Art and Design Education*.

Freedman, K. (1993, April). *Representations of art*. Paper presented at the meeting of the American Educational Research Association.

Freedman, K. (1994). Interpreting gender and visual culture in art classrooms. *Studies in Art Education*, *35*(3), 157-170.

Freedman, K. & Relan, A. (1992). Computer graphics, artistic production and social processes. *Studies in Art Education*, *33*(2), 98-109.

Gardner, H. (1991). *The unschooled mind: How children think and how schools should teach*. New York: Basic Books.

Gessell, A. (1940). *The first five years of life: A guide to the study of the preschool child*. New York: Harper & Brothers.

Golomb, C, (1974). *Young children's sculpture and drawing: A study in representational development*. Cambridge: Harvard University Press.

Hall, G. S. (1911). *Educational problems Vol. 2*. New York: D. Appleton.

Joyce, B., & Weil M. (1986). *Models of teaching*. Englewood, NJ: Prentice-Hall.

Kellogg, R. (1969). *Analyzing children's art*. Palo Alto, CA: Mayfield.

Kershensteiner, G. (1905). Die entwicklung der zeichnerischen begabung (Development of a graphic gift.) Munich: Carl Gerber.

Kincheloe, J. L., & Steinberg, S. R. (1993). A tentative description of post-formal thinking: The critical confrontation with cognitive theory. *Harvard Educational Review, 63*(3), 296-320.

Kindler, A. M. (1994). Children and the culture of multicultural society. *Art Education, 47*(4), 54-60.

Koroscik, J. (1990). Novice-expert differences in understanding and misunderstanding art and their implications for student assessment in art education. *Art and Learning Research, 8,* 6-29.

Langley, P. , & Simon, H. A. (1981)., The central learning in cognition (pp. 361-380). In J.R. Anderson (Ed.), *Cognitive skills and their acquisition.* Hillsdale, NJ: Erlbaum.

Larkin, J. (1981). Enriching formal knowledge: A model for learning to solve textbook physics problems. In J. R. Anderson (Ed.), *Cognitive skills and their acquisition.* Hillsdale, NJ: Lawrence Erlbaum.

Lowenfeld, V. (1947). *Creative and mental growth.* New York: Macmillan.

Lowenfeld, V. (1957). *Creative and mental growth.* (3rd ed.) New York: Macmillan.

Lowenfeld, V., & Brittain, W. L. (1964). *Creative and mental growth* (4th ed.). New York: Macmillan.

Marzano, R. J. (1992). *A different kind of classroom: Teaching with dimensions of learning.* Alexandria, VA: Association for Curriculum and Supervision.

Novak, J. D. (1977). An alternative to Piagetian psychology for science and mathematics education. *Science Education, 61,* 453-477.

Paget, G. W. (1932). Some drawings of men and women made by children of certain non-European races. *Journal of the Royal Anthropological Institute, 62,* 127-144.

Parsons, M. J. (1987). *How we understand art: A cognitive development account of aesthetic experience.* Cambridge, England: Cambridge University Press.

Prawat, R. S. (1989). Promoting access to knowledge, strategy, and disposition in students: A research synthesis. *Review of Educational Research, 59*(1), 1-41.

Resnicke, L. B. (1987). Constructing knowledge in school. In L. S. Lisbon (Ed.), *Development and learning: Conflict or congruence* (pp. 19-50). Hillsdale, NJ: Erlbaum.

Rosenberg, H. (1972). *The definition of art.* New York: Macmillan.

Schaefer-Simmern, H. (1950). *The unfolding of artistic ability.* Berkeley: University of California Press.

Sully, J. (1895). *Studies of childhood.* New York: D. Appleton.

Thorndike, E. L. (1913, November). The measurement of achievement in drawing. *Teachers College Record, 14*(3), 45-82.

Vosniadou, S., & Brewer, W. F. (1987). Theories of knowledge restructuring in development. *Review of Educational Research, 57*(1), 51-67.

Werckmeister, O. K. (1977). The issue of the child in the art of Paul Klee. *Arts Magazine, 52,* 138-151.

Wilson, B., & Wilson, M. (1977). An iconoclastic view of the imagery sources of the drawing of young people. *Art Education, 30*(1), 5-11.

SUBJECTS AND THEMES IN CHILDREN'S UNSOLICITED DRAWING AND GENDER SOCIALIZATION

Research on the subjects and themes of Western children's unsolicited drawing has been undertaken, albeit erratically, for over a century. Data has been gathered by survey, document analysis, and case studies of individual children. The research effort has been sustained throughout by the belief that children's preferred subject matter reveals children's real interests and developmental needs. Drawings have been regarded as objectifications of developmental preoccupations.

The single most striking feature of this research is the remarkable consistency of subject preference, gender differences, and thematic concerns. These findings are consistent despite varied research methodologies, sampling techniques from different Western countries (notably from North America, England and Australia), different theoretical positions, and different pedagogical ambitions.

If children's developmental needs are evident in their drawing preferences, this consistency appears to suggest that the nature of childhood in Western societies has not fundamentally changed over the past century. Moreover, an historical study, which commences its analysis from the early 1700s, suggests that the concerns of contemporary children revealed through their subject preferences are of even longer standing.

Historical perspective
Most of the surveys were conducted around the turn of the century. Although some specific subjects have been superseded, the general picture is consistent with more recent observations. All surveys indicate children's in-

PAUL DUNCUM

terest is in both ordinary life and fantasy as well as in peaceful scenes and in strong physical action (Ballard, 1912, 1913; Burroughs, 1962; Duncum, 1986; Gallagher, 1896-97; Lukens, 1896-97; Maitland, 1895; Munro, Lark-Horovitz & Barnhart, 1942; Potter, 1968; Roberts, 1916). Typical everyday subjects of children's drawings, as reported, include studies of animals, trains, ships, plants, and still life although by far the most favored subject was the human figure, sometimes represented in a satirical mode. The portrayals of ordinary events included going to school and wearing a dunce cap, cooking, and gathering around Christmas trees. Fantasy images included, for example, children going to picnics where there are illimitable spreads and eatables. Giants attack them occasionally and they get run over by strange horses and carriages. They have hair-breadth escapes from being dashed to pieces off ledges careening with frightful velocity down perpendicular hills (Ballard, 1913).

All surveys found strikingly different gender preferences. Ballard (1913), for example, noted that boys typically drew ships, vehicles, and, to a lesser extent, weapons, whereas girls drew flowers and houses. Boys favored machines, transport, and battle while girls favored "growing things."

The spread of subject matter choices listed above is strikingly similar to that derived from a historical study drawn from biographies and autobiographies of 35 children born between 1724 and 1900 (Duncum, 1986). The majority of these individuals drew representations of human figures; slightly less than half drew animals, violent subjects, caricatures, or burlesques; less than a third drew landscapes and buildings, ships or trains; only a handful drew grotesques and sexual subjects while nearly half drew a range of miscellaneous, mostly everyday objects. Eugene Delacroix, for example, drew medieval warriors brandishing swords; John Ruskin drew landscapes and cathedrals; Toulouse-Lautrec and George Stubbs drew horses and dogs; Aubrey Beadsley created malicious caricatures of his teachers; Kathe Kollwitz drew her family; Washington Allston drew Vesuvius erupting; and Diego Rivera drew train wrecks and collisions with bodies strewn around.

Recent studies of theme preferences in spontaneous drawings

These subject matter preferences are confirmed by numerous, more contemporary observations and case studies of individual children (eg. Beck 1928; Duncum, 1986; Eng, 1957; Fein, 1976; Feinburg, 1973; Gardner, 1980; Hildreth, 1941; Pearson, 1993; Robertson, 1989; Wilson, 1974; Wilson & Wilson, 1976). Spontaneous drawings by boys explore themes such as transport vehicles, trains, rockets, imaginary machines, battle scenes, usually involving warfare of all kinds and often concentrating on explosions and the line of fire. Boys' drawings are also concerned with sport themes. Girls have a characteristic preference for houses and a particularly consistent preference for horses. Where the surveys indicate similarities, in an overwhelming preference for the human figure, the case studies show that boys create male superheroes, often pop stars, and sometimes humorous and utterly weird characters. Girls draw idealized teenage girls often wearing fashion clothes. Where boys tend to draw wild beasts, girls tend to draw pet animals.

Both these gender preferences and interest in everyday life as well as fiction were consistent even among the children who drew unsolicitedly in a World War II concentration camp (Volavková, 1978). Girls drew "nature which they remembered" (p. 63), flowers and butterflies, ballerinas and pretty little cottages with flower gardens. Boys drew details of the local hilly landscape decked with stream boats and warships, detective stories, battles, revelries, and adventures. They also drew pictures of their everyday life, "of SS men, ghetto guards, of carts drawn by human beings, of burials or executions" (p. 64).

Of course, there are exceptions to theme gender differences, with individual boys drawing houses, women in fashion clothes, and horses. Romaine Brooks, for example, was found drawing fierce monsters, and Kate Greenaway, massacres (Duncum, 1986). But these exceptions only highlight the extent of the pressures of socialization.

The focus of the numerous studies on unsolicited drawing has been to observe male and female preferences, not to account for them. These studies have been singularly silent on gender specific socialization. However, if the recently developed gender schema theory (Santrock, 1992) is applied, it is possible to understand these preferences as guided by an internal mechanism to conform to gender-based standards and stereotypes. According to this view, an active construction of gender is developed though socially determined gender preferences. Usually without being consciously aware, children select their subjects in accord with what they conceive to be the appropriate subjects for their gender, and consequently they find these rewarding.

The process of socialization to drawing itself, as a valued social activity which confers status on the child as an artist, is mentioned by several studies (Wilson, 1974, 1976; Duncum, 1986). Pearson (1993) refers to such social status among peers as cultural capital. Thus, it seems possible to say that gender preferences indicate an awareness of, as well as constitute a contribution to, gender capital.

Prolific drawers, children who draw consistently, even obsessively, often tend to specialize in a limited number of subjects: horses (Fein, 1974), superhero stories (Wilson, 1974), trains (Hildreth, 1941), domestic scenes (Eng, 1957), muscle men (Pearson, 1993), battle and sport (Feinburg, 1973; Robertson, 1987). In each of these reported cases, the children's preference conformed to the gender stereotype.

Over the past century some subject preferences have changed. Lindstrom (1957), for example, noted that bomb explosions were replacing volcanoes in scenes of violent destruction, while Lark-Horovitz, Lewis & Luca (1974) observed that trains had given way to spaceships. They also noted that while early surveys indicated a strong preference for landscape among both genders, and, among girls, of plant drawings, ornamental designs, and still lifes, these subjects were no longer common. The authors also suggested that landscape, as a setting for narrative adventures, had given way to space in children's drawings. They noted that with greater leisure and affluence there appears nowadays to be a far wider range of subjects.

However, changes in subject preferences do not appear to signal fundamental shifts of interest; rather, they seem to suggest stable orientation to underlying themes. An interest in volcanoes and rocket launchings seems compatible with an interest in sudden, violent action. Trains, ships, and rockets are all methods of transport and, as mechanical objects, can be thought of as icons of power. Furthermore, many contemporary subjects have underlying thematic similarities. For example, sports and battles both involve winning, physical action, teamwork, and rule-making (Feinburg, 1973).

Themes, gender, and development
The relation of subject preferences to thematic, gender, and developmental concerns has been examined through both speculations about individual subjects (Duncum, 1986) and case studies of specific children (Feinberg, 1973; Hildreth, 1941; Wilson, 1976). Intellectual lenses have included various approaches in developmental psychology (Gardner, 1980; Feinburg, 1973), learning theory (Duncum, 1986; Wilson & Wilson, 1977), and structuralism (Wilson & Wilson, 1979, 1980).

Speculations have been made suggesting a link between common subject matter preferences in children's drawings and their broad thematic concerns. Duncum (1986), for example, pointed to the possibility of an association of the subject matter of horses with children's interest in nurturance, procreation and power. Similarly, Hildreth (1941) indicated a possible association with the subject matter of trains and general themes of adventure, mystery, and virility, while Feinburg (1973) suggested the association of battle and sport with motion, a displacement of energy, physical action, social interaction, rule-governed behavior, and a sense of efficacy and personal power. Some of these subject matter-broad concern associations appear gender specific. For example, the association of horses with nurturance and procreation in the case of girls' drawings has no clear parallel in subject matter preferences of boys. It seems that for boys, horses do have other associations which have specific parallels with rockets, trucks, battle, and sport, namely a mastery of power, virility, and strong physical action. It seems to me this suggests that in some cases gender differences may in fact be deeper than the mere choice of subject matter indicates. Boys and girls may draw what appears to be the same subject matter for a very different reason or purpose due to their gender socialization.

Themes in children's drawings have been demonstrated to be related to developmental preoccupations of the middle childhood years. Duncum (1986) has employed a number of developmental lenses in furthering this argument. From a Piagetian position, middle childhood was a time of increasing socialization involving decentring, cooperation, and the submission of the self to rules (Santrock, 1992). For Freud (1938) it was opportune for cultural achievement, while for Social Learning theorists it is apposite for developing a sense of self-efficacy through rule learning (Bandura, 1977). From a life-span developmental perspective (Veroff & Veroff, 1980), middle childhood can also be viewed in terms of such social incentives as assertion through images of competence and power and even benign aggression where the intention is to defend territory or rights (Duncum, 1986). The frequent satirical drawings of middle childhood can be viewed in terms of what Elkind (1974) called the cognitive conceit of childhood (Duncum, 1980). From a general cognitive psychology perspective, Gardner (1980) sums up these characteristics in relation to unsolicited drawing with reference to a general sense of well-being through learning social norms and skills building.

The oeuvre of individual children, which has been examined in terms of interwoven themes, lends support to the fit between thematic content and development. Feinburg (1973) links her son's battle and sport drawings with the need to successfully resolve what Erikson (1963) sees as the chief task of middle childhood: the achievement of a sense of competence. Battle and sport share the goals of winning, harnessing energy, and producing a result, and are seen by her as an objectification of a struggle to achieve mastery. Similarly, Robertson (1987) sees her adolescent son's drawing of the same subjects in terms of Erikson's (1963) chief task of adolescents; identity formation. A quest for identity is said to have subsumed other themes such as sex, power, violence, and family life. Among the children studied by Duncum (1986), Matthew drew many battles between "goodies" and "baddies." A number of interrelated themes emerged from this work: fairness, action, friendly social relations, and rule making. Matthew's themes were linked because, although his goodies eventually won, the goodies and baddies were fairly evenly matched and conflict was conducted according to rules that ensured the action continued for some time. Friendship was important because the goodies relied upon their friends to defeat the baddies' superior force. Thus, Matthew's interest in violence involved a defense of rights as well as rule making.

At a more abstract level, Wilson and Wilson; (1979, 1980) have examined themes in a variety of structural terms. First, employing Propp's classifications of the themes of "villainy nullified" and "lack liquidated," (in Sutton-Smith, Botvin, & Mahony, n.d.) the authors analyzed unsolicited narrative drawings of North American boys and girls. The organizing structure of many of these narrative drawings was the age-old theme of the journey or the odyssey. These narrative drawings were capable of assimilating a wide range of perceptions, actions, and ideas of the most profound interest to children such as growth and metamorphosis, birth and death, trials and success.

Wilson and Wilson; (1980) also claimed that unsolicited drawings show evidence of a "burgeoning construction of and an orientation" (p. 277) to four kinds of realities or themes, as described by Kreitler and Kreitler (1972). These themes are labeled as common, archaeological, normative, and prophetic. Common themes include generally shared observations and beliefs about the veridical world we all inhabit. Examples include drawings of pet animals, people, and houses, as well as stories about daily rhythms, such as going to school and playing. Archaeological themes involve the various conscious and unconscious levels of personal traits, beliefs, and feelings, which in turn encompass archetypal motifs, myths, and legends. While many drawings conform to well established narrative patterns such as "villainy nullified," modifications are often made. For example, one child based his drawings on an old television series of Batman and Robin, but instead of resorting to violence to resolve conflicts, he invariably used verbal wit or gadgetry (Duncum, 1986). Normative themes concern beliefs about social rules and norms and, as noted above, battle and sport pictures are rule governed. Other examples include crime and punishment, socially recognized triumphs, rewards, and achievement. Wilson (1974) explained one boy's renditions of a superhero's adventures in terms of the child's interest in concepts of duty, friendship, and moral obligation. Prophetic themes incorporate the anticipation of events to come, beliefs, and wishes about goals and the future. Examples include young children acting out adolescent or adult roles such as young girls getting dressed for adolescent parties and boys driving powerful trucks.

Many of the themes children use have long been interwoven into myths, legends, and fairytales (Gardner, 1980, Wilson & Wilson, 1979). Today, they are also interwoven into the popular media from where they are often derived and recycled by children according to their predispositions and dispositions.

A century of, albeit erratic, research shows that many subject preferences have remained stable, and where they have changed the underlying themes appear to be the same. Clear gender preferences are apparent in both general subjects of drawings and their specific treatment, although overlaps do occur in some cases. However, even where differences are observable at the level of specific subject matter preferences, it appears that underlying thematic content is at least as similar as divergent. For middle childhood, the broad themes of power, competence, rules, and social relations are clearly common to both girls and boys. It is possible to conclude that while the thematic content of drawings varies to some extent along the gender lines, the general themes explored in children's imagery conform to the major preoccupations of life phases of these youngsters.

References

Ballard, P. B. (1912). What London children like to draw. *Journal of Experimental Pedagogy, 1*(3), 185-210.

Ballard, P. B. (1913). What children like to draw. *Journal of Experimental Pedagogy, 2*, 127-129.

Bandura, A. (1977). *Social learning theory.* Englewood Cliffs, NJ: Prentice Hall.

Beck, W. (1928). *Self-development in drawing, as interpreted by the genius of Romano Dazzi.* New York: Putnam's Sons, Knickerbocker Press.

Burroughs, L. D. (1962). The content of children's spontaneous drawings. Proceedings of the Conference of Art Teacher Training Centres (pp. 12-21). Conference of Art Teacher Training Centres.

Duncum, P. (1986). Middle childhood spontaneous drawing from a cultural perspective. Unpublished doctoral dissertation. The Flinders University of South Australia.

Gardner, H. (1980). *Artful scribbles: The significance of children's drawings.* New York: Basic Books.

Elkind, D. (1974). *Children and adolescents.* Oxford, England: Oxford University Press.

Eng, H. (1957). *The psychology of child and youth drawing.* London: Routledge & Kegan Paul.

Erikson, E. H. (1963). *Childhood and society* (2nd Edition). New York: W. W. Norton.

Fein, S. G. (1972). *Heidi's horse.* Pleasant Hill, CA: Exelrod Press.

Feinburg, S. G. (1973). Combat in child art. Unpublished manuscript. Tufts University. Boston, MA.

Freud, S. (1938). *The basic writings of Sigmund Freud.* (A. A. Brill, Ed. and Trans.). New York: The Modern Library.

Gallagher, M. (1897). Children's spontaneous drawing. *The North Western Monthly, 8*, 130-134.

Hildreth, G. (1941). *The child mind in evolution.* New York: Kings Crown Press.

Kreitler, H., & Kreitler, S. (1972). *Psychology of the arts.* Durham, NC: Duke Universtiy.

Lark-Horowitz, B., Lewis, H., & Luca, M. (1974). *Understanding children's art for better teaching* (2nd. ed.). Columbus, OH: Charles E. Merril.

Lindstrom, M. (1957). *Children's art: A case study of normal development in children's models of visualisation.* Berkeley, CA: University of California Press.

Lukens, H. T. (1896-97). A study of children's drawings in the early years. The Pedagogical Seminary, 4(1), 46-68.

Maitland, L. M. (1895). What children draw to please themselves. *The Inland Educator, 1*, 77-81.

Munro, T., Lark-Horovitz. B., & Barnhart, E. N. (1942). Children's art abilities. Studies at the Cleveland Museum of Art. *Journal of Experimental Education, 11*(2), 97-155.

Pearson, P. (1993). Who cares about "Ninja Turtles?: Image making in the life of Iati. Australian *Art Education, 17*(1), 14-22.

Potter, M. J. (1968). A study of the private drawing of children. Unpublished diploma of art education dissertation, College of Art and Design, Birmingham, England.

Roberts, T. T. (1916). *A study in children's interests: Being the account of an investigation of the favourite topics of Sydney children as revealed by their preferences in drawing.* Sydney: William Applegate Gullick, Government Printer.

Robertson, A. (1987). Development of Bruce's spontaneous drawings from six to sixteen. *Studies in Art Education, 29*(1), 37-51.

Santrock, J. W. (1992). *Life-span development* (4th ed.). Duburque, IA: Wm. C. Brown.

Sutton-Smith, B., Botvin, G., & Mahony, D. (n.d.). Developmental structures in fantasy structures. Paper No. 9. Teachers College, Columbia University.

Veroff, J., & Veroff, J. B. (1980). *Social incentives: A life-span developmental approach.* New York: Academic Press.

Wilson, B. (1974). The superheros of J.C. Holtz: Plus an outline of a theory of child art. A*rt Education, 24*(8), 2-7.

Wilson, B., & Wilson, M. (1976). Visual narrative and the artistically gifted. *The Gifted Child Quarterly, 20*, 432-447.

Wilson, B., & Wilson, M. (1977). An iconoclastic view of the imagery sources of the drawing of young people. *Art Education, 30*(1), 5-11.

Wilson, B., & Wilson, M. (1979). Children's story drawings: Reinventing worlds. *School Arts, 78*(8), 6-8.

Wilson, B., & Wilson, M. (1980). Cultural recycling: The uses of conventional configurations, images and themes in the narrative drawings of American children. In J. Condus, J. Howlet & J. Skull (Eds.). *Arts in cultural diversity.* Sydney: Holt, Rinehart & Winston.

GRAPHIC DEVELOPMENT IN ARTISTICALLY EXCEPTIONAL CHILDREN

This chapter addresses the nature of graphic development in "exceptional" children, and the relationship between early exceptional performance and adult artistic recognition. The term "graphic development" will be used to refer to the systematic changes which can be observed in the child's acquisition of graphic skills, techniques and conventions (Arnheim, 1974; Goodnow, 1977; Luquet 1927). "Artistically exceptional children" are those who draw precociously and who produce large numbers of drawings (Winner & Pariser 1985). Many of the drawings produced by such children are more technically or expressively advanced than the drawings of their peers. We will refer to three groups of children for illustrative material: 1) Children who suffered from neurological and/or psychological anomalies and who produced numerous remarkable drawings; 2) children who were artistically precocious, but who did not, or who have not yet achieved significant artistic recognition; and 3) childen who drew precociously and achieved broad recognition as mature artists.

This discussion of artistic exceptionality is framed within Csikszentmihalyi's (1988) systems model of creativity. This social psychologist insists that creativity should be understood as an emergent phenomenon, something which requires three elements: the participation of a specially endowed individual within a "domain" of knowledge, and the ratification and support of that individual by the "field." "Domain" refers to the intellectual skills and knowledge which the person is mastering (Feldman, 1980). Domains of knowledge can be as diverse as plumbing and microsurgery, as popular as fly-casting or as arcane as the lives of the saints. The field is the social

DAVID PARISER

organization which provides support systems for apprentices. Becker's (1982) description of an "art world" comprising artists, curators, critics, aesthetes, teachers, audiences, galleries, journals, etc, is an example of the field in which visual artists operate.

Csikszentmihalyi's (1988) model helps to frame our examination of the artistic development of exceptional children. Children are "exceptional" only if they excel in a culturally defined and valued domain, and if representatives of the field acknowledge their superlative performance. Keeping this model in mind, it should come as no surprise that in some cultures, the very notion of "specially able" children is viewed with misgiving. Russian and American attitudes towards training artistically gifted children are quite different (Hurwitz, 1976). In a study by Tobin, Wu, and Davidson (1989) on day care, researchers asked Japanese teachers to comment on the notion of childhood giftedness. The teachers interviewed clearly acknowledged differences among the children they taught. But the teachers found the resource implications which follow from the idea of "giftedness" unpalatable. As one teacher put it, "How sad that by age three or four a child might already be labeled as having less chance for success than some of his classmates" (p. 25).

The cognitive development of gifted children is of interest for its own sake (because of the delightful and astounding work which such children produce) and because of what it may tell us about the way in which the brain is organized. A fundamental and unresolved question about the development and structure of the brain is whether it develops in a unified or modular fashion (Feldman, 1980). Contemporary proponents of the monolithic view, Neo-Piagetians such as Case (1992), Dennis (1987) and Porath (1988), have argued for system-wide changes in the cognitive apparatus. Stages in cognitive development are presumed to be system-wide, affecting all aspects of intellectual functioning. Theorists such as Gardner (1983) make a case for modular intelligences. For this reason, gifted children are of special interest as their uneven intellectual profiles are more easily explained by invoking a modular rather than a monolithic model of the human brain.

Gould (1992) uses a description of the 8-year-old Mozart as an opportunity for exploring the concept of mental modularity. According to an 18th century observer, Mozart displayed a mixture of childlike and adult traits. His technical wizardry and invention at the keyboard were stunning, but his behavior in other respects was unremarkably childlike. This is a typically uneven profile for gifted children. Gould (1992) cites this observation of cognitive unevenness as a basis for inferences about the modular structure of the human brain and the mechanisms of evolution. Similarly, Clark and Zimmerman, (1992) argue that most artistically exceptional children have "well-developed drawing skills, high cognitive abilities, affective intensity, and interest and motivation" although, the authors add, these traits "may or may not be present at the same levels in any student at any given time" (p.2).

The works of Tannenbaum (1983) and Clark and Zimmerman (1992) are two of the comprehensive and scholarly presentations which attempt to define the intellectually exceptional child. Tannenbaum gives an overview which includes the history of interest in the gifted child, various definitions, and the connections between giftedness and adult performance. The author proposes four categories of "talent" or gift, scarcity, surplus, quota and anomalous. Although he claims that there is no hierarchy involved in this listing it is clear from the definitions advanced that not all talents are equal. His listing is based on an asessment of how badly certain talents are needed by society. Scarcity talents are abilities which are always in short supply and which are of vital importance to society, the sorts of talents which one sees at work in the actions of great leaders and scientists who address problems of health and justice. The arts are labeled as "surplus" talents, that is, talents which are less urgently needed by society at large. It is clear that when Tannenbaum (1983) uses the term "society" he has in mind modern Western technologized society. Thus his categories for "giftedness/exceptionality" would have to be revised if the term "society" were to include non-Western and less technologized cultures. Consistent with Csikszentmihalyi's model, Clark and Zimmerman (1992) suggest that qualities which are considered highly indicative of talent in one culture may be irrelevant in another.

We will now take a look at the three categories of exceptional children and examine aspects of their graphic development: 1) Child artists with neurological or psychological problems, such as Nadia Chomyn (Selfe,1977), David Downes (Morgan,1981), Stephen Wiltshire (Wiltshire, 1991), Kiyoshi Yamashita (Lindsley, 1965), Yoshihiko Yamamoto (Morishima, 1974), and Shyoichoro Yamamura (Motsugi, 1968); 2) Children who demonstrated a surprising ability in graphic work at an early age, such as Wang Yani, a Chinese wunderkind (Feldman & Goldsmith, 1989; Ho, 1989; Tan, 1993), and an Israeli child, Eytan (Golomb, 1992); (In many cases we do not know if these individuals are "bound for artistic glory"); and 3) Children who we know were destined for significant artistic recognition, i.e., Lautrec, Picasso, Klee (Pariser, 1987), Munch (Carroll, 1992), and Millais (Warner, 1981).

It should be noted that these three categories are ordered according to the three elements in Csikszentmihalyi;'s model of creativity. The first group of children have remarkable "built-in" skills which are extremely useful for mastering aspects of the domain of artistry, but these children are cut off from much of the field itself. The second group of children have innate skills and master portions of the artistic domain with ease; they are also well connected with teachers and mentors in the field. The third group of children possess excellent innate skills, develop superb mastery of the relevant artistic domain, and are well connected with the field. As adults, children from this third group have gained recognition from the field and have also succeeded in reshaping and restructuring the domain itself.

Child artists with diagnosed psychological problems

The work of children like Nadia Chomyn, David Downes, Stephen Wiltshire (all of whom have been diagnosed as having varying degrees of autism) is characterized by a rapid and very early grasp of realistic drawing techniques such as foreshortening, perspective, and line control. These children are so technically accomplished that their work appears almost miraculous. In the case of Nadia Chomyn, psychologists refused to believe that a child of four had made the drawings which they were examining. Nadia's work poses real problems for all theories of graphic representation because her skill at accurate rendering seems at variance with her otherwise low level of cognitive functioning (Arnheim, 1992; Pariser, 1981). In two cases, those of David and Nadia, anecdotal evidence (Morgan, 1981; Selfe, 1977) suggests that neither of these children passed through a "scribbling stage." At least there is no record of their having scribbled with marking implements for as long a period as most of their agemates. This absence of the scribbling stage is certainly unusual as this stage is one of the most widely observed features of graphic development. All children start to draw by making random marks and scribbles on the page, prior to drawing recognizable objects. It may be that Nadia and David passed through the scribbling stage very fast, i.e. within a matter of hours or days, thus leaving little evidence of this stage. Alland, (1983) reports observing a child, who had never drawn previously, pass from scribbling to recognizable representations within a few hours.

What is most striking about the drawings of children like David and Nadia is the phenomenal and early grasp which they show of the relation of line to form. At an age when most children are still drawing simple shapes, Nadia was producing articulated and optically complex drawings of horses and other animals. (These animal drawings were based on images from picture books. All observers agree that Nadia's versions of these banal images are virtuoso graphic performances.) David specialized in architecture and produced detailed studies of buildings late in his fifth year. Stephen (Wiltshire, 1991), who has been diagnosed as autistic, continues to draw architectural details and panoramas with uncanny ability. Here again, the hallmarks of his exceptional performance are the prolific nature of his work and the perspectival "realism" of his imagery. I am not aware of how Stephen acquired his knowledge of perscival rendering, but there is no mention made of instruction.

Thus, the drawings of Nadia, David and Stephen all bespeak an innate capacity for and a driving fascination with optically accurate drawing. These three children share a number of features in their drawing development. They all seem to have reached an early "plateau" in development. For example, Nadia never went beyond the level of drawing which she achieved in her fifth and sixth year (Henley;, 1988). She did not experiment with other styles and she adhered to her limited subject matter. Stephen Wiltshire's drawings of cities are all marvelously well executed. He was given a tour of European and Russian cities as a way of recognizing and stimulating his talent. Yet, Oliver Sacks, in his preface to the book of Stephen's drawings, expresses doubts as to whether or not Stephen's work will develop beyond the very high technical level which this young artist has presently achieved. Of the three children, David seems to be the most experimentally inclined. He has studied the work of Turner, an artist whose style seems much at variance with David's preferred linear approach.

An interesting feature shared by Nadia and David is that they are graphically competent only when using a very narrow range of implements. Because both children are focused on linear drawing they are distressed and derailed when required to use a thicker and less controllable marking implement such as a paintbrush. Under these circumstances both children are reduced to making unrecognizable blobs.

The work of three retarded (or possibly autistic) Japanese artists (Lindsley, 1965; Morishima, 1974; Motsugi, 1968) is very instructive, for here we are able to observe how these children from a non-Western aesthetic context have their visual talents shaped. Lindsley documented the case of Kiyoshi Yamashita, a mentally retarded boy who was trained as an artist and who achieved great success. Morishima describes the training and work life of Yoshihiko Yamamoto. Yoshihiko started to draw by copying cartoons, but soon impressed his teachers with his capacity to work from classical Japanese prints and drawings. He eventually began to produce high skill in his prints and drawings. A third child artist, Shyoichoro Yamamura, documented by Morishima, made finely skilled fingerpaintings of insects. The images he created, and those made by the other two Japanese artists, are a far cry from the "realistic" renderings of Nadia and Stephen.

With these three Japanese children we may observe how cultural influences are grafted onto and shape an underlying psychological condition. Morishima notes that each child had his preferred subject matter, Kiyoshi: scenery, Yoshihiko: buildings, and Shyoichoro: insects. In this respect, the Japanese child artists and the British child artists share the "specialist" label. The training of the Japanese children differs, however, from that of their Brit-

ish counterparts inasmuch as they received extensive and painstaking instruction. The acquisition of skills required teaching. This was not the case with
Nadia.

In terms of graphic development, the examples of Nadia, Stephen and
the others, provide evidence that there are some mechanisms pre-established
in the human nervous system necessary for artistic activity. In some cases, as
with Nadia, the mechanism is so finely tuned and so well primed that it takes
no overt teaching or modeling to mobilize the ability. In other cases, the per-
ceptual-motor mechanism needs human contact for it to be cajoled into life.
Sacks (1987) describes such an instance in his essay on "The Autist Artist."
He reports here that through encouragement a withdrawn/autistic young man
was persuaded to sketch. Sacks uncovered a hidden resource in the young
man, a resource which helped the patient to re-enter the social world. The
selectivity with which these children choose their subject matter, and their
investment of effort reflect the personal significance of their art activity. They
certainly enjoy what they do, but most of these children remain limited to a
narrow repertoire of style and subject matter.

Gifted children whose adult artistry is yet to be recognized

In this category we find "normal" children who produce work which is
far in advance of their agemates. Zimmerman (1990) and Robertson (1987)
examined collections of drawings left behind by their own children. Both of
these longitudinal studies of artistically gifted children found no evidence of
developmental anomalies. Consistent with Porath's (1988) findings there was
acceleration of graphic development and significant and consistent productivity. Zimmerman's (1990) and Robertson's (1987) studies further corrobo-
rate the notion that even gifted children use much the same sources for skill
acquisition as less gifted or "average" children.

Golomb (1992) identified three Israeli children who developed exceptional artistic specializations: Varda, Amnon, and Eytan. She found that in all
three cases there was a record of stage-appropriate, rapid, and technically
striking graphic growth governed by the progressive differentiation of form,
color and space. Eytan's work is perhaps the most spectacular. Where the two
other children are colorists with an "Expressionist" flavor to their work, Eytan
is a draftsman. His development is easy to trace because we can look at his
collected drawings and observe the early achievement of spatial representation.

Eytan's work constitutes further proof of stage-wise development in
the drawing histories of exceptionally able children. Eytan's parents claim
that he never scribbled at all, but that he began to make simple forms almost
immediately. At age 2, he began drawing recognizable outlines of figures and

mechanical devices, but with no suggestion of depth or volume (most children at two are barely making marks on the page). By age 3, he was exploring volume and rendering the multiple faces of an object. The rapidity with which Eytan acquired and/or invented these representational systems is most impressive. Equally impressive is the fact that he moved through the stages of spatial representation in exactly the same sequence as other, older children. He mastered orthogonal, then oblique and isometric projection and, finally, began to experiment with one and two-point perspective. The path is well-trodden, but it is the speed with which Eytan traveled it that makes him special.

Given the great expanse of human artmaking, it seems reasonable to assume that there exists a multiplicity of culturally favored representational systems (e.g., Hagen, 1985). Each requires a different set of innate abilities in the child and is judged according to a different set of qualitative criteria. Traditional Chinese graphic art, for example, emphasizes such issues as line quality, saturation of the ink, energy of the stroke, where the stroke begins and ends, and the way in which the stroke composes the space around it. These dimensions can be identified and discussed by visually literate connoisseurs as easily as aspects of perspective and projective geometry. Being able to create images which embody these special linear qualities requires the gift of visual organization, fine motor control, and planning. The issues of spatial rendering and "optical realism," which are so central to some Western notions of exceptional child art, are not particularly relevant to traditional Chinese art forms.

According to Tan (1993), a sizeable proportion of Chinese children have mastered the techniques of traditional brush painting and calligraphy at a very young age, i.e., 3-4 years old. One such child who has received high praise in the West for her brushpainting ability is Wang Yani (Ho, 1989). She demonstrated a similar level of productivity and precocious activity as Eytan but in a style and context which foregrounds the painted image. According to Tan (1993), Yani produced some 10,000 brushpaintings by the age of 17, or approximately 700 per year.

Wang Yani revealed her interest in art at 3 years of age by daubing marks on her artist father's Western-style oil paintings. She achieved fame within China and abroad for her prolific and lively images of monkeys and other animals. These monkeys were produced according to a formula for the sequence of brush strokes (Tan, 1993). What distinguishes them is the vitality and skill with which the creatures are depicted, the interaction depicted among the various animals and the composition of the pictures. The use of such formulaic animals, which is standard practice in the creation of traditional brushpaintings, raises an important issue for comparison between Chinese/

Asian and Eurocentric notions of artistic exceptionality, that of "originality." One of the most important criteria invoked by Western connoisseurs for judging the quality of children's artwork is "originality, authenticity," the notion that the child has freely invented and used forms of his/her own devising (Lowenfeld & Brittain, 1970). Even though it is now common knowledge that children borrow copiously and promiscuously from the media and each other (Wilson & Wilson, 1982), "originality" remains a criteria which is invoked ahead of technical mastery in Western judgments of the artistic worth of a child's work. Chinese connoisseurs of traditional brush paintings are not nearly as concerned with the derivative nature of the image which a child produces. It is expected that the child will copy from the works of acknowledged masters as a way of acquiring the standard sequence of strokes. Originality is reserved for the venerable artist, not the neophyte and certainly not the child. Solomon (1993) states, "originality was reserved for old age, when you might make changes so slight that they were almost invisible" (p. 49). The traditional Chinese calligraphic or representational image may be thought of more as a "performance" where the score is known and consulted. Thus, the question of originality, which looms very large in Western eyes, is of much less consequence in judging the excellence of exceptional Chinese children's work than, for instance, the "lifelike quality" or *ch'i* of the image (Pariser, 1991b).

Of interest in considering Yani's work is that her calligraphy is not at the same level as her painting skills. Knowledgeable viewers (Andrews, 1989; Gotze,1985; Tan,1993) have commented that her calligraphy, which is considered an integral part of the painting, is at a low level of skill and does not change or improve over time. This is an intriguing observation for it suggests that Yani, like many of the other children who are considered exceptional, is a "specialist" with a fairly narrow range of exquisite competence. An additional feature of Yani's development, which links her artistic growth with that of the other children we have discussed, is that the record shows that she acquired increasingly complex techniques for handling brush and ink over time. Thus, instead of seeing her move through a series of stages in the mastery of spatial and three-dimensional representation, as is the case with Eytan, we can see her move through stages in the skilled use of brush and ink. Here again, we witness the shift from simple to complex which is a fundamental feature in all children's acquisition of skills and techniques.

Gifted children with high skill levels who, as adults, are recognized by the field and who shape the domain

Art educators, art historians and psychologists have looked at the juvenilia of famous artists. The work of Murray (1991), Paine (1987), Porath (1988), and Thomson (1981) on Lautrec's childhood and adolescent work; Carroll's (1992) examination of Edvard Munch's juvenilia; Warner's (1981) review of Millais' childhood drawings; and my own on those of Klee, Lautrec and Picasso (Pariser, 1987, 1991b, 1995) all provide illustrations of how children destined for artistic renown develop their skills. Collections of childhood and adolescent drawings have been preserved and documented for these four artists: Klee (see Glaesemer, 1973), Lautrec (see Dortu, 1971), Munch (see Carroll, 1992), Picasso (see Museu Picasso, 1984; Zervos, 1932, 1949, 1950).

It is evident from the record that Klee, Lautrec, Munch and Picasso passed through the "normal" developmental stages of drawing as I outlined them earlier. For example, Klee and Lautrec passed through a stage of representation in which objects are depicted by "adding together" simple forms. At age 5 or 6, both boys drew steam trains and used the same addition of simple circular schemata to render the locomotive and wagons (see Pariser 1991a). As in the artwork of many other children, drawings by Lautrec and Klee contain figures at many levels of proficiency. For instance, some of Lautrec's earliest drawings contain images of horses, carriages and birds. The horses and carriages are drawn with considerable skill, with an inflected and comprehensive line, while the birds, being of less interest and therefore less practiced, are rendered in a schematic manner. When it comes to learning how to use perspective and to rendering objects with volume and shadow, Millais seems to have been more than the equal of Picasso. At the age of 9, Millais made a stunningly proficient study of a Roman bust (Warner, 1981, p. 13). Picasso was not to achieve this sort of mastery until a few years later. It is not possible to tell from Warner's discussion of Millais if he acquired realistic drawing skills in the standard sequence. In the cases of Klee, Lautrec and Picasso, it is possible to tell that they acquired academic drawing skills in a standard sequence.

One element of graphic development that is particularly salient is that all five children made extensive use of the images which surrounded them. Like all children, Klee, Lautrec, Munch, Millais and Picasso copied from various sources and for various purposes. For example, Picasso imitated cartoons, postcards, and the caricatures he saw in the press. In early adolescence he began to study and copy Old Master images. He also had a phenomenal ability to imitate and to work in the style of a given artist. When he came to Paris at the turn of the century, he made an "original" Lautrec as homage to the artist whom he admired. Without a doubt he could have been a master forger. As an adolescent, Klee made laborious studies of calendar tear sheets. He copied these images in order to learn how to render details of architecture and costume. At the same time, Klee also studied copybooks, books with pictures which were intended for imitation. Munch copied popular images of

Native Americans as did Millais. Lautrec made careful studies of the oil paintings which were hung in his chateau (Murray, 1991). He also copied from and
studied the work of a popular satirist named Grandville.

In conformity with Wolf and Perry's (1988) description of graphic development, Klee, Lautrec, Munch and Picasso experimented with a variety of
styles and renditions of a given subject. In Picasso's schoolbooks one can
find two versions of his favorite subject: the bull. There are cartoon-like images and carefully modeled studies. Lautrec cultivated a serious style of drawing which he learned from his artistic uncles and his first teacher, Princeteau,
but he also dabbled in a caricatural style which he acquired from the popular
press. Lautrec also experimented with distortions. For example, in his Greek
grammar we find an oddly elongated elephant scurrying past a thicket of Greek
words. In late childhood and adolesence, Klee also indulged in several stylistic variations. He drew fantasies and grotesques in a Jugendstil manner, worked
in a more academic manner in his landscapes, and demonstrated ability in
scientific drawing (there is a carefully rendered dissection of a snail in
multicolored ink from this period in his life).

Klee, Lautrec, Munch and Picasso explored all sorts of visual conventions which served as the basis for graphic activity and learning. The work of
Duncum (1984) confirms that, over a period of two centuries, many European children destined for artistic renown used many of the same sources and
reference points in learning drawing techniques.

The drawing record left by four of these artists reveals that not every
sketch they made was touched with genius. There are childhood drawings by
Klee, Lautrec, Munch and Picasso which are labored and awkward. There is
no suggestion that the authors of these particular sketches are bound for artistic glory. In fact, there is evidence that all four artists experienced an aesthetic
slump in the production of their work. This slump, which conforms to the "U-
Curve" in aesthetic development (Davis, 1993; Gardner & Winner, 1982), is
a typical event in the graphic development of most Western children. In many
cases, children do not persevere in their artwork beyond this point. As we
know, in the cases of Klee, Lautrec, Munch and Picasso, this slump was only
a temporary slowdown in a lifetime of artistry. For many other children, early
adolescence is the graveyard of visual activity. It remains to be seen if this U-
curve in aesthetic development is an artifact of Western aesthetic criteria or is
a more universal phenomenon (Pariser,1994).

Connections between exceptional childhood drawings
and adult performance

An intriguing aspect of looking at this last group of exceptional children is that we can assess the way in which these individuals acquired competence in a domain and how this was translated into acceptance by the field.

The first point is that the themes and experiments which were initiated in childhood and early adolescence seem to return in the mature work. For example, Munch's adult love of narrative images seems to have been cultivated in his childhood work (Carroll, 1992). Staaller (1986) examined Picasso's adolescent sketchbooks and claims that the invention of Cubism can be traced back to Picasso's childhood experiments with distortion. In Lautrec's case, certain discrete images, first glimpsed in his sketchbooks and schoolbook doodles, can be clearly recognized in his mature work, such as a sketch of a face drawn on the inside cover of his French-Latin Dictionary which has many of the expressive features found in his portrait of La Goulou (a Montmartre singer), *Linger Longer Lou* (1898). Likewise, some of his schoolboy doodles of horses are almost identical with the monumental images of horses which he presents in such works as *Le Cirque Fernando* (1888), and *The Jockey* (1899).

A theme which announces itself very early in Klee's work and which persists undiminished throughout his lifework is his love of the natural world (Verdi, 1984). An interrupted connection between childhood and adult work is at the level of a personal/thematic issue: music. An important breakthrough occurred for Klee on his trip to North Africa where he began to integrate color into his work. Klee likened color to visual music. His childhood training was as a musician and he even played in the Berne symphony at the age of 12, suggesting that he had great musical talent. In spite of the fact that Klee's immediate family did not encourage his visual-artistic interests, he continued to draw with the support of his uncle and grandmother. At the age of 19, Klee committed himself fully to the study of the visual arts by going to Munich. The discovery and use of color "as music" several years after his formal training may have been a way of reintegrating the two divergent aspects of his artistic nature, the musical and the visual.

With Lautrec and Klee, we have examples of Gardner's (1993) "ten-year rule." Gardner claims that the ground is often prepared for creative breakthroughs by at least a decade of intensive involvement and mastery of the field. In Lautrec's case, 10 years separates his expressive schoolboy sketches of horses and his first major painting, *Le Cirque Fernando*, where three figures dominate the scene: a slightly sinister ringmaster and an equestrienne standing on a powerful horse. The anatomy and posture of this horse are strikingly similar to that of a horse drawn in Lautrec's schoolboy notebook. It is also the expression of the two drawings which links them accross 10 years of work. With Klee, the issue is not one of a 10-year period during which technical skills were perfected, but of a period of time after which the artist reintegrated an aspect of his childhood training into his creative life.

Thus, with all four artists there are thematic and technical threads which link earlier and later work. One connection is puzzling by virtue of its absence: the connection between precocious mastery of academic drawing and the style of the mature work for which the artist is recognized by the field.

A general point to be made is that there is no clear connection between the rapid mastery of academic drawing techniques (as required by the artistic field of the late 19th Century) and the mature work for which the four artists were recognized by the field. Klee, Lautrec, Munch and Picasso achieved varying degrees of competence in the rigors of academic drawing. However, not one of these four owes his standing as an artist to the excellence with which he mastered techniques of rendering.

Lautrec's case is particularly instructive. His first Parisian drawing teacher (Bonnat) commented that Lautrec's drawing was "atrocious." Lautrec never won a prize from the Ecole des Beaux Arts de Paris. Such recognition would have ratified him as a bona fide artist of the first order. It is evident that the very features which contemporary viewers find so striking in Lautrec's work—its satirical bite, the energy of line, the animated compostion—all of these features were lost on the gatekeepers who applied their stuffy standards to the field of academic painting. Along the same lines, if we consider the work for which the field has recognized Picasso and Klee and Munch, we note that mastery of realistic conventions and the study of plaster casts are a far cry from the work for which these three are famous.

By contrast, Millais (Warner, 1981) is an example of a precocious child whose early mastery of classical drawing techniques *does* have a bearing on the style of the mature work for which he became famous. Millais' mature work was right in the mainstream of the 19th century academic tradition and his Pre-Raphaelite canvases relied heavily on the techniques in which he excelled as a child. Millais would seem to illustrate the fate of a nontransgressive (therefore temperamentally nonmodernist) artist, one who was moulded by and who adhered to the aesthetic paradigm of his day.

Conclusion

The evidence presented in this chapter suggests seven common characteristics in the graphic productions of artistically gifted children:

1. There is ample evidence of developmental movement from simple to complex forms and techniques.
2. The acquisition of spatial conventions for rendering three-dimesional space and volume proceeds in a recognized and unsurprising sequence.
3. In almost every case cited there is evidence of a certain uneven specialization.

4. With the exception of some autistic/abnormal child-artists, there is evidence of exploration of different graphic genres.

5. Where the record is detailed enough, we can find evidence of a period when the child had to struggle with technical issues and where much visual spontaneity was lost.

6. The connection between exceptional childhood performance and adult achievement is tenuous. Many gifted children do not go on to adult success (see Bamberger, 1982; Feldman, 1982; Feldman & Goldsmith, 1986).

7. It is evident from looking at prolific and precociously able children from Western and non-Western cultures (Tan, 1993) that volume of work is often associated with artistic exceptionality.

As we have seen from the childhood sketches of the four modernist artists (Klee, Lautrec, Munch and Picasso), mastery of "realism" and perspective in childhood is a poor predictor of the style and nature of mature artistic production. Early acquisition of realistic rendering skills may indicate the presence of some sort of generalized artistic ability, but although realistic/academic drawing skills are placed at the pinnacle of exceptional drawing ability, such skills are of little value in predicting the nature of mature artistic activity in modern artists. Such skills are also irrelevant to the development of aesthetic competence in cultures which value aesthetic dimensions other than the realistic depcition of space and volume. We need to rethink the properties of artistic giftedness in the light of the sorts of images which diverse cultures and social strata recognize as art. Second, we need to restructure our notion of graphic development (Atkinson, 1991; Costall, 1993; Pariser, in press, b; Wolf & Perry, 1988) so that realistic drawing skills are not seen as the supreme artistic good, the pinnacle of artistic achievement, but simply as one of several possible vectors for the course of artistic development.

Acknowledgment
     Some of my research cited in this chapter was supported by grants from Concordia University, the Social Sciences and Humanities Research Council of Canada, and the Spencer Foundation Small Grants program.

References

Alland, A. (1983). *Playing with form: children draw in six cultures*. New York: Columbia University Press.

Andrews, J. (1989). Wang Yani and contemporary Chinese painting. In W. Ho (Ed.), *Yani: the brush of innocence* (pp. 39-50). New York: Hudson-Hills Press, in association with the Nelson-Atkinson Museum of Art, Kansas City, Missouri.

Arnheim, A. (1974). *Art and visual perception; A psychology of the creative eye. (The New Version)*. Berkeley, CA: University of California Press.

Arnheim, R. (1992). *To the rescue of art: 26 essays*. Berkeley, CA: University of California Press.

Atkinson, D. (1991). How do children use drawing? *Journal of Art and Design Education, 10*(1), 57-72.

Bamberger J. (1982). Growing up prodigies: The mid-life crisis. In D. Feldman (Ed.), *Developmental approaches to giftedness and creativity*, no. 17. San Francisco, CA: Jossey Bass.

Becker, H. (1982). *Art worlds.* Berkeley, CA: University of California Press.

Carroll, K. (1992). *Beginnings:The work of young Edvard Munch.* Unpublished paper, The Maryland Institute College of Art.

Case, R. (1992). *The mind's new staircase: Exploring the conceptual underpinnings of children's thought and knowledge.* NJ: Erlbaum.

Clark, G., & Zimmerman E. (1992). Issues and Practices Related to Identification of Gifted and Talented Students in the Visual Arts. Storrs, CT: The National Research Center on the Gifted and Talented.

Costall, A. (1993). *Conflicting images of innocence and corruption in the valuation of child art.* Paper given at the Twenty Third Annual Symposium of the Jean Piaget Society; Values And Knowledge. Philadelphia.

Csikszentmihalyi, M. (1988). Society, Culture and Person: A Systems View of Creativity. In R. Sternberg (Ed.), *The nature of creativity; Contemporary. psychological perspectives* (pp. 325-340). New York: Cambridge University Press.

Davis, J. (1993). *Drawing's demise: U-Shaped development in graphic symbolization.* Paper given at the Society for Research in Child Development Biennial Meeting, New Orleans.

Dennis, S. (1987). *The development of children's art: A Neo Piagetian interpretation.* Unpublished doctoral dissertation. Ontario Institute for Studies in Education (OISE), University of Toronto.

Dortu, M. (1971). *Toulouse-Lautrec et son oeuvre. 6 vol.* New York: Collector's Editions.

Duncum, P. (1984). How 35 children, born between 1724 and 1900, learned to draw. *Studies in Art Education, 26*(1), 93-102.

Feldman. D., & Goldsmith, L. (1986). *Nature's gambit: Child prodigies and the development of human potential.* New York: Basic Books.

Feldman. D., & Goldsmith, L. (1989). Wang Yani: gifts well-given. In W. C. Ho (Ed.), *Yani: The brush of innocence* (pp. 51-65). New York: Hudson-Hills Press, in association with the Nelson-Atkins Museum of Art, Kansas City, Missouri.

Feldman, D. H. (1980). *Beyond universals in cognitive development.* Norwood, NJ: Ablex Publishing.

Feldman, R. (1982). *Whatever happened to the quiz kids?* Chicago: Chicago Review Press.

Gardner, H. (1983). *Frames of mind: The theory of multiple intelligences.* New York: Basic Books.

Gardner, H. (1993). *Creating minds; An anatomy of creativity seen through the lives of Freud, Einstein, Picasso, Stravinsky,Eliot ,Graham and Gandhi.* New York: Basic Books.

Gardner, H., & Winner, E. (1982). First imitations of artistry. In Strauss (Ed.), *U-shaped development.* New York: Academic Press.

Glaesemer, J. (Ed.). (1973). *Paul Klee: Handzeichnungen I. Kinderheit.* Bern, Switerland: Kunstmuseum.

Golomb, C. (1992). *The child's creation of a pictorial world.* Berkeley, CA: University of California Press.

Goodnow, J. (1977). *Children drawing*. Cambridge, MA:Harvard University Press.

Gotze, H. (1985). *Wang yani: Pictures by a young chinese girl*. Munich, Germany: Prestel.

Gould, S. (1992). Mozart and modularity: How could a mere child be so transcendent in one arena but so ordinary in all other ways? *Natural History*, No. 2, 8-16.

Hagen, M. (1985). There is no development in art. In N. Freeman & M. Cox. (Eds.), *Visual order* (59-77). Cambridge, England: Cambridge University Press.

Henley, D. (1988). *Nadia revisited: mollification of regression in the Autistic Savant Syndrome*. Unpublished paper, Art Institute of Chicago.

Ho, W.C. (1989). *Yani: The Brush of Innocence*. New York: Hudson Hills Press.

Lindsley, O. (1965). Can Deficiency Produce Specific Superiority? The Challenge of the Idiot Savant. *Exceptional Children, 31*, 225-232.

Lowenfeld, V., & Brittain, L. (1970). *Creative and mental growth (5th.ed)*. New York: Macmillan.

Luquet, G. (1927). *Le dessin enfantin*. Paris: Alcan.

Morgan. M. (1981). David Downes drawings from 4 to 10 years. In S. Paine (Ed.), *Six children draw* (pp. 23-38). Toronto: Academic Press.

Morishima, A. (1974). Another Van Gogh of Japan. The superior artwork of a retarded boy. *Exceptional Children*, 41 (October), 92-96.

Motsugi, K. (1968). Shyochan's drawings of insects. *Japanese Journal of Mentally Retarded Children*. No.119, 44-47

Murray, G. (1991). *Toulouse-Lautrec: The formative years, 1878-1891*. New York: Oxford University Press.

Museu Picasso. (1984). *Cataleg de pintura I dibuix Picasso*. Barcelona, Spain: Ajuntament de Barcelona.

Paine, S. (1987). The childhood and adolescent drawings of Henri de Toulouse-Lautrec (1964-1901). Drawings from 6 to 18 Years. *Journal of Art and Design Education, 6*(3), 297-312.

Pariser, D. (1981). Nadia's drawings:Theorizing about an autistic child's phenomenal ability. *Studies in Art Education, 22*(2), 20-31.

Pariser, D. (1987). The juvenile drawings of Klee, Toulouse-Lautrec and Picasso. *Visual Arts Research*, 13(20), (Fall), 53-67.

Pariser, D. (1991a). Normal and unusual aspects of juvenile artistic development in Klee, Toulouse-Lautrec and Picasso: A review of findings and directions for future research. *The Creativity Research Journal, 3*(1), 51-65.

Pariser, D. (1991b). *What does giftedness mean in the context of chinese Visual art? Chinese artists look at drawings by a prolific chinese child-artist, Wang Yani.* Presented at the 12th Annual Ethnography in Education Research Forum, University of Pennsylvania.

Pariser, D. (1994). *Are Goodman's symptoms of the aesthetic contagious? A cross-cultural look at the U-curve in aesthetic development.* Paper given at the International Association for Empirical Aesthetics. Montreal.

Pariser, D. (1995). Not under the lamppost: Piagetian and Neo-Piagetian research in the arts: A review and critique. *Journal of Aesthetic Education*.

Pariser, D. (in press b). Lautrec: Gifted child-artist and artistic monument. connections between juvenile and mature work. In C. Golomb (Ed.), *The development of gifted child artists: Selected case studies*. New Jersey: Erlbaum.

Porath, M. (1988). *The intellectual development of gifted children: A Neo-Piagetian approach.* Unpublished dissertation. Ontario Institute of Studies in Education (OISE), University of Toronto.

Robertson, A. (1987). A case study of the development of Bruce's spontaneous drawings from 6 to 16. *Studies in Art Education, 29*(1), 37-51.

Sacks, O. (1987). *The man who mistook his wife for a hat and other clinical tales.* New York: Harper and Row Publishers.

Selfe, L. (1977). *Nadia: a case of extraordinary drawing ability in an autistic child.* London: Academic Press.

Solomon, A. (1993, December 19). Not just a yawn but the howl that could set China free. *New York Times Magazine,* pp. 41-72.

Staaller, N. (1986). Early Picasso and the Origins of Cubism. *Arts Magazine, 61*(1), pp. 80-90.

Tan, L. (1993). *A case study of an artistically gifted Chineses girl:Wang Yani.* Unpublished Masters Thesis, Concordia University, Montreal.

Tannenbaum, A. (1983). *Gifted children.Psychological and educational perspectives.* New York: MacMillan Publishing.

Thomson, R. (1981). Henri de Toulouse-Lautrec, Drawings from 7 to 18 Years. In S. Paine (Ed.), *Six children draw* (pp. 38-49). London: Academic Press.

Tobin, J, Wu, H., & Davidson, D. (1989). *Preschool in three cultures.* New Haven: Yale University.

Verdi, R. (1984). *Klee and nature.* New York: Rizzoli.

Warner, J. (1981). John Everett Millais drawings from 7 to 18 years. In S. Paine (Ed.), *Six children draw* (pp. 9-23). London: Academic Press.

Wilson, B., & Wilson, M. (1982). *Teaching children to draw: A guide for teachers and parents.* New Jersey: Prentice Hall.

Wiltshire, S. (1991). *Floating cities: Venice, Amsterdam, Moscow, Leningrad.* London: Michael Joseph Ltd.

Winner, E. (1982). *Invented worlds: the psychology of the arts.* Cambridge Mass.: Harvard University Press.

Winner, E. & Pariser, D. (1985, December). Giftedness in the visual arts. Items (Social Science Research Council) 39(4), 65-69.

Wolf, D., & Perry, M. (1988). From endpoints to repertoires. New conclusions about drawing development. *Journal of Aesthetic Education, 22*(1), 17-35.

Zervos, C. (1932). *Pablo Picasso* (Vols.1-33). Paris: Editions Cahiers d'Art.

Zervos, C. (1949). *Dessins de Pablo Picasso. 1892-1948.* Paris: Editions cahiers D'Art.

Zervos, C. 1950. Oeuvres et Images Inédités de la Jeunesse de Picasso. *Cahiers d'Art, 25*(2), 277-334.

Zimmerman, E. (1990). *A case study of the childhood art work of an artistically talented young adult.* Paper given at the 98th annual convention of the Amercan Psychological Association, Symposium, The Development of Gifted Child Artists, Boston.

REPRESENTATIONAL CONCEPTS IN CLAY

THE DEVELOPMENT OF SCULPTURE

Over the last 100 years, children's graphic representations have received much attention as psychologists and educators have pondered over the nature of graphic development and the principles that best account for its course. Depending on the investigator's theoretical orientation, cognitive, social, affective, and cultural factors have been highlighted, and perspectives on child development are well represented in this volume.

Despite much productive research in the domain of drawing, no clear consensus has been reached regarding the course of development, the nature of the progression, the validity of a stage conception, and the goals or end-states of graphic development. The early drawings are flat two-dimensional representations that seem to show little regard for the objective form, size, proportion, color, and orientation of the real life model. These drawings elicit diverse interpretations regarding the child's intentions, aesthetics, cognitive status, and skill level that might account for the universally observed characteristics of child art. With few exceptions (see Arnheim, this volume, and Golomb, 1992), investigators have assessed the two-dimensional drawings of children in terms of an hypothesized standard of realism and declared them deficient. Deviations from realism are interpreted as symptoms of conceptual immaturity, a deficit that is supposed to be overcome with the growth of logical and spatial reasoning. In this view, the drawer strives for a close correspondence (in terms of photographic realism) between his perception of objects as solids extended in three-dimensional space and their graphic representation. Regardless of the author's specific assumptions about the relationship between perception and representation, whether a perceived scene can

CLAIRE GOLOMB

be simply translated onto paper, or its translation requires a more complex set of analytical and constructive processes, the notion that mature cognition demands a realistic representation has been adopted by Piagetians, neo-Piagetians, and the British school that has analyzed children's drawings in terms of task demands and production deficits (Cox, 1992; Freeman, 1980; Freeman & Cox, 1985). These authors tend to minimize the nature of constraints that characterize the two-dimensional medium of drawing and the role of cultural variables. They share the assumption that two dimensional representations are primitive constructions that do not adequately represent the three-dimensional object, but reflect the child's incomplete and distorted conception.

It is somewhat paradoxical that drawing, a medium that lacks the third dimension, has been the focus of studies that examine the child's evolving three-dimensional representational conceptions, and that work in the three-dimensional medium of clay has lagged behind. The reasons for this neglect are not difficult to discern: clay is a technically difficult medium, and the collection and preservation of children's fragile clay figures make special demands on the investigator. The few studies devoted to modeling with clay have examined a limited range of issues. Their focus has been the human figure and the number and kind of parts of which it is composed. The development of three-dimensional strategies of representation and the issue of balance in sculpture have not been addressed (Brown, 1975; Golomb, 1974; Grossman, 1980). Modeling a human poses the problem of constructing an upright standing figure whose long and spindly legs must support a substantial torso. The technical difficulty of creating a well-balanced figure is an important aspect that needs to be considered in the study of modeling or sculpting. The practice of focusing on a single task, namely the human figure, provides only limited information on children's representational conceptions. In the case of the human figure, the frontal aspects are the most important and informative ones: they define the character of the person, his or her gender, affect, and intentionality. In sculpture as in real life, humans relate most directly through their senses which privilege what is in front of them, a tendency which favors the representation of the canonical frontal view. If we want to understand children's evolving representational conceptions, we need to consider the nature of the task, the skill level that is demanded for representing an upright standing figure, the conditions that facilitate or impede attention to diverse sides of the modeled figure, the child's definition of the task and his or her overall cognitive competence.

Representational Strategies and Task Variables

With these considerations in mind, we designed a study that explored the child's representational conceptions in clay (Golomb & McCormick, 1995). We were interested in studying this development in its own right, as children's first steps in sculpting; we also hoped to shed light on issues that pertain to drawing. Our study focused on the emergence of three-dimensional concepts as seen in the modeling of upright standing figures and their multiple sides. In selecting a set of objects to be modeled, we considered the object's complexity, symmetry, and the technical difficulty of balancing the figure. We selected eight tasks that varied along these dimensions: a cup, table, man, woman, person-bending-down, dog, cat, and turtle. The cup and the table are objects that are relatively simple in structure; they can be easily balanced, and they are symmetrical in terms of their sides. The cup can be modeled by turning the ball of clay, indenting its center, and flattening its bottom to make it stand. The table requires more planning in the modeling of separate parts and their attachment to yield a balanced upright standing structure.

By comparison with the cup and the table, animals are more complex in terms of the number and arrangement of their different parts. They are, however, relatively stable in structure, with bodies resting on four legs placed perpendicular to the horizontal axis of the body, which might favor their being modeled in an upright posture. Animals are also quite symmetrical with two major sides (the long sides) near duplicates of each other. Instead of a dominant canonical view, there is in four-footed animals a competition between frontal and side views which might enhance the intention to represent more than a single side of the creature.

The human is the most complex figure in this set of tasks. Its structure is mostly organized along the vertical axis, and its relatively disproportionate parts make it difficult to achieve balance. By contrast with animals, the dominant sides or regions of the human figure are quite distinct, with marked differences between its front and back sides, which calls for the representation of frontality. In the case of the figure bending down, the added specification of modeling a human in action calls the child's attention to posture, and thus tends to facilitate upright representation and attention to multiple sides.

We assumed that the factors of complexity, symmetry, and balance are closely related to the child's modeling of diverse objects, and that such three-dimensional representational strategies as modeling a standing figure and its multiple sides are more likely applied to tasks that are relatively simple in structure, symmetrical, and easily balanced. In terms of our specific tasks, this meant that we expected that three-dimensional modeling scores on the cup and the table would exceed those for the animals, which in turn would exceed the scores on the person bending down, with man and woman figures scoring the lowest. Since we were interested in developmental issues, we included a broad range, from age 4 years through age 13.

Developmental Trends in Modeling

Overall, the data support our predictions regarding the modeling of upright standing or upright held figures and their rotation to permit work on multiple sides. Such procedures were most prominent on the cup and the table, followed by the modeling of animals, the person bending down, and tapered off with the man and the woman figures.

Nearly all the subjects modeled the cup and the table three-dimensionally, and demonstrated effective use of such spatial concepts as "in," "under," "top," and "side." The cup was rounded on the outside, hollowed out in the inside, and free standing. Although the younger children modeled their cup crudely, they succeeded in portraying the three-dimensional character of the object. Likewise, the majority of the children constructed the table in a three-dimensional manner. Faced with the problem of legs collapsing under the weight of the table top, many children inverted the object so that its flattened slab rested on the table with legs extending upwards, explaining that it could be turned upside down after the legs had dried. Thus, on the two tasks that were relatively simple in structure, symmetrical, and balanced, almost all of the children, including the youngest, created three-dimensional representations, with upright intention as one of the defining attributes of three-dimensionality. The majority of children also modeled upright standing or upright held animals (83%), closely followed by the person bending (79%); the percentage of upright male and female figures was significantly lower (57%). In general, upright intention increased with age for all the figures, with the exception of man and woman. On the latter, preschoolers had the highest upright intention (71%), followed by the kindergartners (68%), with all others trailing behind. Closer examination of the modeled figure revealed a positive relationship between upright posture in man and woman tasks and their degree of figural differentiation (complexity). As the human figures increased in detail, children found it harder to make the figure standing, and resorted to a horizontal posture, thus avoiding the problems of balancing the figure in a vertical position. Horizontality in these figures is a compromise solution: the figure is more detailed in its structure but is resting on the table top. In the person-bending task, the inclination to place the figure horizontally is countered by the strong demands for the verticality implied in the instruction (see Figures 1, 2, 3).

On the animal tasks, the child's intention to model an upright figure finds an easier expression: these figures can be balanced on four legs that provide a stable base for the body (see Figures 4, 5, 6).

Our results reveal an unsuspected competence in our youngest subjects and indicate that some attributes of three-dimensionality, uprightness and attention to multiple sides, are understood early on, even by preschoolers. Even

Figure 1
Upright standing humans. Artist is a boy, age 4.8.

Figure 2
Woman and man placed horizontally; person-bending-down to pick up a ball modeled in upright posture. Artist is a boy, age 9.8.

Figure 3

Woman and man. Figures are more differentiated and show greater detail; they are placed horizontally on the table. Artist is a girl, age 10.3.

Figure 4

Animals, standing upright. Artist is a boy, age 4.8.

Figure 5
Seated cow. Artist is a girl, age 8.11.

Figure 6
Animals in upright posture. Artist is a boy, age 10.1.

the youngest children in this study were inclined to consider more than a single side of the object, especially in the case of animals. The tendency was to create an upright standing animal with its head and body orientation clearly differentiated (frontal orientation for head, side orientation for body), with some attention to the underside of the body and the modeling of front and hind legs. We found few so-called "mixed views" that align head and body on a single side or plane, a system of representation which is quite common in children's drawings. Of equal interest is the finding that the dimensionality scores that assess three-dimensional aspects of the representation, level off during the middle childhood years.

Representational Models and Figural Differentiation

One-dimensional models composed of unattached snakes or pieces of clay were extremely rare, and stick figures were few in number. In general, stick figures were modeled by older children, from eight years on. A two-dimensional outline or graphic model composed of thin strips of clay appeared infrequently, and was mostly confined to preschoolers and kindergartners. The solid but flattened figure was employed more frequently (between 10 - 26% on the various tasks) but was unrelated to the age of the child. The great majority of our children created three-dimensional models that were held upright, free standing, or standing with some support. Overall, figural complexity increased with age, and development progressed from a global, one-unit figure to more differentiated ones. Figural differentiation scores also tended to level off during the middle childhood years and the representational models of humans and animals of this age group tend to be quite similar to the clay sculptures of untrained adults.

Construction styles involved two strategies: (a) internal subdivision of the lump of clay by pinching, pulling, and subtracting clay from a single unit; (b) addition of separately modeled parts. The majority of figures were constructed by a process of addition of separately modeled parts. Construction style was not related to the age of the children. The temporal order in which parts were modeled was also independent of the construction style. The majority of human figures were constructed in a top-to-bottom sequence; next came the inverse order of bottom-to-top, followed by a sequence that began with the body first. The sequence differed for animals, and the majority of animal figures were modeled with the body as the first part.

Summary and Conclusion

Our major question concerned the development of three-dimensional concepts in modeling with clay. Our results indicate that when children become representational in this medium, approximately at five years of age, they exhibit some basic three-dimensional understanding, witness their attention to the volume of a figure, its upright stance, and attention to multiple sides. The flattened, horizontally placed human figures appear to be a somewhat later development, a function of both practice with the medium and the ambition to create a more complex and differentiated figure. Even then, however, the tendency to work horizontally is counteracted on the person-bending and animal tasks that override it. It is most striking to observe the differential treatment which the same child applies to our eight tasks (see Figures 7a, 7b).

Thus, the previously held notion that the singular attention to frontal aspects of the human figure denotes the child's conceptual limitation seems no longer tenable. Children seem to approach modeling with an incipiently three-dimensional conception that becomes gradually refined and differentiated, provided the child is exposed to this medium and experiments with various tasks and possibilities.

We had predicted that young children's modeling of objects that are simple in structure, symmetrical, and easily balanced, would reveal an early three-dimensional conception and representational competence. We expected to find evidence for the child's intention to model figures in an upright fashion, and some attention to the multiple sides of the figures. Indeed, the cup

Figures 7a & b—Diverse models for humans and animals. Artist is a boy, age 9.6.

Figure 7a
*Graphic models of humans; the figures of the woman, man, and person-bending-down are
outlined with strips of clay placed horizontally on the table top.*

Figure 7b
The animals are modeled in upright posture.

and the table met all these conditions; they were modeled three-dimensionally and not flattened. Animals that are relatively symmetrical in structure and potentially balanced, came next in terms of standing posture and attention to sides. Finally, the human figure, which is complex in structure, asymmetrical in terms of front and back sides, and difficult to balance, was less likely modeled in an upright fashion, and attention focused mostly, though not exclusively, on its frontal aspect.

We found very little support for the view that the early and primitive representations are merely the product of cognitive immaturity, and much evidence that the young artist struggles with problems older children must also confront: how to create a satisfying representation in a medium that puts a premium on balance, uprightness, and the modeling of multiple sides, all of which require great skill and practice.

Beyond a delineation of some of the principles that underlie representational development in the three-dimensional medium of clay, these findings also suggest that the analysis of drawing can benefit from an understanding of development in modeling. The constraints of the graphic medium can best be understood when we compare a child's performance in two- and three-dimensional media and thus differentiate between medium-specific and conceptual constraints on the representation. In the two-dimensional graphic medium, animal drawings often display so-called "mixed views": the body drawn in side-view with the frontal view of the head rotated into the same plane as the body. This juxtaposition of differentiated views, most commonly interpreted as a sign of conceptual immaturity, is an exceedingly rare occurrence on our modeling tasks and calls into question the adequacy of its interpretation in drawing. Similar reasons apply to the so-called "transparencies" in drawing and line "overlap" that highlight both the constraints of the graphic medium on the representation and also the child's visual thinking. They provide us with a record of the child's problem solving strategies and also reflect the child's lack of familiarity with so-called "tricks of the trade" that create the appearance of three-dimensional space. The study of representational development in both drawing and modeling can provide a more comprehensive account of the principles that underlie the performance in each medium.

References

Brown, E. V. (1975). Developmental characteristics of clay figures made by children ages three through eleven years. *Studies in Art Education, 16*(3), 45-53.

Cox, M. (1992). *Children's drawings.* London: Penguin Books.

Freeman, N. L. (1980). *Strategies of representation in young children's drawings.* London: Academic Press.

Freeman, N. L., & Cox, M. (Eds.). (1985). *Visual order.* Cambridge, England: Cambridge University Press.

Golomb, C. (1974). *Young children's sculpture and drawing.* Cambridge, MA: Harvard University Press.

Golomb, C. (1992). *The child's creation of a pictorial world.* Berkeley, CA: University of California Press.

Golomb, C., & McCormick, M. (1995). Sculpture: The development of three-dimensional representation in clay. *Visual Arts Research, 21*(1), 35-50.

Grossman, E. (1980). Effects of instructional experience in clay modeling skills on modeled human figure representation in preschool children. *Studies in Art Education, 22*(1), 51-59.

WHAT POTENTIAL DO YOUNG PEOPLE HAVE FOR UNDERSTANDING WORKS OF ART?

Some of my fondest memories as a young girl are of the times I spent looking at works of art. On occasion I was able to persuade my family to make the 100-mile round trip from my hometown in Kenosha, Wisconsin, to visit the Art Institute in Chicago. There were more frequent visits to the local public library where I discovered artworks (reproductions) from all over the world. I am uncertain why works of art captured my attention at a young age. My family was not especially interested in art, nor do I have memories of ever studying works of art in elementary school. However, I do recall admiring the very large reproductions of paintings on display in my junior high art classroom, despite the fact that my art teacher rarely talked about them.

This attraction to works of art has preoccupied me as a researcher in art education. Over the past several years, I have studied art viewers, young children through adults, to discover how they interpret and form understandings of art. In this chapter I will make observations about art learning based on the findings of my ongoing research and related studies of cognitive development. Much of this discussion focuses on some of the problems that inexperienced art viewers confront in developing greater expertise. I will also discuss theoretical issues that have emerged from my research as they relate to more recent views of cognitive learning theory. So as not to lose sight of the object of these research findings and theoretical issues, I will provide a point of reference to particular works of art.

JUDITH SMITH KOROSCIK

Background to the Problem

My early study of artworks was not altogether serendipitous. I saved my weekly allowance to take bus trips to the adult public library because I found it had a far more extensive collection of art books than the children's library. I also discovered that browsing library shelves was only one way to locate works by certain artists. Learning how to use the card catalog through self-instruction felt like striking gold. Not only did it allow me to find reproductions of particular artworks, it led me to books about the artists' lives and to the stories behind their work. My curiosity grew as I learned how artists made works of art. I also wanted to know why artists chose to make their work look one way instead of another, where they got the ideas for their work, and how their work developed over time.

I remember struggling at age 11 to find the relationship between two sculptures that were identified as Michelangelo's in one of the library reference texts I was studying. I no longer remember what two sculptures they were, but I do remember my failure to understand why these two artworks were by Michelangelo. It seemed only reasonable to me that an artist's later work should somehow resemble his or her earlier work. Yet these two works did not seem to share any family resemblance beyond similar biblical themes. My puzzlement over this stylistic question lasted for months.

I looked through all available texts on Michelangelo's work, but they offered no explanation that was comprehensible to me. I then discovered that my grandfather had a copy of Irving Stone's (1961) novel about Michelangelo, *The Agony and the Ecstasy.* To an 11-year-old, Stone's book promised to be a good source of information about the artist and the development of his work. I was determined to read the entire 664-page volume in order to answer questions about Michelangelo's style, including my question about the stylistic characteristics of his early and later work. Stone's novel took me weeks to read. Simultaneously, I carefully studied numerous reproductions of the artist's sculptures.

It was only after a great deal of effort that I found my original impressions to be correct. The two sculptures identified as Michelangelo's in my early study of his work were not in fact both by Michelangelo. I discovered that the works had been mislabeled in the original text. This came as a complete surprise because it never occurred to me that the information contained in books could be wrong. I was delighted by this discovery because my puzzlement over Michelangelo's work was resolved at long last. It seemed equally important to me that I had found ways to search for a resolution on my own. This experience also gave me some degree of confidence that I could do the same thing again with other works of art.

These childhood memories reveal something important about the nature of art learning and the potential young people have for understanding artwork. As an art educator, I realize that not all young people make the kind of discoveries I did as a young girl. I also now recognize that educational interventions could have greatly enhanced what I was able to discover on my own. My art teachers seemed unaware of my deep interest in works of art, and they seemed to lack strategies for fostering art understandings. The same problem can be found among art educators today because we are mostly at a loss for answers to three fundamental questions about art learning:

1. What does it mean when we speak of understanding works of art?
2. What are the potential understandings of a work of art?
3. What constraints are prevalent in the development of art understandings?

I will try to provide some answers to these questions. In addressing the latter question, I will make numerous references to common patterns of misunderstandings that arise when studying mathematics, science, computer programming, chess, and social studies among other domains. As far removed as these disciplines may be from the visual arts, there is evidence that similar patterns of misunderstandings occur in the development of art understandings.

The Multiple Facets of Understanding Works of Art

We can tackle the first question by distinguishing cognitive processes that come into play when someone tries to interpret a work of art. When I set out to understand why two sculptures by Michelangelo did not seem to "go together," I made certain conscious and unconscious decisions that guided my study. The end result is that my knowledge of Michelangelo's life and work expanded—I knew more. But knowing more was only one facet of my cognitive development. Equally important, but less often considered, is that facet of cognition that led me to make choices about what to look at and search for while viewing and thinking about works of art. For instance we might ask: How did I come to question the lack of family resemblances between two artworks that were identified as Michelangelo's? Why did I think an artist's later work should in some way look like his earlier works? What made me think that reading about the artist's life would give me clues to understanding the stylistic characteristics of his sculptures? Why did I think that books would provide answers to all of the questions I asked? Why did I ask questions about this artist's work in the first place when I could have just as easily worked at memorizing factual information to impress my family, friends, and teachers?

These are significant questions because they help us delineate at least three interrelated facets of cognition that come into play in the acquisition and transfer of art understandings (Koroscik, 1992b, 1993). One facet concerns the extensiveness of the viewer's existing *knowledge base*. This is the extent to which a person has accumulated knowledge, skill, and experience that have some bearing on the artwork he or she is attempting to interpret and understand. Another facet pertains to the viewer's choice of *knowledge-seeking strategies* (or *search strategies*). Strategic knowledge provides a person with a set of cognitive steps that guides the construction of new understandings, that directs the search for new knowledge, and that enables the person to apply previously acquired knowledge, skill, and experience. A third facet of cognition encompasses a person's *dispositions* toward learning. Dispositions are sometimes described as the "habits of mind" that influence a person's willingness to learn and seek new understandings (Katz & Raths, 1985; Prawat, 1989). "In motivational theory, dispositions are thought to account for the frequent disparity between what individuals are capable of doing in ideal situations and what they actually do in more normal contexts" (Prawat, 1989, p. 3).

These three facets of cognition come into play when knowledge, skill, or experience acquired in one context is transferred to another learning situation. *Transfer* is "the ability to draw on or access one's intellectual resources in situations where those resources may be relevant" (Prawat, 1989, p.1). Transfer is so central to the learning process that it is considered to be the hallmark of intellectual development (Bransford, Sherwood, Vye, & Rieser,1986). For transfer to occur, a person must be able to activate the contents of his or her existing knowledge base when search strategies call for that knowledge, skill, or experience. Moreover, a learner must be willing to learn.

Intellectual development hinges upon the inextricable relationship between these facets of cognition. Without a rich knowledge base to draw upon, understanding is limited whether the viewer is a child or an adult. The same is true if a person has an inadequate repertoire of search strategies or a poor disposition towards learning. A person can broaden his or her knowledge base through rote memorization, but knowledge acquired in this way is often later forgotten or ineffectively transferred. Providing students with a repertoire of search strategies without developing their knowledge base is not fruitful either. Nor will students build deep understandings if they are highly motivated but ill-equipped because their knowledge base and/or knowledge-seeking strategies are lacking.

Potential Understandings of Artworks

Artworks can be especially demanding for young people to understand because their meanings are typically ill-defined and subject to multiple interpretations.

Today, a work of art is understood to be a very complex set of signals and meanings, sometimes contradictory and always relative, embedded in the object not only at the moment of its creation (and then not always consciously by its creator) but also by its subsequent life and by what we bring to it from other times and places. (Rossen, 1989, p. 122)

This variability makes it difficult for art educators to set achievable yet challenging goals for student learning. Developmental research can help teachers set realistic expectations about their students' capacity to understand works of art through instruction. To date, researchers have paid most attention to gathering descriptive evidence of how children respond to works of art at various ages or developmental stages (e.g., see Gardner, 1970, 1972; Parsons, 1987). This evidence provides essential information about cognitive development from early childhood through adolescence and adulthood. However, there is very little evidence to use in predicting a young person's full potential to interpret and understand art. By full potential I mean that development which can only be achieved through disciplined inquiry and educational intervention of some kind.

Researchers are only beginning to understand why young people fail to reach their full potential. In order to establish what that potential may be, we can look to persons who possess the highest levels of art expertise. Development can be viewed as a novice-to-expert process wherein expectations for novice understandings of a discipline are set relative to understandings acquired by discipline experts (Prawat, 1989). Novice/expert comparisons help us identify possible understandings, and they can also help us explain the roadblocks novices may experience in developing deep understandings in a discipline. The term, *novice* not only applies to most children, it also refers to any person, regardless of age, whose understandings are underdeveloped.

A useful way of thinking about novice/expert differences is to conceptualize them along developmental continua in terms of a person's knowledge base, knowledge-seeking strategies, and dispositions. Figure 1 provides a learning model in which these comparisons are represented. Continua are used here to represent differences in the degree of cognitive development, not dichotomies between novices and experts.

least relevant	THE LEARNER'S KNOWLEDGE BASE All of the accumulated knowledge, skill, and experience a student currently possesses, including what the learner already knows about the material being studied.	most relevant

transfer

least effective	THE LEARNER'S CHOICE OF KNOWLEDGE SEEKING STRATEGIES The cognitive steps a student takes to construct new understandings, to seek new knowledge, and to apply previously acquired knowledge, skill, and experience.	most effective

transfer

low motivation	THE LEARNER'S DISPOSITIONS The motivational factors or "habits or mind" that influence the learner's willingness to learn and seek understandings.	high motivation

Figure 1
A Cognitive Model of Art Learning

The basic idea is that a viewer's expertise differs from one work of art to the next, and understandings of those artworks vary from one viewer to the next. These differences can be represented as the intersection of the three continua shown in Figure 1. For instance art critic/historian, Linda Nochlin, possesses a highly developed and relevant knowledge base for interpreting and understanding George Seurat's painting, *Sunday Afternoon on the Island of La Grande Jatte* (1884-86) (Nochlin, 1989). She also possesses effective knowledge-seeking strategies and is favorably disposed (highly motivated) to study the painting.

Nochlin's understandings far surpass my own, even though I am fairly knowledgeable about Seurat's work. The knowledge base, knowledge-seeking strategies, and dispositions I now possess and use for interpreting the painting reflect far greater expertise than when I first saw the painting as a young girl. But age alone cannot account for this development difference. If age was the principle factor, Linda Nochlin and I would have independently come to interpret the painting at a similar depth. But admittedly, her interpretations are far more developed than my own. I will cite a few examples to illustrate this point below.

In general, the differences between novices and experts are both quantitative and qualitative (Chi, Glaser, & Farr, 1988). Experts possess a far more extensive knowledge base and much more effective knowledge-seeking strategies than novices. However, their expertise is domain-specific (Koroscik, 1990). For instance, Linda Nochlin cannot be said to be an expert in fields outside art history/criticism, such as mathematics and computer programming.

Novice/expert differences have captured the attention of many cognitive psychologists and educational researchers who seek to explain why intellectual development varies from person to person. Some of the most prevalent differences have been summarized by Chi et al. (1988) as follows:

1. Experts excel mainly in their own domain.
2. Experts perceive large meaningful patterns in their domain.
3. Experts are fast; they are faster than novices at performing the skills of their domain, and they quickly solve problems with little error.
4. Experts have superior short-term and long-term memory.
5. Experts see and represent a problem in their domain at a deeper (more principled) level than novices; novices tend to represent a problem at a superficial level.
6. Experts spend a great deal of time analyzing a problem qualitatively.
7. Experts have strong self-monitoring skills. (pp. xvii-xx)

Constraints to Developing Art Understandings

Recent studies in cognition also give a good deal of attention to identifying roadblocks to intellectual development, i.e., what causes a novice learner's understandings to remain underdeveloped (e.g., see Bransford, et al, 1986; Covington, 1992; Feltovich, Spiro, & Coulson, 1993; Glaser, 1988; Perkins & Simmons, 1986; Prawat, 1989). This research seeks to explain why students sometimes form misunderstandings that inhibit cognitive growth. We now know that those problems can be a function of an inadequate knowledge base, weak knowledge-seeking strategies, a poor disposition to learn, or some combination of all three facets of cognition (see Table 1).

A more specific explanation of what can interfere with transfer and understanding is discussed below, using Seurat's painting of the *Grande Jatte* as a point of reference. I have talked about this painting before (Koroscik, 1992a) and have chosen to do so again because the work is often included in elementary and secondary art curricula, and it is commonly featured in published instructional resource materials and textbooks. Another reason for making reference to the *Grande Jatte* is that it is a very well-known painting but not one that art educators tend to discuss in any depth (i.e., most published references refer to the painting as an example of *pointillism* and nothing more).

When I first saw the original painting as a 12-year-old, I remember being fascinated with its dotted brushstrokes. I was amazed at the magnitude of the painting and its countless dots. I had no doubt that this was an important painting (after all, it was so big, and only important paintings are selected to hang in museums), but I could not help question why the artist chose to paint this way. I had tried it (pointillism) myself, but the experience only added to my uncertainty.

Although I cannot be sure that my classmates experienced the painting in quite the same way, these childhood memories are representative of a rather unsophisticated understanding of the work. That assessment can be explained by considering a range of problems that often differentiate novice understandings from those formed by persons with greater expertise. To illustrate those differences, I will quote art viewers of various ages and expertise below. Quotations by art critics and historians are drawn from the published literature. Statements by less experienced art viewers come from a variety of sources (some of which are synthesized below), including my research with children and adults, written statements by my undergraduate students, published statements by children, and interviews conducted by my students with their friends, family, and other volunteers ranging in age from preschool through adulthood.

Problems with the Learner's Knowledge Base	Problems with the Learner's Knowledge-Seeking Strategies	Problems with the Learner's Dispositions	Problems with Transfer
Naive Concepts	Myopic Search Patterns (Tunnel Vision)	Perseveration, Guessing, or Quitting	Near vs. Far Transfer
Underdifferentiated Concepts	Disoriented Search Patterns	Conservative Tendencies	Hugging vs. Bridging
Garbled Knowledge	Ritual Patterns	Performance vs. Mastery Orientation	
Compartmentalized Concepts			

TABLE 1
Common Constraints to Understanding

Problems with the Learner's Knowledge Base

Naive concepts. Differences in understandings possessed by novices and experts are in part due to the depth and breadth of their existing knowledge of art concepts and procedures. When this knowledge is lacking, naive preconceptions often impede the acquisition of new understandings (Perkins & Simmons, 1988). Unless a student comes to understand that a painting like the Grande Jatte can be interpreted as having multiple layers of meaning, some of which can even seem conflicting, the student will fail to discover and comprehend alternative meanings.

A naive understanding of the *Grande Jatte* can be exemplified by the student who interprets the painting as a happy scene in a park. This interpretation makes good sense to someone with the preconception that people in a park must be having a good time.

Persons with extensive knowledge of art and Parisian life in this period have interpreted the painting differently. They have argued that upon first viewing the painting, it appears to be a pleasant scene of family life. However, the work can also be interpreted as an anti-utopian allegory as discussed by an early art critic:

> The painting depicts a middle-class Sunday morning (sic) on an island in the Seine near Paris; and that is just the point; it depicts this merely with scorn. Empty-faced people rest in the foreground, most of the others have been grouped into wooden verticals like dolls from the toybox, intensely involved in a stiff little walk. Behind them is the pale river with sailboats, a sculling match, sightseeing boats—a background that, despite the recreation going on belong more to Hades than to a Sunday....[The painting is about] endless boredom, the little man's hellish utopia of skirting the Sabbath and holding onto it, too; his Sunday succeeds only as a bothersome must, not as a brief case of the Promised Land. (Bloch, cited in Nochlin, 1989, p. 133)

Underdifferentiated concepts. Another constraint to understanding stemming from the learner's knowledge base is the prevalence of underdifferentiated concepts. Novices can observe subtle details in paintings (Parsons, 1987). However, they are often ill-equipped to distinguish important details from unimportant ones, and they tend to lose sight of these discriminations during concept formation (Perkins & Simmons, 1988). What typically results are oversimplifications, e.g., my childhood understanding that Seurat's painting was only made to show how dotted brushstrokes could be used to make pictures.

Underdifferentiated concepts are easier to understand than complex ones, but they constrain the learner from grasping essential differences between related concepts. The result is that subsequent learning is constructed atop overgeneralizations.

On a more sophisticated level, students with underdifferentiated concepts about 19th century Western art might fail to understand differences between the *Grande Jatte* as a Post-impressionist painting and Impressionist works such as Pierre-Auguste Renoir's painting, *At the Moulin de la Galette* (1876). These advanced students might not grasp any significant differences because like Renoir and other Impressionists, Seurat painted in dabs of color, and he painted the same subjects, i.e., artist studios, circus scenes, people in outdoor cafes, harbors, and seashores. Advanced students might also fail to observe that Seurat actually rejected the casual, relaxed approach of the Impressionists; he did not depict the "fleeting moment," but instead he wanted to show permanence and exactness (Kielty, 1964).

Other differences have been noted by art scholars. For instance, Nochlin is but one art scholar who distinguishes the use of dotted brushstrokes in the *Grande Jatte* from Impressionist paintings. The following quotation reflects the kind of differentiation commonly made by persons with high degrees of expertise about Seurat's work and this period in Western art history.

[The] historical presence of the painting is above all embodied in the notorious dotted brushstroke—the petit point—which is and was the first thing everyone noticed about the work—and which in fact constitutes the irreducible atomic particle of the new vision. For Seurat, with the dot, resolutely and consciously removed himself as a unique being projected by a personal handwriting. He himself is absent from his stroke; there is no sense of the existential choice implied by Cezanne's constructive brushstroke; of the deep, personal angst implied by Van Gogh's; nor of the decorative, mystical dematerialization of form of Gauguin. The paint application is matter-of-fact, a near- or would-be mechanical reiteration of the functional "dot" of pigment. (Nochlin, 1989, p. 135)

Garbled knowledge. A third problem that may be attributed to the learner's knowledge base can best be described as garbled knowledge (Perkins & Simmons, 1988). When a novice's knowledge base contains oversimplifications, that knowledge is incomplete and typically inaccurate. Those newly acquired understandings are predictably confused or mistaken in some way. It is a common occurrence for novices to get the facts wrong and make mistakes in remembering what they have previously learned. Most easily detected are blatant mistakes and misconceptions, such as the conclusion that Seurat was an Italian Renaissance painter or that he was a prolific painter throughout his long career.

Subtle forms of garbled knowledge can also occur. For example, intelligent novices might confuse stylistic concepts of realism and naturalism. In such instances, they would be unable to dispute the claim that "Seurat was concerned with naturalism as shown in his choice of realistic colors." By comparison, art scholars would not confuse naturalism with realism. While many agree that the *Grande Jatte* is a realistic painting, they argue that it is not naturalistic (House, 1989; Piper, 1981). In order to emphasize the *Grande Jatte's* anti-naturalistic style, scholars have compared the painting to Seurat's later work, *The Models* (1888), in which three female nudes are depicted in the artist's studio against the backdrop of the *Grande Jatte*. That juxtaposition is discussed by one art historian as follows:

> Its figures, their lines relaxed and cursive, are juxtaposed with the wooden figures in the *Grande Jatte,* shown on the studio wall next to them. This contrast plays on oppositions between nature and artifice: the *Grande Jatte's* figures assume the artificial guise of fashion in order to appear in the "natural" setting of the island; next to them are three nudes who can only reveal their natural selves in the ultimately artificial circumstances of posing for "art" in a painter's studio. Judging from the opposition Seurat made here, the stiffness in the *Grande Jatte* cannot be treated as an internal stylistic development in Seurat's art, but must be seen as a calculated, expressive device conceived for that particular project.... Both the modeling of the figures and the handling of the paint emphasize that the picture is a fiction. (House, 1989, p. 129)

Compartmentalized concepts. The novice's knowledge base can also contain compartmentalized concepts that constrain transfer and understanding (Perkins & Simmons, 1988). Cognitive research shows that an expert's knowledge base seems to be organized around a more central set of understandings than a novice's (Prawat, 1989). This organizational structure connects key ideas and procedures in meaningful ways—which in turn improves later access and transfer of that knowledge. By comparison, a novice's knowledge base is typically organized as rigid and isolated cognitive structures. That organizational structure limits the novice's ability to grasp relationships between two or more related concepts even when some knowledge of each concept is already possessed.

In the case of the *Grande Jatte,* students might compartmentalize the use of dotted brushstrokes from any understandings they might have about the artwork's expressive meanings. Their knowing that the artist used pointillism (or divisionism) does not imply knowledge of how expressive meanings are conveyed through dotted brushstrokes. By comparison, expert understandings reflect an integration of observations about the painting's formal characteristics and the painting's possible meanings as exemplified in this statement by Nochlin (1989):

> It is through the pictorial construction of the work—its formal strategies—that the anti-utopian is allegorized in the *Grande Jatte*...In Seurat's painting, there is no interaction between the figures, no sense of them as articulate, unique, and full of human presences. The Western tradition of representation has been undermined, if not nullified, here by a dominant language that is resolutely anti-expressive, rejecting the notion of a hidden inner meaning to be externalized by the artist. Rather, in these machine-turned profiles, defined by regularized dots, we may discover coded references to modern science, to modern industry with its mass production, to the department store with its cheap and multiple copies, to the mass press with its endless pictorial reproductions. (p. 133-135)

Problems with the Learner's Knowledge-Seeking Strategies
    Myopic search patterns (tunnel vision). Novices typically employ search strategies that are unidimensional due to the rigid structure of their knowledge base. Because they lack cognitive flexibility that permits elaboration on a single conceptual theme, their responses to art tend to be relatively short in duration.

    When scholars study the *Grande Jatte,* they look at and beyond the painting. This broad search strategy includes examining "the literature, criticism, popular imagery, and pictorial traditions of the period in order to suggest ways in which the painting embodies the social, class, and familial tensions of the newly developing urban world" (Rossen, 1989, p. 113). By comparison, an adult novice may look at the painting and conclude that, "I see it as a view of a nice sunny day in the park, no more, no less."

    Disoriented search patterns. When novices approach understanding something, they are often at a loss over what to search for. They typically use arbitrary criteria to guide the direction of their search, often following a path of least resistance. When one path is perceived as leading to a dead-end, a novice will frequently "change his or her mind" and randomly set out in a new direction.

An example of this search pattern can be found in someone who responds to the *Grande Jatte* and remarks, "I am not sure what other artists may have influenced Seurat to paint this way. It is hard to say for sure." These statements suggest that the viewer has some doubts about how one might go about discovering who influenced Seurat. Such uncertainty is likely to be accompanied by a random choice of search strategies, whereas as art scholars have been more deliberate and methodical in seeking new understandings of the painting. The scope of those expert search patterns is exemplified in the following statement:

> First, [historians] have investigated the physical context of the island of the *Grande Jatte* itself, located on the river Seine in the suburbs northwest of Paris. Second, they have tried to define the painting's social context by determining what types of people are represented in it. Third, they have examined its institutional context as a manifesto for an artistic splinter group that was first presented in the independent forum of the final Impressionist group exhibition. And fourth, they have looked at its critical context, at the ways in which the painting was received when it was first exhibited. (House, 1989, p. 116).

Ritual patterns. The development of deep understandings can also be constrained by the adoption of formula-like strategies that are symptomatic of a learner's lack of sensitivity to deep structures of the discipline (Perkins & Simmons, 1988). Unlike naive patterns of misunderstanding, ritual patterns are common among advanced learners who have acquired an extensive knowledge base of the discipline. An advanced learner can appear to have acquired sophisticated understandings, yet actually approach learning in a rigid, ritualistic way. Consequently, the advanced student can struggle to employ effective search strategies in novel learning situations even though his or her knowledge base is more than adequate.

This problem can be seen in art education when advanced students adopt strategies for responding to art without comprehending their purpose nor limitations. For example, students might be taught to use the principles of design to analyze the formal properties of an artwork, then automatically employ this strategy even when an art viewing problem calls for the interpretation of meanings. Teaching art students to use a four-step art criticism method, i.e., description, analysis, interpretation, and judgment (Feldman, 1973) or aesthetic scanning (Broudy, 1988) can impede the development of understandings when these methods are used in a rote and purposeless manner. In such instances, it is predictable that students will lose track of what they are actually searching for.

In contrast expert scholars, such as art historians, recognize that interpretations change over time as more contextual evidence comes to light and as theoretical paradigms shift within their discipline. As such, their methods for seeking new interpretations are always subject to change as House (1989) explains:

> The historian's task is to seek the range of meanings that can be found in a work at a particular historical moment and to highlight the assumptions that underlie the various ways in which it has been interpreted, both in the past and in the present....It is the life of the work, not the life of the artist, that must command our attention. (pp. 130-1)

Problems with the Learner's Dispositions

Perseveration, guessing, or quitting. Depth of understanding is also limited by the learner's motivation to pursue it (Covington, 1992; Prawat, 1989). The willingness of a learner to proceed can be expressed in at least three ways: (1) to persevere with greater or lesser effort, (2) to guess, or (3) to give up (Perkins & Simmons, 1988).

For example, if asked why a woman dressed like the one on the left in Seurat's painting is fishing (from *Art & Man,* 1985 edition), a novice might respond as follows:

> I am not certain why a woman would be dressed like that to go fishing, but maybe if I look harder at the painting I will discover the answer....Maybe she didn't have time to go home after work to change her clothes before going to the park....I just don't know.

On occasions when novices are uncertain of what to do next, they guess. Some guesses are better than others but are alike in reflecting strategies that proceed without confirmation (Perkins & Simmons, 1988).

Experts are far more willing to persevere, and they typically proceed on the basis of contextual information because it can provide a means to inform and confirm their interpretations of an artwork. For example, scholars suggest that the social significance of being seen on the island is a possible reason why the woman's somewhat formal attire may have been the norm (Clayson, 1989; House, 1989). Scholars also call into question the fact that the woman is unchaperoned, and they suggest that during the mid-1880s an unchaperoned woman may be interpreted to be in a morally compromised position (House, 1989). This interpretation is based on contextual evidence, including comparisons to other paintings that make reference to the pun in French on *pêcher* (to fish) and *pécher* (to sin).

Conservative tendencies. Novices also tend to approach learning by confirming preconceived ideas and personal biases, sometimes to reflect peer group consensus. On the other extreme, many novices blindly adopt authoritative conclusions without question, operating on the belief that if something is written in a book, it must be true. At the same time they may be steadfast in their belief that "modern art is really dumb" or assume that "good art should have pleasing subject matter." This "spirit of conviction" contrasts the "spirit of exploration" that typically characterizes expertise (Perkins & Simmons, 1988). For instance, it is quite common for art scholars to continuously challenge the boundaries of the discipline when they revisit such paintings as the *Grande Jatte.*

Performance vs. mastery orientation. The relationship between strategy and disposition can also be seen in a novice's tendency to approach learning with either a *performance orientation* or *mastery orientation* (Prawat, 1989). A novice with a performance orientation is inclined to get the job done as quickly as possible. In such instances, learning serves as a means to an end and not an end in and of itself. The learner is disposed to ask, "Can I do it?" when approaching an opportunity to acquire new understandings. Someone with a mastery orientation would instead ask, "What will I learn?" In the case of studying the *Grande Jatte,* a performance-oriented student might ask, "Will the final exam contain any items about the *Grande Jatte?*" A mastery-oriented student might approach studying the painting with the following thoughts in mind:

> I am curious about why Seurat chose to use dotted brushstrokes given the subject matter of this painting. It is interesting that he used dots to create "hard edge" effects in order to stiffen the figures and to create a sense of social conformity. I know that Seurat was influenced by a number of 19th century French painters, but I wonder who was influenced by his work? In particular, it would be interesting to find out if Seurat influenced any women artists. There are several more questions that come to my mind about this painting and the artist.

Problems with Transfer

Near (low road) vs. far (high road) transfer. Of fundamental importance in learning and development is the process of transferring skill or knowledge acquired in one learning context to new situations (Perkins & Salomon, 1988). The development of deep understandings within a domain requires that learners use their cognitive resources flexibly to find connections across contexts (Prawat, 1989). Novices more often transfer knowledge on the basis of superficial similarities, i.e., *low road* or *near transfer.* But as novices develop greater expertise, they see past these superficial similarities to find deeper analogies, i.e., *high road* or *far transfer* (Perkins & Salomon, 1988).

The following cases illustrate how transfer differs in degree and how those differences affect the understanding of the *Grande Jatte.* The first is a comparison between Seurat's painting and a parody that accompanied a 1990 *Business Week* article on the opening of Euro-Disneyland. The parody replicates the original painting: however, all of the men, women, and children on the island are transformed into Disney characters, the most prominent of which are Mickey and Minnie Mouse.

Near transfer (by an adult novice): "The [Disney parody] is humorous. I could identify with the characters because I grew up with Walt Disney cartoons....Mickey and Minnie Mouse, the Little Mermaid, Donald Duck...I found myself comparing the original Seurat to the Walt Disney replica."

Far transfer (by an adult novice with a more advanced understanding): "I thought of the Disney parody as humorous at first, but then began to think of [the creator] as someone who can take a serious painting and then just play with it. This led me to think of Marcel Duchamp and his works and the criticism he received, which finally led me to think of the Disney parody as a form of art."

In a second example of near and far transfer, we see that scholars are not dissuaded from looking for relationships among earlier artworks that bear no stylistic or expressive similarity to the *Grande Jatte.* Nochlin (1989) compares Seurat's painting to an earlier work, *Scared Grove* (c. 1884), by Pierre Puvis de Chavannes. A novice art viewer is typically unprepared to see any relationship between the two paintings even after viewing the *Grande Jatte* in comparison to the Disney parody.

Near transfer by an adult novice: "I can see how the Disney illustration pokes fun at Seurat's painting, but I don't see that the painting by the other artist, *Sacred Grove*, had anything to do with the *Grande Jatte.*"

Far transfer by an art scholar: "From a certain standpoint, the *Grande Jatte* may be considered a giant parody of Puvis's *Sacred Grove*, calling into question the validity of such a painting and its relevance to modern times—in both form and content. For Puvis's timeless muses and universalized classical setting and drapery,

Seurat substituted the most contemporary fashions, the most up-
to-date settings and accessories....in the mode of modern urban-
ity rather than that of pastoral antiquity." (Nochlin, 1989, p. 138)

Conclusion

In this chapter, I have outlined some of the reasons why the development of art understandings can be attributed to a young person's knowledge
base, choice of search strategies, and dispositions toward learning. These facets of cognition coalesce as transfer in different ways with every art encounter, not in some generic manner nor to the same degree in all art viewing
situations. For instance, a novice art viewer may find it nearly impossible to
transfer relevant knowledge to one work of art but be quite successful with
another. The same is true for the choice of search strategies and dispositions.
Thus, gauging a young person's development in understanding works of art
requires consideration of what that individual is actually attempting to understand (i.e., the particular artworks under study as well as the context for that
study).

My own early understanding of the *Grande Jatte* serves as a good example of how development can be constrained by the lack of educational
intervention. I remember struggling to understand what the painting was about
and why the artist chose to paint with dotted brushstrokes. The only search
strategy I knew to employ was to keep staring at the dots in search of meaning. Although I knew that Seurat used pointillism, I did not understand the
concept of pointillism nor did I grasp any meaningful relationship between
pointillism and the "dot paintings" made in my junior high art class. Perhaps
if my art teacher had taught me to promote transfer, I would have come closer
in bridging my own observations of people and city life to the painting, certainly not with the expertise articulated by Linda Nochlin and other art scholars, but in personally deep and meaningful ways. At the very least, I might
have come closer to understanding that Seurat's choice of dotted brushstrokes
relates to the expressive content of the painting. I might have also come to
understand that a painting can offer multiple layers of meaning for interpretation. My development could have been enriched easily because, at the time, I
was genuinely disposed (in fact, down-right determined) to understand Seurat's
painting.

When developmental research examines *how* artworks are understood
and *what* can be understood from art viewing experiences, the outcome of
that research can be useful for art teachers. As researchers gather more evidence of potential learning problems, teachers will have more information at
their disposal for designing curricula to meet specific student needs. For example, by assessing gaps in a student's knowledge base and knowledge-seeking strategies, a teacher could promote "near transfer" by "hugging" new cur-

riculum content close to the learner's existing knowledge (Perkins & Salomon, 1988). "Far transfer" could be promoted by "bridging" seemingly distant concepts on the basis of "key ideas" or other meaningful abstractions to guide the learner's choice of knowledge-seeking strategies (Koroscik, 1992b; Perkins & Salomon, 1988; Prawat, 1989). Young people are more likely to become favorably disposed to understanding a work of art if they perceive transfer to be easily within their reach.

It is important for art educators to recognize that "transfer is potential, not automatic" (Covington, 1992, p. 210). One reason to examine novice/expert differences is to explore that potential. Another reason is to detect, diagnose, and remedy any problems associated with transfer. By comparing a young person's understanding to others, of lesser and greater expertise, we are better able to identify any factors that may constrain further development. The use of novice/expert comparisons does not imply that young people should be expected to think like adults, nor does it imply that scholarly interpretations of artworks are unquestionable. Quite the contrary, art scholars often offer interpretations that invite question, and sometimes they articulate controversial interpretations for the sole purpose of opening discussion and debate (Heller, 1994).

As more art teachers bring artworks into the classroom for study, it becomes increasingly evident that young people are far more capable of developing deep understandings than once thought possible. However, art educators are not quite sure how much to expect from their students nor what curricular interventions are most effective for fostering advanced understandings and far reaching transfer. More research, particularly empirical research, is needed to fully answer these questions. Theorizing about the development of art understanding is important, but it is also essential that we gather evidence from observation and experiments in classrooms, galleries, and wherever artworks are shown to confirm and extend theory and to inform practice.

Reference Note
This chapter is an expanded and updated version of a paper presented by the author at the annual meeting of the American Educational Research Association (AERA), Boston, April 1990 and a presentation to the Illinois Alliance for the Arts Education (IAAE) at Northern Illinois University, August 1990. Proceedings of the AERA Arts and Learning Special Interest Group program were published in *Arts and Learning Research, 8* (1), 6-22.

References

An American in Paris. (1990, March 12). *Business Week,* 60-64.

Bransford, J., Sherwood, R., Vye, N., & Rieser, J. (1986). Teaching thinking and problem solving: Research foundations. *American Psychologist, 41* (10), 1078-1089.

Broudy, H. S. (1988). *The uses of schooling.* New York: Routledge.

Chi, M. T. H., Glaser, R., & Farr, M. J. (Eds.). (1988). The nature of expertise. Hillsdale, NJ: Lawrence Erlbaum.

Clayson, S. H. (1989). The family and the father: The *Grande Jatte* and its absences. *The Art Institute of Chicago Museum Studies, 14* (2), 155-164.

Covington, M. V. (1992). *Making the grade: A self-worth perspective on motivation and school reform.* New York: Cambridge University Press.

Feldman, E B. (1973). The teacher as model critic. *Journal of Aesthetic Education, 7* (1), 50-57.

Feltovich, P., Spiro, R., & Coulson, R. (1993). Learning, teaching, and testing for complex conceptual understanding. In N. Fredericksen, R. Mislevy, & I. Bejar (Eds.), *Test theory for a new generation of tests.* Hillsdale, NJ: Lawrence Erlbaum.

Gardner, H. (1970). Children's sensitivity to painting styles. *Child Development, 41,* 813-21.

Gardner, H. (1972). The development of sensitivity to figural and stylistic aspects of paintings. *British Journal of Psychology, 63* (4), 605-615.

Glaser, R. (1988). Cognitive science and education. *International Social Science Journal, 115,* 21-44.

Heller, S. (1994, August 17). Art historian and provocateur: Colby College's David Lubin shakes up the world of American art studies. *The Chronicle of Higher Education,* pp. A9, A14.

House, J. (1989). Reading the Grande Jatte. *The Art Institute of Chicago Museum Studies, 14* (2), 115-131.

Katz, L. G., & Raths, J. D. (1985). Dispositions as goals for teacher education. *Teaching and Teacher Education, 1,* 301-307.

Kielty, B. (1964). *Masters of painting: Their works, their lives, their times.* Garden City, NJ: Doubleday.

Koroscik, J. S. (1990). The function of domain-specific knowledge in understanding works of art. Inheriting the theory: New voices and multiple perspectives on DBAE. Los Angeles: J. Paul Getty Trust.

Koroscik, J. S. (1992a). A comparative framework for designing visual art curricula. Arts Education Policy Review, 94 (1), 17-22.

Koroscik, J. S. (1992b). Research on understanding works of art: Some considerations for structuring art viewing experiences for students. *Finnish Journal of Education Kasvatus,* 23 (5), 469-477.

Koroscik, J. S. (1993). Learning in the visual arts: Implications for preparing art teachers. *Arts Education Policy Review,* 94 (5), 20-25.

Nochlin, L. (1989). Seurat's Grande Jatte: An anti-utopian allegory. *The Art Institute of Chicago Museum Studies, 14* (2), 133-153.

Parsons, M. J. (1987). *How we understand art: A cognitive developmental account of aesthetic experience.* New York: Cambridge University Press.

Perkins, D. N., & Salomon, G. (1988). Teaching for transfer. *Educational Leadership,* 46 (1), 22-32.

Perkins, D. N., & Simmons, R. (1988). Patterns of misunderstandings: An integrative model for science, math, and programming. *Review of Educational Research,* 58 (3), 303-326.

Piper, D. (1981). *Looking at art.* New York: Random House.

Prawat, R. S. (1989). Promoting access to knowledge, strategy, and disposition in students: A research synthesis. *Review of Educational Research, 59* (1), 1-41.

Rossen, S. (Ed.) (1989). *The Art Institute of Chicago Manual Studies, 14*(2).

Stone, I. (1961). *The agony and the ecstasy: A novel of Michelangelo.* Garden City, NJ: Doubleday.

CROSS-CULTURAL RESEARCH IN AESTHETIC DEVELOPMENT: A REVIEW

> We live between what our body tells us and what we have to know in order to function, there is a vacuum we must fill ourselves, and we fill it with information (or misinformation) provided by our culture. The boundary between what is innately controlled and what is culturally controlled in human behavior is an ill-defined and wavering one. (Geertz, 1973, p. 50)

The idea of culture is central in the understanding of how children develop aesthetically. Kroeber and Parsons (1958) defined culture as transmitted patterns of values, beliefs and ideas influencing human behavior and the objects produced by this learned behavior. Cultural experiences such as language, the arts, religious and moral practices predominantly determine the mental experiences which are possible for human beings (Best, 1985). McFee (1986) suggested that art operates in the two aspects of culture identified by Triandis (1980, 1992) which are the objective elements (the objects made by peoples) and the subject elements (their value systems, roles, and attributes). Both the objects made by children as well as their perceptions, responses, and values about art need to be studied in cross-cultural research.

It is our belief that all of these definitions and ideas about culture add further support to current postmodernist stances about the intricate relationship between art and its cultural context. Cross-cultural researchers in the visual arts need to be sensitive and cognizant of both the formal and informal learnings which occur from merely being a member of a particular culture and to be careful to avoid the focus of the modernist movement on Western art and its reluctance to consider the cultural learning of other societies and groups of people. Efland, Stuhr and Freedman (1990) reminded us that the fundamental postmodern issue in the arts questions the predominance of the

CONNIE NEWTON & LARRY KANTNER

Western viewpoint while promoting the notion of pluralism in which the meaning of art objects of all cultures must be understood within the context of their origin. Grieder (1985) dispelled the modernist notion that artists in foreign cultures produced primitive art leading to the limited attention paid to the cultural learnings of those artists. The postmodern theories of art have tremendous implications on cross-cultural research and necessitate that both art and aesthetic response to art must be examined as forms of cultural expression.

According to Witkin and Berry (1975), the primary purpose of cross-cultural research is to determine the universality of a phenomenon documented in the research of a single culture. However, cross-cultural research can also examine new phenomena in both a behavioral and cultural context. Triandis (1980) offered a slightly broader definition in which cross-cultural research is concerned with the study of behavior and experience as it occurs in different cultures, is influenced by culture, or results in changes in existing cultures. Cross-cultural research enables the study and possible understanding of the relationship between certain cultural and behavioral variables (Hardiman & Zernich, 1985a). Allison (1980) cautions that any consideration and comparison between cultures must recognize that all cultures are in a continual state of change with considerable variation between the degree and type of change and the kinds of influences contributing to change.

Breslin (1983) denoted the strategy of seeking known cultural universals which provide continuity across cultures as "etic" analysis and distinguished the alternative strategy of seeking out cultural variables which require specific and unique attention as "emic" analysis. Berry and Dasen (1974) suggested a combination of and balance between the etic and the emic approaches to cross-cultural research, and Breslin (1983) stated that this combination is essential to fully understand a concept within its cultural context. Lovano-Kerr (1983) discussed the etic and emic as two emerging trends in a research agenda: assessing the generality of theories originating in Western industrialized cultures by subjecting them to cross-cultural testing and formulating approaches to account for cross-cultural differences.

Behaviors, skills, and concepts in art making, perceiving, responding to, and valuing art are complex perceptual and cognitive processes. Comparative cognitive psychology focuses on understanding the variability or difference as a function of culture and the universal uniformities or cross-cultural consistencies in the cognitive processes (Berry & Dasen, 1974). Thus, cross-cultural developmental studies focusing on both cognition and perception provide implications for cross-cultural research in artistic and aesthetic development. Glick (1975) defined the study of cognition as the examination of how an individual comes to have organized knowledge. Glick further explained that cognition is viewed from a dual perspective, describing the particular processes involved at different age levels and identifying specific etiological factors which determine their development. Glick considered biological factors, physical environment, social environment, and sociocultural factors, such as language and education, as the determinants of development.

Early studies in cross-cultural developmental research utilized Piagetian theory in the search for universals between cultures. Piaget's theory centered around the notion that cognitive development occurs throughout a set sequence of universal stages. Within his theoretical framework, cultural variables are not influential on the sequence of states but, rather, upon the age in which children attain each state. Dasen (1972) reviewed a large number of cross-cultural studies which were grounded in Piaget's theory. These descriptive studies resulted in the conclusion that the sensorimotor, concrete operational, and formal stages in cognitive development are applicable universally across cultures. Dasen, however, stressed the need for further quasiexperimental research to link these findings to specific cultural factors. Much of cross-cultural research utilizing Piagetian theory is vulnerable to criticism for utilizing Western theory, research paradigms, instrumentation and methodology in an attempt to find universal similarities in non-Western cultures with little attempt to understand the culture or its influence on child development.

Some recent cross-cultural research has relied on other theories, particularly Vygotsky's (1978) theory which focuses on the sociocultural context of development. Vygotsky posited that higher mental processes are a result of social interaction, particularly with more experienced members of society. According to him, an individual's learning efforts are embedded in both an interpersonal and institutional context of culture.

What is the value of cross-cultural research that is concerned with the aesthetic development and issues related to aesthetic response? Clearly, such research provides a comprehensive look at human development. It is a means to seek the etic and the emic and to understand better the effects of enculturation and acculturation. Such research helps us to know who we are as part of the human race, as members of a culture, and as individuals.

Children Perceiving and Responding to Art

As educators in the arts we are concerned with how people develop aesthetic awareness, how their past experience affects how they experience works of art. We need to know how each society enculturates its young into using its own aesthetic view of reality. (McFee, 1978: 45-46)

Most cross-cultural research in children's artistic and aesthetic development has been focused on art making. However, it is essential to also examine how children respond to art from a developmental cross-cultural perspective. Aesthetic experience involves complex aspects of human behavior including perceptions, attention to and discrimination of sensory information, values, emotions, interpretations of meaning, and the intricate relationships of all these factors to each other. Chapman (1978) delineated these dimensions of aesthetic experience as perceiving qualities of art, interpreting perceptions as sources of meaning, and judging the significance of the perceptual experience.

The ability to perceive and respond to works of art is a complex cognitive process involving, in part, the ability to decode and interpret pictorial cues in imagery. Werner (1979) warned us this is indeed a learned ability by stating

> cross-cultural research...has made us aware...that the reading of pictures is far from an automatic or innate ability, and that it is like the reading of words, an end product, a skill of some complexity. (p. 159)

Interpretation of Space in Two-Dimensional Imagery
The ability to interpret visual imagery, abstractions in particular, is dependent on being able to decode pictorial cues. One such task involves the ability to perceive and interpret depth in two-dimensional imagery. Mundy-Castle (1966), studying 5-and 10-year-old children in Ghana, and Hudson (1960), who researched aesthetic responses of other African children, both found that young children in these populations had difficulty with spatial or depth interpretation. Dawson (1967), who studied children in West Africa, concluded that decoding and interpretative abilities were affected by cultural influences and experiential opportunities. In a later study, Dawson (1974), found 3-year-old children in China were capable of decoding three-dimensionality in pictures, attributing this ability to culture and experience with decoding imagery. According to Werner (1979), such ability involves reading cues and is developed over time with increased exposure to imagery.

Miller (1973) reviewed cross-cultural perception studies and concluded experience with three-dimensional depth dues is a culturally learned phenomenon, and seeing three-dimensionally in the real world does not automatically transfer to decoding depth cues in two-dimensional images. Glick (1975), in reviewing related studies, summarized cultural differences between groups in the degree to which three-dimensional responding to two-dimensional materials occurred.

McFee (1978), in her discussion of cross-cultural differences in perception of pictures, indicated a number of cultural differences in experiences with pictorial images. In particular, she brought attention to the fact that the amount and type of experience in simply looking at and decoding pictures affects the ability to recognize objects; that the familiarity of the culture with objects and ideas in the images also influences perception; and that the degree of strictness of the culture affects individual openness and ability to recognize depth cues. Obviously, those perceptual cues which are difficult for children in a particular culture to decode and interpret are culturally biased. For example, many cultural differences exist in the use of space or depth cues within works of art in different stylistic and historical periods.

Aesthetic Sensitivity
Numerous cross-cultural studies have focused on color sensitivity and preference. Some researchers in studies involving children from Japan, Phillipines, and Mexico, for example, have found red to be a highly preferred colour, followed by green and blue, with yellow and white among the least preferred (Garth, Ikeda & Langdon, 1931; Garth & Collado, 1929; Gesche, 1927). Using more complex stimuli, Ramkisson & Bhana (1985) investigated the responses of 9- and 12-year-old students in India using free and matrix classification with results supporting the developmental theories of Piaget and Inhelder (1967). However, some matrix behaviors were manifested earlier than would be expected from these developmental theories.

Experimental or psychological aesthetics have made numerous contributions to cross-cultural comparisons in aesthetics. Berlyne (1980), a pioneer in this field, reviewed cross-cultural studies which involved the use of both genuine works of art (analytic stimuli) as well as artificial, or synthetic stimuli and concluded that the one objective thus far in cross-cultural research

> is to ascertain how far findings obtained from subjects from the predominant cultures of Europe and North America can be generalized to other populations, or...to what extent there are universals in the domain of psychological aesthetics. (p. 353)

Berlyne conducted numerous cross-cultural studies examining exploratory and verbal responses to visual patterns (e.g., Berlyne, 1975; Berlyne, Robbins, & Thompson, 1974) and investigated judgments of similarity and aesthetic preferences (Berlyne, 1976). Child and his associates conducted extensive research to test the hypothesis of the existence of universal aesthetics (Child, 1964; Anwar & Child, 1972; Haritos-Fatouros & Child, 1977). Numerous similarities across cultures were revealed through their work thus establishing some cross-cultural consistency.

However, the preponderance of studies in experimental aesthetics has almost exclusively been concerned with responses of adults or older subjects thereby providing little insight into aesthetic development. Young children have been studied primarily as a counterpoint in explorations of adult responses as related to those of experts (Child, 1962, 1964). Also, there has been a lack of consistency in sampling procedures across cultures. Child et al (1968b), for example, studied children in grades 2 and 6 from the U.S., but adult subjects from Japan, Puerto Rico, Ecuador, and Peru.

In other cross-cultural studies in aesthetic response, Chan, Eysenck and Götz (1980) found considerable similarities in aesthetic reactions of Japanese, Hong Kong, and English children. Berlyne (1980) described another study by Machotka (1966) with French and American children aged 6 to 18 in which he found similarity between cultures in both preference and verbal reasons. Eysenck (1988), assuming an objective basis for the concept of beauty, conducted numerous cross-cultural experiments. He concluded that there is evidence of both a considerable degree of objectivity and some degree of relativism. In another study, Iwawaki, Eysenck, and Götz (1979) found few differences between Japanese and English children; however, 11-year-old Japanese children scored higher than their English counterparts on selected tasks. Eysenck (1988) discussed a study by Götz, Boring, Lynn, and Eysenck (1979) in which he concluded that possibly one of the reasons that formal or informal training had little to do with the results

> is the fact that children and adults growing up in different cultures obtain scores similar to those of the children and adults growing up in the same culture as the originator of the test, and the artists who constituted the panel whose decisions endorsed the choice of items. (p. 142)

Conducting a series of cross-cultural developmental studies involving children from Kuwait, Sweden, Taiwan, and the U.S., Newton (1992a) investigated cultural similarities and differences of 10-year-old children. Kantner & Newton (1993) utilized a factor analysis to examine the influence of culture on the multidimensional nature of aesthetic responses of three age levels. Newton (1992b) also examined developmental changes in aesthetic response to different media in a cross-cultural study. In all of these studies, cultural similarities emerged suggesting certain universals. However, numerous cultural differences were also discovered.

Kuo (1993) conducted a cross-cultural empirical study involving 7-, 9-, 11-, 13-, and 15-year-old Chinese and American students to investigate the achievement in three disciplines within the realm of art appreciation: art history, art criticism, and aesthetics. Results of this study indicated transcultural stability in knowledge about art and art judgments using global stimuli, but some cultural differences emerged as well. American students at all stages of cognitive development achieved higher mean scores in the art appreciation survey than Chinese students. Also, differences were found between the five developmental levels with older subjects able to perform with significantly greater accuracy.

Due to the sparcity of studies exlploring the phenomena relative to aesthetic development in a cross-cultural perspective, it is appropriate to examine a number of comparable studies exploring responses of subjects in different single cultures. Several researchers addressed developmental questions regarding young children's attitudes towards and preferences for works of art. Most of these studies examined similar properties of art (subject matter, color, and style) as essential to response and explored their significance in aesthetic judgements and classifications. Obviously, these comparisons need to be done with caution due to the variety of methodological approaches and variations in the stimuli employed.

Studies of Aesthetic Preferences
Bou and Lopez (1953) examined preferences for style among elementary-aged children in Puerto Rico and found that children preferred more realistic illustrations. No gender differences were found in this study. Machotka (1966) analyzed justifications provided by French boys for their stylistic preferences and found that realism was the dominant criterion. The significance of realism as a preference predictor increased with age, with younger children choosing paintings for their subject matter and color. Goude (1972) utilized a multidimensional scaling approach to investigate the formation of perception of art and the variation occurring during development among 8-, 10-, 12-, 14-year-old Swedish children. He concluded that younger children base their similarity judgments on fewer dimensions than older subjects. He also noted that the role of motif (content) component diminishes with age while attraction to the emotion and composition components increases with age.

Bell and Bell (1979) studied Australian children's responses to 20th century painting and found a more multidimensional nature of preference (color, representation, and complexity) without a definite preference for representational art. The notion of a multidimensional nature of aesthetic preference was further confirmed by Kindler (1993) in her study exploring preferences for realism in art among Canadian First Nations children.

Several studies were conducted in Great Britain. Rump and Southgate (1967) investigated aesthetic preferences of 7-, 11-, and 15-year-old children and found that younger subjects preferred realistic depictions of familiar objects and bright colors, and they provided egocentric justifications of their choices. O'Hare and Cook (1983) investigated 5- to 11-year-old children's sensitivity to modes of color in art and concluded that children demonstrate sensitivity to the four color modes (heraldic, pure, harmonic and gradation) only in the middle childhood years. O'Hare and Westwood (1984) investigated the sensitivity of 6- and 10-year-old children to formal and stylistic properties of line drawings by analyzing subjects' classificatory responses with multidimensional scaling. They found little evidence for line sensitivity in 6- and 7-year-old children.

Gebotys and Cupchik (1989), studying 6-, 9-, and 12-year-old Canadian students, examined cognitive and affective aspects of aesthetic perception and found "6-year-old children had a stronger affective response to the art works" while cognitive responses increased with age (p. 55). It was also found that cognitive and affective aspects, or "emotionality and cognition in the aesthetic responses of children" (p. 55), are relatively independent.

Most of the above studies with children from various regions of the world correspond to numerous developmental studies conducted by researchers in the U.S. investigating variables, such as subject matter and style, affecting aesthetic response (e.g., Hardiman & Zernich, 1977, 1985b; Newton, 1989; Kindler, 1990). Many developmental studies were founded on the Piagetian theory of cognitive development. For example, Parsons, Johnston and Durham (1978) incorporated the works of Piaget, Kohlberg and Selman in their investigation of developmental stages by analyzing responses to questions about art. Other researchers, including Gardner and his associates of the Project Zero, studied children's creative, perceptive, and responsive behaviors without the confines of established developmental theories (Gardner, 1972; Gardner, Winner, & Kirchner, 1975; Silverman, Winner, & Gardner, 1976; Winner, Rosenblatt, Windmueller, Davidson & Gardner, 1984).

Although it is difficult to make direct comparisons because of different methodological procedures, some commonalities of abilities at particular ages can be observed when studies from different countries and cultures are examined. Subject matter and color seem to be universally significant dimensions shaping aesthetic preferences, particularly among younger children. Also, the ability to discriminate style has been documented to develop by the age of 10 or 11. Taunton (1982), in her review of numerous studies investigating the relationship between stimulus characteristics such as familiarity and complexity on preference and attention behaviors, acknowledged an ability shared by children over 10 years of age to distinguish between attending and preference judgments with a consistency in preferences. "Attending behaviors" refers to the subjects' abilities to perceive and respond to certain dimensions of the stimuli such as complexity and familiarity whereas "preference behavior" is simply what subjects like or dislike (p. 99). It should be noted that most of the developmental studies examined subjects' responses without special training sessions to determine the natural maturation of aesthetic response.

Several studies in empirical or experimental aesthetics that are not cross-cultural offer possibilities for extensions in the cross-cultural realm. Neperud and Serlin (1984) examined certain proportional and semantic bases thought to underlie children's aesthetic responses using the Fibonacci sequence. This sequence, described as originating in Arabic countries but introduced to Europe during the 13th century, has intrigued aestheticians and scholars for centuries. The results of this study indicated that younger subjects had higher evaluation of all stimuli than older subjects with the possible interpretation pointing to innate foundations of aesthetic preference in young children.

Neperud, Serlin, and Jenkins (1982) validated semantic and graphic scales for visual rating and found the evaluative, potency, and activity factors to be unaffected by the race of the viewer. If certain graphic symbols could be validated with similar meanings across cultures, the graphic differential as a measurement instrument could potentially alleviate the problems of language and verbal fluency for future cross-cultural research. However, this would require determining whether unique learning experiences and/or cultural interactions with children in different cultures would cause them to decode the graphic differential symbols in different ways.

Although numerous studies with age as an independent variable have investigated the covariance of various dimensions of art stimuli, a clear developmental understanding of the complex nature of aesthetic response is not apparent. As indicated earlier, very few cross-cultural studies have been concerned with developmental changes in aesthetic responses. Comparisons of children's perceptions and responses to aesthetic stimuli across multiple studies are difficult due to different variables under investigation, methodological and procedural variations, and varying theoretical bases for the studies. Thus, we are left with small isolated pieces of information about a very complex process. Consequently, it is impossible to claim with confidence that there are indeed universal trends in the development of aesthetic response corresponding with chronological age. The variability and extent of cultural influence or the discrepancies existing between and within cultures need to be further examined.

Issues and Problems in Cross-Cultural Research

Researchers interested in pursuing this path of inquiry may benefit from the advice of Boyer (1984) and Eisner (1979) who critically observed that cross-cultural research in this area has been focused primarily upon universal similarities rather than cultural differences in aesthetic behaviors. Boyer (1983)

presented several limitations observed in experimental aesthetics: the need
for clarity and clearer definition of terminology, a greater use of nonverbal
measures along with verbal measures, more individual flexibility and opportunity for choices in response instruments, and expansion of the focus of the
studies beyond dimensions of stimuli to variables such as motivation, processes, environment, and viewer intention. Boyer's final recommendation was
the consideration of more qualitative approaches.

Berlyne (1980) predicted a future phase in experimental aesthetics with
the primary task establishing correlations between cultural characteristics and
characteristics of aesthetic preference while continuing to seek reasons for
them. He stated that this would require objective measurement, objective
methods of classifying cultures, and measuring their selected attributes.

In direct contrast to experimental aesthetics researchers' focus on the
idea of universality of aesthetic response, Bourdieu (1968) presented a perspective which emphasized the sociological and cultural influences on learned
decoding patterns of aesthetic perception. An anthropological perspective has
been proposed by Young (1982) who offered the following definition of aesthetic response:

The aesthetic response is intimately connected with the creative
processing of information associated with the formal properties
of the external world...includes the act of perception itself and
extends to the rearrangement of such formal properties in artifacts, in order to exert greater control over the environment (p. 5).

A more socio-scientific definition of aesthetics relates biological, psychological, cultural, and social aspects of the aesthetic response. McFee (1978)
questioned whether aesthetics (primarily Western) can be considered universal. While convinced of the universality of aesthetic experience, she recom-
mended that researchers develop more understanding of the aesthetic values
of many more cultural systems, paying particular attention to the cultural influences on aesthetic perception and response. Similarly, Hart (1993) urged
an embracement of pluralist aesthetics based upon the premise that different
aesthetics are in operation in different cultures.

Research concerned detecting universal behavior is limited if researchers are simply duplicating single culture studies (predominantly Western) in
other cultural settings (predominantly non-Western). This type of research
provides little understanding about the universal and culturally relative variables in child development in art. Eisner (1984) urges researchers to examine

comparisons and contrasts of important development concerns in art rather than to pursue research that merely expands an existing study by collecting data in another country.

There are numerous other problematic issues facing the cross-cultural researcher. Glick (1975) discussed several methodological problems in cross-cultural investigations and identified three concerns which should be addressed. Glick stressed the need for

establishing comparable familiarity of materials when different groups are employed; establishing equivalences of communication and translation when different language groups are used; and establishing motivational comparability among differently motivated and oriented groups. (p. 608)

Selection of materials, media, stimuli, types of instructions, and kinds of tasks ultimately center around the notion of familiarity. If any of these procedures are biased toward one culture, then familiarity becomes an uncontrolled variable which, with great probability, can affect the results of the study.

In cross-cultural research, communication problems often occur in the introduction, instructions for the tasks, and the translation of language and responses. Very few cross-cultural studies can escape the need for translating language for observation, research instruments, and measurements. The process of back-translating has become a common practice in sociological, anthropological, and some psychological studies. Back-translating involves asking an individual fluent in both languages and familiar with the subject and variables under investigation to translate from the first to the second language. Then, another bilingual person working independently translates these back to the first language. The resultant two language versions are compared and differences are scrutinized. Osgood (1965) utilized existing sets of data by applying back-translations in examining cross-cultural attitudes and meanings attributed to concepts. Breslin, Lonner and Rhorndike (1973) discussed several cross-cultural studies utilizing back translation and suggested limiting vagueness, metaphors and colloquialisms.

Language also influences and complicates cross-cultural research in other ways. McFee (1980) reminded us that the universal working definition of aesthetic experience is difficult because it means so many different things in different cultures. A Native-American participant in the 1992 Discipline-based Art Education and Cultural Diversity Conference noted, for example, that "the word 'art' does not exist in her language, but is infused in many other concepts such as religion, science, and family" (Getty Center for Education in the Arts, 1992, p. 105).

It is extremely imperative that cross-cultural researchers utilize procedures, materials, stimuli, tasks, and measurement instruments which are not culturally or ethnically biased (Hui & Triandis, 1985). The mere act of collecting drawings or aesthetic responses from children in other cultures utilizing a Western bias in the stimuli and criteria for analysis does not provide significant insight in cross-cultural understanding of child development in art. Breslin (1983) summarized this issue by advocating a set of methodological guidelines which do not impose the researcher's cultural standards in gathering data in another culture. Collaborative research involving researchers indigenous to the studied cultures (e.g., Kindler & Darras, 1994; Kindler, Darras & Kuo, 1994) offers a possible solution to some of these issues.

Concluding Remarks

Reflecting on the early work of developmental psychologists in cognition and perception, the work of cultural anthropologists, and more recent efforts of art educators, the quest for an understanding of the aesthetic development of children in making and responding to art in a cross-cultural perspective is paramount. Developmentalists defined mental and visual growth in invariant stages with a predetermined end-point. Art educators tended to follow with their more descriptive analysis of the graphic features. These were the universalists who, through their theoretical stance, saw a strong consistent similarity in the innate graphic development of the child. Many of today's developmentalists, although in general agreement with a natural unfolding of development, recognize the importance of cultural and environmental factors in artistic and aesthetic growth.

With the cultural factor beginning to play a decisive role in the minds of many, developmental theory is being called into question with increasing repetition. Do the Piagetian tasks, for example, represent culture-free tests? Bernat (1992) suggests that researchers now recognize the inaccuracy of Piaget's description of cognition of the young children without, however, considering it totally false. Many theoreticians use the universal concept to provide a base for further speculation. For example, Pariser (1994) suggested that the

> Wolf and Perry [1988] proposal (a developmental mechanism which accounts for the origins of diverse styles through multiple graphic options or endpoints) could easily be incorporated into Golomb's Gestalt framework and could provide researchers with an exciting agenda; namely, to demonstrate cross-culturally that within each of the multiple streams of graphic development outlined by Wolf and Perry, and across cultures, the basic laws of Gestalt development hold true. (p. 60)

Furthermore, the writings of Vygotsky (1978), Bruner (1983), and Cole, Gay, Glick, and Sharp (1971), which place social mediation as the primary factor in development, are influencing more and more our understanding of artistic and aesthetic development. With the introduction of Vygotsky's concept of the "zone of proximal development," the influence of adults and more advanced peers is now being more seriously considered. No longer is the child regarded as the Piagetian insular thinker, but one who thinks within a social context. This concept is very important to the cross-cultural researcher as it emphasizes the role of social mediation in development.

Wolf (1987), a developmental psychologist, provided an insight into the question of the viability of developmental studies. She stated, "I think the (developmental) studies are valuable for casting up possibilities for learning, necessities for learning, rather than absolute sequences of any kind" (p. 23).

The vital importance of multicultural and cross-cultural research is to promote a greater understanding of diverse cultures and to explore the role of art in multicultural education (Kantner, 1983). Rogoff & Morelli (1989) stated that

The potential from research on cultural groups around the world as well as down the street lies in its challenge to our system of assumptions and in the creative efforts of scholars to synthesize knowledge from observations of differing context of human development. Such challenge and synthesis is fruitful in the efforts to achieve a deeper and broader understanding of human nature and nurture. (p. 347)

While research provides us with insights into cultural differences and similarities, one must keep in mind that these findings should not tempt us to unconsciously stereotype cultures, groups, or individuals or promote ethnocentrism and/or xenophobia. Through enculturation, an individual becomes the carrier of culture if the culture is to be maintained and respected. As Disanayake explained to the delegates of the 1993 Getty Seminar:

Eskimos are not better than Mbuti pygmies, or Italians better than Greeks, although we can ask whether one cultural system serves universal human species needs better than another. But emphasizing one society's arts as intrinsically superior to another's on some dogmatic scale of values will only generate strife. It is more important for representatives of each culture to realize...that species-centrism embraces and precedes culture-centrism for only within a larger awareness of our common needs and heritage can we constructively appreciate the differences in individual cultures...(I am) convinced that the arts, if properly introduced can serve as an ideal avenue for 'Harmonizing' the compelling claims of diverse and warring cultures. (p. 17)

Hofsetede (1980) predicted that the survival of mankind is predicated on the successful interaction between "others" acting together.

In our postmodern world, this appreciation for the diversity found in "others" is not only of value, it is essential. Cross-cultural researchers, in considering the similarities and differences in children's artistic growth, should continue to be guided by the advice given by Rousseau: "Begin then by studying your pupils more thoroughly, for it is certain you do not know them" (in Korzenik, 1979).

References

Allison, B. (1980). The relationship between child arts and their cultural foundations. *Journal of Aesthetic Education, 14*(3), 59-79.

Anwar, M. P., & Child, I. L. (1972). Personality and esthetic sensitivity in an Islamic culture. *The Journal of Social Psychology, 87,* 21-28.

Bell, R., & Bell, G. (1979). Individual differences in children's preferences among recent paintings. *British Journal of Educational Psychology, 49,* 182-187.

Berry, J. W., & Danson, T. R. (Eds.) (1974). *Culture & cognition: Readings in cross-cultural psychology.* London: Methuen & Co.

Berlyne, D. E. (1975). Extension to Indian subjects of a cross-cultural study of exploratory and verbal responses to visual patterns. *Journal of Cross-Cultural Psychology, 6,* 316-330.

Berlyne, D. E. (1976). Similarity judgment and preferences of Indian and Canadian subjects exposed to Western paintings. *International Journal of Psychology, 11,* 43-55.

Berlyne, D. E. (1980). Psychological aesthetics. In H.C. Triandis & W. Lonner (Eds.), *Handbook of cross-cultural psychology, 3,* (pp. 323-362). Boston: Allyn and Bacon.

Berlyne, D. E., Robbins, M., & Thompson, R. (1974). A cross-cultural study of exploratory and verbal responses to visual patterns varying in complexity. In D.E. Berlyne (Ed.), *Studies in the New Experimental Aesthetics: Steps Toward an Objective Psychology of Aesthetic Appreciation.* Washington, DC: Hemisphere.

Best, D. (1985). Concepts and culture. *Journal of Multi-Cultural and Cross-Cultural Research in Art Education, 3*(1), 7-17.

Bou, I., & Lopez, D. (1953). Preferences in colors and illustrations of elementary school children of Puerto Rico. *Journal of Educational Psychology, 44,* 490-496.

Bourdieu, P. (1968). Outline of a sociological theory of perception. *International Social Science Journal, 20,* 589-612.

Boyer, B. A. (1983). An examination of experimental aesthetic research related to the visual perception of painting. *Visual Arts Research, 9*(1), 34-40.

Boyer, B. A. (1984). *Critical issues in developing cross-cultural research.* Paper delivered at XXV World Congress, International Society for Education through Art, Rio de Janeiro, Brazil.

Breslin, R.W. (1983). Cross-cultural research in psychology. *Annual Review of Psychology, 34*, 363-400.

Breslin, R., Lonner, W., & Rhorndike, R. (1973). *Cross-cultural research methods.* New York: John Wiley & Sons.

Bruner, J. S. (1983). *In search of mind.* New York: Harper and Row.

Chan, J., Eysenck, H., & Götz, K. (1980). A new visual aesthetic sensitivity test: Cross-cultural comparisons between Hong Kong children and adults, and English and Japanese samples. *Perceptual and Motor Skills, 50*(3), 1385-1386.

Chapman, L. H. (1978). *Approaches to art education.* New York: Harcourt, Brace, & Jovanovich.

Child, I. L. (1962). Personal preferences as an expression of aesthetic sensitivity. *Journal of Personality, 30*, 496-512.

Child, I. L. (1964). Observations on the meaning of some measures of esthetic sensitivity. *The Journal of Psychology, 57*, 49-64.

Child, I. L., Iwao, S., Briddell, D., Fintzelberg, N., Garcia, M., Hetata, F., Most, S., Ning, L., & Sewall, S. (1968b). *Art preferences in culturally varying groups.* Washington, DC. Office of Education Bureau of Research, 1-35. (ERIC DOC).

Cole, M., Gay, J., Glick, J. A., & Sharp, D. W. (1971). *The cultural context of learning and thinking.* New York: Basic Books.

Dasen, P. R. (1972). Cross-cultural Piagetian research: A summary. *Journal of Cross-Cultural Psychology, 3*(1), 23-39.

Dasen, P. R. (1974). Cross-cultural Piagetian research: A summary. In J. W. Berry & P. R. Dasen (Eds.), *Culture and cognition: Readings in cross-cultural psychology* (pp. 409-424). London: Methuen & Co.

Dawson, J. (1967). Cultural and physiological influences upon spatial perceptual processes in West Africa. *International Journal of Psychology, 2*, 115-128.

Efland, A. D., Stuhr, P., & Freedman, K. (1990). *Postmodern art education: The next challenge.* Unpublished manuscript.

Eisner, E. W. (1979). Cross-cultural research in art education: Problems, issues, and prospects. *Studies in Art Education, 21*, 27-35.

Eisner, E. W. (1984). Cross-cultural research in art education: Problems, issues, and perspectives. In R.W. Ott & A. Hurwitz (Eds.), *Art in education: An international perspective* (pp. 39-52). University Park, PA: Pennsylvania State University Press.

Eysenck, H. J. (1988). Personality and scientific aesthetics. In F.H. Farley & R.W. Neperud (Eds.), *The Foundation of Aesthetics, Art, & Art Education* (pp. 117-162). New York: Praeger.

Gardner, H. (1972). The development of sensitivity to figural and stylistic aspects of paintings. *British Journal of Psychology, 63*, 605-615.

Gardner, H., Winner, E., & Kirchner, M. (1975). Children's conceptions of the arts. *Journal of Aestheic Education, 9*, 60-77.

Garth, T. R., & Collado, I. R. (1929). The color preferences of Filipino children. *Journal of Comparative Psychology, 9*, 397-404.

Garth, T. R., Ikeda, K., & Langdon, R. M. (1931). The color preferences of Japanese children. *Journal of Social Psychology, 2*, 397-402.

Gebotys, R. J., & Cupchik, G. C. (1989). Perception and production in children's art. *Visual Arts Research, 15*(1), 55-67.

Geertz, C. (1973). *The interpretation of cultures.* New York: Basic Books.

Gesche, I. (1927). The color preferences of one thousand one hundred and fifty-two Mexican children. *Journal of Comparative Psychology, 7,* 297-311.

Getty Center for Education in the Arts. (1992). Affinity group summary reports. In *Discipline-based Art Education and Cultural Diversity.* Los Angeles: J. Paul Getty Trust, 21-44, 105-107.

Glick, J. (1975). Cognitive development in cross-cultural perspective. In F.D. Horowitz (Ed.), *Review of Child Development Research, Vol. 4,* (pp. 595-654). Chicago: University of Chicago Press.

Götz, K., Boring, S., Lynn, R., & Eysenck, H. (1979). A new visual aesthetic sensitivity test (VAST), I. Construction and psychometric properties. *Perceptual and Motor Skills, 49,* 795-802.

Goude, G. (1972). A multidimensional scaling approach to the perception of art II. *Scandinavian Journal of Psychology, 13*(4), 272-284.

Hardiman, G. W., & Zernich, T. (1977). Influence of style and subject on the development of children's art preferences. *Studies in Art Education, 19*(1), 29-35.

Hardiman, G. W., & Zernich, T. (1985a). Cross-cultural research in the visual arts: An overview. *Journal of Multicultural Research in Art Education, 3*(1), 19-24.

Hardiman, G., & Zernich, T. (1985b). Discrimination of style in painting: A developmental study. *Studies in Art Education, 26*(3), 157-162.

Haritos-Fatouros, M., & Child, I. (1977). Transcultural similarity in personal significance of esthetic interests. *Journal of Cross-Cultural Psychology, 8*(3), 285-298.

Hart, L. (1993). The role of cultural context in multicultural aesthetics. *Journal of Multi and Cross Cultural Research in Art Education,* 5-18.

Hofstede, G. (1980). *Culture's consequences, international differences in work-related values.* Beverly Hills, CA: Sage Productions.

Hudson, W. (1960). Pictorial depth perception in sub-cultural groups in Africa. *The Journal of Social Psychology, 52,* 183-208.

Hui, C. H., & Triandis, H. C. (1985). Measurement in cross-cultural psychology: A review and comparison of strategies. *Journal of Cross-Cultural Psychology, 16*(2), 131-152.

Iwawaki, S., Eysenck, H., & Gotz, K. (1979). A new visual sensitivity test (VAST) II. Cross-cultural comparisons between England and Japan. *Perceptual Motor Skills, 49,* 859-862.

Kantner, L. (1983). Editorial. *Journal of Multi-cultural and Cross-cultural Research in Art Education, 1*(1), 4.

Kantner, L., & Newton, C. (1993). *A factor-analysis of cross-cultural comparisons of children's aesthetic responses.* Paper presented at the International Society for Education in Art, Montreal, Canada.

Kindler, A. M. (1990). Classification of nonobjective paintings: Developmental and methodological determinants. *Visual Arts Research, 16,* 1-10.

Kindler, A.M. (1993). Preference for realism in art among First Nations Children. Paper presented at the International Society for Education through Art World Compress. Montreal, August 1993.

Kindler, A. M., & Darras, B. (1994). *A cross-cultural study of young children's understanding of selected visual literacy related functions and concepts.* Paper presented at the National Art Education Association Convention, Baltimore, MD.

Kindler, A. M., Darras, B., & Kuo, A. (1994). *Development of attitudes and beliefs in regard to nature and value of visual arts and acquisition of basic art competencies: A cross-cultural study.* Unpublished research proposal, University of British Columbia, Vancouver.

Korzenik, D. (1979). *Nineteenth century dialogue on international art education: Age grading and curriculum.* Paper presented at the United States Society of Education through Art Conference, Cambridge.

Kuo, A. C. (1993, August). *Theory and practice in art education-art appreciation achievement among students in Taiwan and America: A cross-cultural study.* Paper presented at the International Society of Education through Art World Congress, Montreal, Canada.

Lovano-Kerr, J. (1983). Cross-cultural perspectives on cognition and art: Implications for research. *Journal of Multicultural Reserach in Art Education, 1,* 77-87.

Machotka, P. (1966). Aesthetic criteria in childhood: Justification of preference. *Child Development, 37,* 877-888.

McFee, J. K. (1978). Cultural influences on aesthetic experience. In J. Condous, J. Howlett, & J. Skull (Eds.), *Arts in Cultural Diversity* (pp. 45-52). New York: Holt, Rinehart and Winston.

McFee, J. K. (1980). Cultural influences on aesthetic experience. In J. Condous, J. Howlett, & J. Skull (Eds.), *Arts in Cultural Diversity* (pp. 45-52). New York: Holt, Rinehart and Winston.

McFee, J. K. (1986). Cross-cultural inquiry into the social meaning of art: Implications for art education. *Journal of Multi-Cultural and Cross-Cultural Research in Art Education, 4*(1), 6-16.

Miller, R. J. (1973). Cross-cultural research in the perception of pictorial materials, *Psychological Bulletin, 80*(2), 136.

Mundy-Castle, A. (1966). Pictorial depth perception in Ghanaian children. *International Journal of Psychology, 1,* 290-299.

Neperud, R. W., Serlin, R., & Jenkins, H. C. (1982). Ethnic aesthetics: Blacks' and nonblacks' aesthetic perception of paintings by Blacks. *Studies in Art Education, 23,* 24-30.

Neperud, R. W., & Serlin, R. (1984). The Fibonacci sequence: Proportional and semantic bases of children's aesthetic preferences. *Studies in Art Education, 25,* 92-103.

Newton, C. (1989). A developmental study of aesthetic responses using both verbal and non-verbal measures. *Visual Arts Research, 15,* 76-85.

Newton, C. (1992a). *Developmental changes in children's aesthetic responses.* Paper presented at the International Congress of Psychology, Brussels, Belgium.

Newton, C. (1992b). *A cross-cultural study of developmental changes of children's aesthetic responses to different media dimensions of art stimuli.* Paper presented at the International Congress of Empirical Aesthetics, Berlin, Germany.

O'Hare, D., & Cook, D. (1983). Children's sensitivity to different modes of colour use in art. *Journal of Educational Psychology, 53,* 267-277.

O'Hare, D., & Westwood, H. (1984). Features of style classification: A multivariate experimental analysis of children's responses to drawings. *Developmental Psychology, 20*(1), 150-158.

Osgood, C. E. (1965). Cross-cultural comparability in attitude measurement via multilingual semantic differentials. In E. Steiner and M. Fishbein (Eds.), *Current Studies in Social Psychology* (95-106). New York: Holt, Rinehart and Winston.

Pariser, D. (1994, April). *An experiment in cross-cultural aesthetics: Testing the notion of u-shaped aesthetic development in a Chinese setting.* Paper presented at the National Art Education Association Convention.

Parsons, M., Johnston, M., & Durham, R. (1978). Developmental stages in children's aesthetic responses. *Journal of Aesthetic Education, 12*(1), 83-104.

Piaget, J., & Inhelder, B. (1967). *The child's conception of space.* New York: Norton.

Ramkissoon, R. D., & Bhana, K. (1985). Free and matrix classification: An experimental investigation of the responses of nine- and twelve-year-old children. *International Journal of Psychology, 20*, 319-328.

Rogoff, B., & Morelli, G. (1989). Perspectives on children's development from cultural psychology. *American Psychologist, 44*(2), 343-348.

Rump, E. E., & Southgate, V. (1967). Variables affecting aesthetic appreciation, in relation to age. *British Journal of Educational Psychology, 37*(1), 58-72.

Silverman, J., Winner, E., & Gardner, H. (1976). On going beyond the literal: The development of sensitivity to artistic symbols. *Semiotica, 18*(4), 291-312.

Taunton, M. (1982). Aesthetic responses of young children to the visual arts: A review of literature. *Journal of Aesthetic Education, 16*, 94-109.

Triandis, H. C. (1980). Introduction to handbook of cross-cultural psychology. In H. C. Triandis & W. W. Lambert (Eds.), *Handbook of cross-cultural psychology Vol. 1*, (pp. 1-14). Boston: Allyn and Bacon.

Vygotsky, L. (1978). *Mind in society.* Cambridge, MA: Harvard Press.

Werner, E. E. (1979). *Cross-cultural child development: A view from the planet Earth.* Monterey, CA: Brooks Cole Publishing Company.

Winner, E., Rosenblatt, E., Windmueller, G., Davidson, L., & Gardner, H. (1984). Children's perception of "aesthetic" properties of the arts: Domain-specific or pan-artistic? Cambridge, MA: Harvard University. *U.S. Department of Education*, 1-53. (ERIC DOC).

Witkin, H. A., & Berry, J. W. (1975). Psychological differentiation in cross-cultural perspective. *Journal of Cross-Cultural Psychology, 6*(1), 4-87.

Wolf, D. (1987, May). The growth of three aesthetic stances: What developmental psychology suggests about discipline-based art education. In *Issues in discipline-based art education: Strengthening the stance, extending the horizons* (pp. 85-100). Seminar sponsored by The Getty Center for Education in the Arts, Cincinnati, OH.

Wolf, D., & Perry, M. D. (1988). From endpoints to repertoires: Some new conclusions about drawing development. *Journal of Aesthetic Education, 22*(1), 17-34.

Young, D. E. (1982). Aesthetic response as coping behavior: An anthropological perspective. *Studies in Art Education, 24*(1), 5-15.

DEVELOPMENT AND PRACTICE

WHAT CAN THE LITERATURE TELL THE TEACHER?

What knowledge is of most worth? Herbert Spencer's teasing question, posed over a century ago, still sums up neatly the central concern of and for the educator. But in order to lead students to the acquisition of worthwhile knowledge, teachers must determine first, what the students are organismically capable of achieving; next, the extent to which their material circumstances will permit them to move in a desired direction; and finally, how learning experiences may be devised to facilitate that movement.

Many forms of arts activity are grounded in the expression of feeling or emotion, and in Western societies education in the arts has included recurring opportunities for self expression. The inherent difficulty of showing that educated sensitivity is qualitatively different from naive emotion has, however, frustrated the creation of defensible sequences of activities exclusively in the realm of the emotions. Cognitive activities that deal with knowledge or strategy acquisition, and which may include affective or sensuous elements, are more likely to provide those unidirectional variations by which educational progress is observed and evaluated.

For the visual arts, organismic development has come to be in part defined as acquiring increasingly efficient perceptual and cognitive strategies that result in increasingly effective ways and means of making and respond-

RONALD MACGREGOR

ing to art. Art education is about learning to look; nature takes care of learning to see. The anatomy that contributes to visual perception is virtually completely operative within the first two years of life. Newborns show discrimination skills that increase rapidly in the day-by-day context of getting around in the world. The preschool or kindergarten teacher should be alert to possible physical defects (myopia, or shortsightedness; nystagmus, or squint; astigmatism, or horizontal or vertical distortion) which might impair visual efficiency. For most children, though, the visual apparatus develops in such a manner that they are able to discriminate light from dark, contour from surface, densely textured from lightly textured areas, moving objects from still objects, so readily that it seems "natural." Long before young persons embark on formal education, perceptual development is, in the physiological sense, well advanced.

What distinguishes older children from their younger counterparts is the relative facility they display in adapting, translating, and transforming visual data—including how they respond to art tasks. Art is used here to describe products of a two-or three-dimensional nature that have a parallel in the valued artifacts of an adult society. Historically, this has not always been the case, and there are cultural exceptions as well. But as a working definition, it will do.

Adaptation, translation, and transformation of visual data into art forms requires the use of areas of the brain not directly accessible to research. Any ideas on how processing of information occurs in the cortex are inferences based on observed behavior. When the behavior of healthy children is compared with the behavior of those with head injuries or those who are otherwise maladapted, a sense of what is "normal" (that is, what may commonly be expected) gradually accumulates. Similarly, the behavior of young children confronted by a task may be compared with that of older children given the same task on such dimensions as speed of execution or complexity of product.

Since researchers operate from particular value stances, their interpretation of findings will vary. Hence, researchers whose primary interest is in differentiation, the progressive addition of detail, will attend to and place importance on different aspects of the child's work than will those whose interests lie in how children acquire new strategies for dealing with visual-spatial problems.

There also exists a body of opinion that holds discussion of cognitive skills such as differentiation to be only part of the much larger question of what it is to be conscious: something, it is argued, that cannot be inferred from counting instances or events. There are differences of opinion on whether cognitive ability is a unified concept or whether several bundles of cognitive skills develop independently of each other. Bearing all these matters in mind, it is probably safest to say that controversies generated around the topic of child development in art are usually less the product of absolute differences in what researchers think is conceivable and more the result of different emphases and interests.

What are students capable of achieving?

The first stages of art making require the assembly of visual data. Differences in light and color among objects in the physical, external world are registered and transported by series of neurons from the eye to the visual cortex at the back of the skull. Neurons are small electrochemical "machines" that produce tiny charges or impulses, so visual data may be said to be encoded as electrochemical charges. To make identification simpler and speedier for researchers, the brain has been divided into numbered areas; those where most visual data are assembled and where decoding probably begins are known as areas 17 and 18. According to researchers such as David Marr (1982), certain neurons in those areas are sensitive to the kind of information associated with edges (i.e. to differences between light and dark); some to density (or, in Marr's term, "blobs"); still others to points. The information these neurons provide is combined by other neurons to create what Marr calls a "primal sketch", which is a rough approximation of an object, but an object re-presented as neural energy and as little like an artist's sketch as the letters d-o-g are like an actual dog. Out of primal sketch material, other combinations of neurons in the brain, including those storing previously acquired information, construct a rough three-dimensional re-presentation that is then further refined by additional memory and experiential input to become recognizable as a particular chair or a special kind of dog. Exactly how one recognizes it as a dog is another, currently insoluble question.

The old argument over whether children proceed from a generalized notion of doggishness to recognition of particular dogs or whether they build a notion of doggishness out of particular dogs they encounter is, according to Marr's model, two parts of reciprocal and evolving relationships among clusters of neurons. When linked to increasingly controlled motor activity on the part of the child, neural information undergoes yet another re-presentation, this time as a mark of enclosure: a roughly circular shape made with a crayon or a pencil or a finger that "stands for" a dog or one particular dog.

From this point, art activity takes on a specific character. The child takes possession of what was formerly a blank space (or, in the case of three dimensional examples, an area of sand or a lump of clay) in the name of a re-presented dog or truck or dad. Thenceforth, building a repertoire of images that re-create experiences in and of the world becomes a priority.

In this, children learn from each other, from their teachers, from what they see on television, in films and in books, from the work of adult artists, from nature, and from their own experiences translated into art forms. As social beings, they wish to be accepted as competent in aspects of what Bruner (1966) has referred to as "knowing how" and "knowing that." Partly because art is an effective vehicle for recording special or important events at a time in life when verbal precision and diversity are not yet mastered, children in the first three grades of school tend to be prolific in output and increasingly individual in their interpretation of topics.

Piaget's (1929) identification of growing up as a progressive facility in getting outside oneself, so that the self-centered world of the newborn eventually is complemented by the ability to see a situation from another person's perspective, has been elaborated and supported by a wealth of research. In art education, Parsons'(1987) identification of five stages that might be anticipated in children's responses to art works recapitulates the Piagetian developmental spiral. From simple statements of "I like" to attention to realism, to a sense that an art work is an expression of its creator's feelings, to the consciousness that an art work has a particular character or style, to a realization that an art work is a part of a historical and cultural tradition: these parallel the general trend among students to move, in the art they produce, from recording events of personal significance to trying to get things to "look right," to creating work designed to elicit a particular emotional or sensuous or intellectual reaction from the viewer.

To what extent do circumstances permit movement in desired directions?

This question might more properly be phrased in terms of the constraints that circumstances impose upon development in desired directions. Though it would simplify matters educationally if all children were predictably at the same stage in cognitive competency at any one time, the everyday world of child development is out-of-step and rather haphazard.

One source of variation involves those art forms commonly used in art classrooms to furnish evidence of development on the part of children. Drawing is perhaps the most popular form used by researchers, but its inherent limitations may provoke the wrong surmises. As an example, consider the belief traditionally held that children's preferences for vertical and horizontal lines over diagonals was a consequence of not being ready developmentally to deal with drawing obliques. In a series of experiments, Naeli and Harris (1976) showed that children cued in on the line provided by the perimeter of the page, using it as a template for drawing contours. When the children were provided with pages cut diagonally, they drew oblique lines readily, and when circular-shaped pages were provided, they achieved roughly equal levels of success in drawing squares and diamonds.

A second set of constraints arises from conventions that are applied voluntarily by the children themselves. Things are "done" or "not done". In Artful scribbles, Howard Gardner (1980) described how he asked his daughter, whose drawings of the human figure had arms that sprouted from the waist, whether they reflected what she saw. She reassured him that she was fully aware of where arms fitted anatomically, but said of her drawings, "I know that's not the way you want to do it, Dad...But that's the way I want to do it, at least for now." (1980, p. 73).

Cox (1992) reports a similar instance of children knowing more than their drawings may tell in some children's persisting use of "tadpole" figures, wherein head and torso share the same circular form. In her words, "Tadpole drawers have little or no difficulty in producing a conventional human figure if all the body parts are provided ready made and can be easily identified" (p. 47).

Another persisting and frequently documented occurrence among younger children is a reluctance to use overlap in their drawings. Goodnow (1977) presents examples to show that children are prepared to leave out arms or legs entirely, rather than deal with the problem of overlap. More recently, though, English (1987) conducted a study in which two preschool children who had been taught to use a Macintosh Colorpaint program used overlap freely in their image creation. It would seem that, whatever the reasons for the avoidance of overlap in drawing, these do not carry over into computer-generated graphic forms.

A third group of constraints is external, in that children have no control over them. They are manifested in the degree of access that children may have to reach a particular level of performance.

Access may be differentiated along social and cultural lines. The importance that art has in the eyes of parents is sometimes translated into the amount of support children receive, and the attitudes they, in turn, develop. In a study of Nepalese children's art, Kaneda (1994) reported that as foreign goods have flooded country markets, "the village people now feel their local hand-made products are inferior and not valuable. Children do not emulate their parents because their parents are no longer making objects" (p. 23). Children's creative output, once characterized by spontaneous doll-making, building model carts, and decorating mud walls, is now channeled into copying the Nepalese flag.

Teachers may unwittingly inhibit opportunities for some students by assuming that the teaching model they are using is universally suitable. This is particularly true in situations where the the prevalent mode in a community is to arrive at a solution by consensus, and the imported educational model to which the children are subjected is based on competitiveness, independence, and the cultivation of individuality. A pioneer study by Wolcott (1967), documenting his experiences as a teacher in a Canadian Indian school, recounts the frustration he and his classes experienced over homework. The older children habitually did the younger children's homework, so Wolcott was never able to determine how the younger children were progressing. "The children's attention focused on the task to be done...and with their combined resources they accomplished the task. As the teacher I felt I had accomplished little when I found the papers assigned to beginners had been completed by pupils twice their age" (p. 105).

How well cooperative models work in formal education, and what effects they might have on how children develop, are matters that have been tried from time to time, but not usually documented in any systematic way. Non-Western teaching methods may result in different learning patterns, and in differences in how those learnings are manifested in art products, but evidence of these in research terms is slight compared with the material assembled in Western societies.

Arguments on how students are excluded from access to learning on cultural grounds may be extended to various economically deprived groups. During preschool years, economic differences may mean lack of opportunity to attend playschool, so that some children are already disadvantaged in the first year of formal schooling. They may lack opportunities in their homes to encounter a variety of learning experiences, or to work with learning materials. They may suffer lower levels of health and nutrition than those in better economic situations, to the detriment of their energy and stamina. The result of economic disadvantage is not a difference in the sequence of development, but rather, impoverishment in the images these children produce and in the repertoire they accumulate. Anyon (1981), and other critical theorists have described teachers' expectations about the performance of economically differentiated students as sometimes having the air of self-fulfilling prophecies.

A further set of constraints imposed on moves in desired directions arises from ambiguity on the part of art educators about the preferred form of a developmental art program. In an extensive review and analysis of studies conducted over a 30-year period, Haanstra (1994) identified two major directions that have been pursued in children's development in art. The first takes as its focus the improvement of visual/spatial abilities; the second, increased facility in aesthetic perception. As part of this study, Haanstra held interviews with seven art educators who have been cited extensively. All of them were critical of experimental studies conducted within the field in the past. Some, though, felt that greater refinement in methods and design could result in more useful information to guide practice, while others felt that the increasing weight of anecdotal evidence on the central role of interpretation and reflection rendered experimental studies obsolete.

This lack of consensus among experts: indeed, the fundamental schism in their positions, is echoed in Haanstra's analysis of the collected studies. Though, he says, the effects of perceptual training, particularly in regard to ability to distinguish figure from ground, are most visible among young (4-6 yrs.) children, there is little compelling evidence that this is widespread or continuing. At the same time, lack of an agreed-upon definition of aesthetic perception inhibits the collection of material in stable categories and indeed, begs the question of what kind of consistent behavior may legitimately be expected of any group or class exposed to teacher influence.

How may facilitative learning experiences be devised?

The models described by Kindler and Darras (Kindler & Darras, this book) and various other contributors to this collection of articles point to confirmation of multi-activity, cross-disciplinary programs for schools, as means to encourage the creation of an art-literate public. Kindler and Darras suggest that learning is like a map: as indeed it is, in the sense that at any one point, learning may be viewed cross-sectionally, or spatially, to determine what are the elements or concepts being explored, and how they interrelate.

Learning is also like a river, though, in that it travels in a direction over time. Its temporal character is reflected over decades in the changing character of research and in shifting classroom preoccupations. While the learning river may flow swiftly at some points and meander at others, there must always be a sense on the part of those who travel on it that it is going *somewhere*, that particular ends are to be served. These ends are the explicit responses to Spencer's question: What knowledge is of most worth? In this collection, the nature of these ends influences the content of the discussion undertaken by Freedman (Freedman, this book) on the difference between experts (those whose social experiences have given them desired competencies) and novices (those who have not yet acquired them).

Part of the difficulty in having teachers achieve familiarity with developmental or growth or acquisition models in art is that often, insufficient occasions exist in schools to discuss art programs in their entirety (for example, from kindergarten through sixth grade). In this respect, programs such as Discipline-based Art Education (Clark, Day, & Greer, 1987) have performed a useful service. To qualify for funding for DBAE program implementation, school districts were explicitly required to propose activities that would re-flect a belief in the potential for systematic student growth in art production, historical knowledge, critical and aesthetic behavior. This had the effect of stimulating teachers to think of art programs rather than isolated experiences, and of cumulative rather than immediate effects.

More recently, the development of visual arts standards as part of the Goals 2000: Educate America Act has resulted in the closest thing to a na-tional model for art education so far created in North America. These stand-ards reflect the collective wisdom of a committee of art educators represent-ing various levels of schooling, of how children manifest progress in learning (Consortium of National Arts Education Associations, 1994).

Divided along three classroom groupings (K-Gr.4; Gr.5-8; Gr.9-12), activities characteristic of each group might be summarized respectively as familiarization, expansion, and application. The curiosity and sponge-like absorption of information displayed by children in the lower elementary grades is embodied in experiences in learning to use tools and media, developing a store of subject matter, and gaining a sense of how art (one's own, and that of others) is one means of externalizing personal ideas, beliefs, and reflections. The search for common structures, and the desire to make connections within and between groups, which are characteristic of students in the middle school years, is marked by an emphasis on what works and what doesn't, how pur-pose defines the kind of art produced, historically and culturally, and how art works represent integrations of visual, temporal, and spatial factors. The up-per grades student's desire to establish an artistic identity, to find a position that is individual without being socially alien, is met by the proposal of ac-tivities that offer challenging problems for which there may be multiple solu-tions, that encourage discussion of validity and values, and that allow for the examination of multiple contexts as means to understand the complexities and contradictions of human society.

The outlines of activities in the Standards document are not radically different from those that have been developed locally, or state-wide, as cur-riculum guides. Many of these guides follow parts of that same general learn-ing sequence. Curriculum guides do not, however, normally contain informa-tion sufficiently comprehensive to be applicable to the range of classes from kindergarten to 12th grade. Nor do they say, as unambiguously as the Stand-ards do: This is what students should know.

A major initiative to place learning experiences within a frame of pro-gressive experiences in production and discussion of art concepts was under-taken by Chapman (1985). The individual, the society within which the indi-vidual creates, and the cultural values to which a society subscribes, form three sources for art experiences that are grouped as Creating Art, Looking at Art, and Living with Art. The developmental path taken by Chapman in the case of creating art moves from basic media skills and experiences centered on family and friends, to the use of combinations of media and exercises in imagination and visual recall, to consideration of different vantage points and the orchestration of technical means to express mood and solve problems. Looking at art begins with acquiring a basic vocabulary useful for description and the expression of opinion, then deals with comparison and contrast and with the cultural origins and functions of art, and so to a final stage in which a sense of historical continuity is created. Living with art originates as awareness of community resources in the natural and constructed environment, expands into the roles taken by artists and designers, and culminates in experiences to show how a variety of arts may flourish in a variety of cultures.

Models that reflect how students acquire knowledge but which are developed from material collected in limited settings may often be encountered in the professional journals. In one instance, Sowell (1993) tackled the problem endemic among junior high school students of how these students may be persuaded to exchange polarized ways of thinking, in which intuitive response for or against predominates, for a state in which they reconstruct meanings from the perspective of others. Sowell married a learning cycle approach developed for the sciences to the Piagetian notion of progressive decentering, to create learning units wherein progress was documented in students' abilities to explore a body of knowledge, sift through the several layers of meaning associated with the material, and apply their understanding of several contexts to interpretation of the work.

The attitude to child development implicit in programs like these reflects a contemporary recognition of the intertwined relationships among persons, events, settings and conditions that result in patterns of behavior, including art behavior. Wilson (Wilson, this book) makes it abundantly clear that art occurs at the intersect of the ideologies and values held by teachers, children, the art world, the world of education and (one surmises), a number of less visible worlds, as well. There is no archetypal "child"; rather, there are groups of children whose differences are as pronounced as their similarities. Development is as much a response to conditions as it is a genetic imperative.

Koroscik has pointed out (Koroscik, this book) that in addition to the improvement of knowledge, students are intimately concerned in learning search strategies (by which, avenues to knowledge are improved) and transfer (by which, connections are made and possibilities are widened). Hence, the increasing importance given in the field to interpretation: of how children explain events in their lives and images in their art, through what they know, how they plan, and how they see beyond the immediate result. The best sources of how children are developing are surely the children themselves, so their interpretive language is at once a confirmation of their knowledge and a vehicle for their development of sensibility. Teachers can be active agents in that interpretive blossoming, helping children bring to consciousness those things that are imperfectly understood or dimly sensed.

Perhaps, through this common focus, researchers and practitioners will forge new relationships for theory and practice, wherein complementarity of contribution erodes and finally replaces the politics of territoriality. Clifford Geertz once posed the anthropologist's question: How is it that we all start out originals and finish up copies? The psychologist's question might be: How is it that we all start out copies and finish up originals? The educator wants to know the answer to both questions, and is grateful for any thoughtful contribution to their solution.

References

Anyon, J. (1981). Social class and school knowledge. *Curriculum Inquiry.* 11(1), 3-42.

Bruner, J. (1966). *Toward a theory of instruction.* Cambridge, MA: Harvard University Press.

Chapman, L. H. (1985). *Discover art* (6 vols.). Worcester, MA: Davis.

Clark, G. A., Day, M. D., & Greer, D. (1987). Discipline-based Art Education: Becoming students of art. *Journal of Aesthetic Education.* 21(2), 129-196.

Consortium of National Arts Education Associations. (1994*). National standards for arts education.* Reston, VA: Music Educators National Conference.

Cox, M. (1992). *Children's drawings.* London: Penguin.

English, M. R. (1987). *The effects of using computer graphics with preschool children.* Unpublished master's thesis. University of British Columbia, Vancouver, Canada.

Gardner, H. (1980). *Artful scribbles.* New York: Basic Books.

Goodnow, J. (1977). *Children drawing.* Cambridge, MA: Harvard University Press.

Haanstra, F. (1994). *Effects of art education on visual-spatial ability and aesthetic perception: Two meta-analyses.* Proefschrift, Rijksuniversiteit Groningen, The Netherlands.

Kaneda, T. (1994). Art activities in now/less industrialized socieites: A case study in Nepal. *Art Education,* 47(1), 20-24.

Marr, D. (1982). *Vision.* New York: Freeman.

Naeli, H., & Harris, P. L. (1976). Orientation of the diamond and the square. *Perception.* 5, 73-77.

Parsons, M.J. (1987). *How we understand art: A cognitive developmental account of aesthetic experience.* New York: Oxford University Press.

Piaget, J. (1929). *The child's conception of the world.* London: Routledge, Kegan Paul.

Sowell, J. E. (1993). A learning cycle approach to art history in the classroom. *Art Education,* 46(2), 19-24.

Wolcott, H. F. (1967). *A Kwakiutl village and school.* New York: Holt, Rinehart and Winston.

CONTRIBUTORS

Rudolf Arnheim is a Professor Emeritus of Psychology, Harvard University, Boston, Massachusetts, U.S.A.

Bernard Darras is an Associate Professor in the Department of Arts and Liberal Sciences, Université de Paris I, Panthèon-Sorbonne, Paris, France.

Jessica Davis is a Researcher in the Development Group, Harvard Project Zero at Harvard University Graduate School of Education, Boston, Massachusetts, U.S.A.

Paul Duncum is a Senior Lecturer in the Faculty of Education, University of Central Queensland, Rockhampton, Australia.

Kerry Freedman is an Associate Professor in the Department of Curriculum and Instruction, University of Minnesota, Minneapolis, Minnesota, U.S.A.

Claire Golomb is a Professor in the Department of Psychology, University of Massachusetts, Boston, Massachusetts, U.S.A.

Larry Kantner is a Professor in the Departments of Art and Curriculum and Instruction, University of Missouri, Columbia, Missouri, U.S.A.

Anna M. Kindler is an Associate Professor of Art Education in the Department of Curriculum Studies, University of British Columbia, Vancouver, British Columbia, Canada.

Judith Smith Koroscik is an Associate Professor and a Dean, College of Arts, Ohio State University, Columbus, Ohio, U.S.A.

Ronald N. MacGregor is a Professor of Art Education in the Department of Curriculum Studies, University of British Columbia, Vancouver, British Columbia, Canada.

Connie Newton is an Associate Professor at the School of Visual Arts, University of North Texas, Denton, Texas, U.S.A.

David Pariser is a Professor in the Department of Art Education, Concordia University, Montreal, Quebec, Canada.

Emiel Reith is an Assistant Professor in the Department of Psychology and Educational Studies, University of Geneva, Carouge, Switzerland.

Brent Wilson is a Professor in the Department of Art Education, School of Visual Arts, Pennsylvania State University, University Park, Pennsylvania, U.S.A.

Index